Women's Work in Soviet Russia

Michael Paul Sacks

5·23·77

Women's Work in Soviet Russia

Continuity in the Midst of Change

PRAEGER SPECIAL STUDIES IN INTERNATIONAL ECONOMICS AND DEVELOPMENT

Praeger Publishers New York Washington London

Library of Congress Cataloging in Publication Data

Sacks, Michael Paul.
Women's work in Soviet Russia.

(Praeger special studies in international economics and development)
Bibliography: p.
Includes indexes.
1. Women—Employment—Russia. 2. Women—Russia—Social conditions. 3. Time allocation. I. Title
HD6166.S2 331.4'0947 75-19813
ISBN 0-275-55790-1

PRAEGER PUBLISHERS
111 Fourth Avenue, New York, N.Y. 10003, U.S.A.

Published in the United States of America in 1976
by Praeger Publishers, Inc.

Printed in the United States of America

To my parents

ACKNOWLEDGMENTS

This book is an updated and substantially revised version of my doctoral dissertation. I am especially grateful to Charles Tilly for his incisive criticism of the dissertation. This had a profound influence on my subsequent work. Irving Louis Horowitz and Alex Simirenko also read the dissertation and provided valuable comments and advice.

I am indebted to the Russian Research Center of Harvard University for providing me with an opportunity to utilize their extensive resources during the acedemic year of 1972-73. I wish to thank Helen Defosses, an associate of the Center, for bringing the dissertation to the attention of the publisher.

John Brewer gave generously of his time to read the entire manuscript and gave extremely helpful and detailed comments. I am also grateful to Norman Miller, another colleague at Trinity College, for his help in revising several of the chapters.

I owe a great deal to my wife Debbie for her efforts to endure the years of work and sacrifice that have gone into the preparation of this book.

CONTENTS

LIST OF TABLES

Table		Page

Table | Page

Table		Page

LIST OF FIGURES

Women's Work in Soviet Russia

CHAPTER 1
THEORETICAL ISSUES

A very striking feature of Soviet society is the extensive and highly diverse employment of women. In Soviet Russia there are more women than men in the labor force. As detailed analysis in a later chapter will show, women are represented in virtually every occupation and in numbers that often far exceed those in other industrialized nations of the world (Mandel 1975). How pre-Revolutionary conditions shaped this development, why female labor-force participation changed and grew during the Soviet period and how women's work roles influenced their family life are the fundamental questions with which this book is concerned. Answering these questions entails an exploration of the relationship between large-scale social change and change in the status of women—a subject of considerable debate.

THE DEBATE OVER WOMEN'S ENTRANCE INTO THE LABOR FORCE

The conflicting arguments of William J. Goode (1963) and Scott and Tilly (1975) clearly illustrate the issues involved in this debate. Two different conceptions of the process of change shape their views of the impact of and impetus behind female employment outside the home.

Goode (1963, p. 56) contends that female employment resulted from "the gradual, logical, philosophical extension to women of originally Protestant notions about the rights and responsibilities of the individual [which] undermined the traditional ideal of 'woman's proper place.'" (It is particularly relevant to note that Goode emphasizes in the same passage the importance of changed cultural definitions in Eastern Europe: "Unquestionably in the Communist nations of Europe the immediate impulse has been ideological.") Also necessary was the emergence of the free market economy, for it provided a social structure that would support this change in values. On the free market "the individual was hired for his own skill with little regard for his family position." Again, what is critical is the change in values: the shift from the application of ascribed to achievement criteria which Goode, following Parsons, sees as a concomitant of industrialization. Similarly, Poston and Johnson (1971) claim that the growing shift from ascription to achievement parallelling industrial development reduces professional occupational segregation by sex.

Scott and Tilly (1975) have fundamental objections to Goode's argument. They see novel patterns of behavior as "less the product of new ideas than of the effects of old ideas operating in new or changing contexts" (p. 42). Their data convincingly show that at least in France, Italy, and Great Britain change in cultural values, as reflected by the extension of political rights, was not directly associated with change in patterns of employment (p. 37):

> First, there was little relationship between women's political rights and women's work. The right to vote did not increase the size of the female labor force, neither did the numbers of women in the labor force dramatically increase just prior to their gaining the vote. Moreover, great numbers of women worked outside the home during most of the nineteenth century, long before they enjoyed civil and political rights. Finally, rather than a steady increase in the size of the female labor force the pattern was one of increase followed by decline.

Values already present in the peasant family were consonant with changes in behavior. Goode (1963, p. 59) also recognized that "women have always worked, in the field and in the home. Even in the cities only a tiny minority of women were allowed to avoid work." Scott and Tilly emphasize the importance of the household as an economic unit to which women were obligated to make a contribution. "Woman's place" involved combining productive and reproductive tasks. With the expansion of industrial opportunities in the nineteenth century, families "sent their daughters out into the labor market as garment workers or domestic servants" (1975, p. 40). Poor married women also took advantage of these novel means to fulfill their traditional obligations. There is no need to posit a change in values to explain this response to industrial development.

In her analysis of female labor-force participation in the United States, Oppenheimer (1970; 1973) proposes a similar model of change. She shows that female participation in the labor force was a product of changes both in the economy and population composition that shaped the supply of and demand for female labor. The change in attitudes of employers toward hiring older and married women appeared to be largely a product of economic necessity and their discovery after hiring such women that they made excellent employees. Oppenheimer, in fact, stresses that the conceptions of what were appropriate occupations for women did not change. The expansion in opportunities for female employment was a product of the growth of the tertiary sector of the economy—an area consisting of occupations in which women were traditionally employed or new occupations of a comparable nature. This is confirmed by Gross's (1968) finding that occupational segregation by sex in the United States has remained almost unchanged between 1900 and 1960. Thus, like Scott and Tilly, Oppenheimer focuses on the changed social conditions that fostered behavioral adaptation—a far cry from Goode's conception of change as stemming from the spread of an altered value system. Am empirical investigation of these issues through the study of developments in Soviet society thus entails an examination of early patterns of female labor-force participation and family obligations, an analysis of the changing economic and demographic conditions that shaped demand and supply, and, finally, consideration of the changing conceptions of appropriate female behavior.

The Relationship between Work and Family Status

Goode (1963) contends that women's entrance into the labor force is associated with an improvement of their position in the family. Employment outside the home is directly tied to a change in the broader values regarding women's rights. An emphasis develops within the family

> on the uniqueness of each individual, so that sex status and seniority are less relevant than the 'human' qualities of warmth, emotionality, character, and so on, which are not based on age or sex. These emphases reduce sex and age-based inequalities among children as well as adults . . . (1963, p. 21).

Goode argues, in addition, that job opportunities and better training for women—products of the "needs of an industrializing system" and the "long ideological debate about rights and opportunities"—will in turn further the development of egalitarianism:

> The woman, like the child, no longer needed to depend on her family elders or males when she wanted to work. Consequently, she achieved an independent basis for her own existence, so that she could, in the larger society as well as within the family, drive a better "role bargain." That is she could achieve a better set of rights and obligations with respect to other statuses (1963, pp. 20-21, 56).

In all fairness it should be noted that Goode is quite aware of the slow pace of change in family relations and the difficulty of interpreting the available data on values and behavior:

> In reality, in all countries there are many women who manage to dominate the men, but it seems likely that in most countries, when the husband tries to dominate he can still do so. Even when the husband performs household chores, his participation means that he gains power—the household becoming a further domain for the exercise of prerogatives in making decisions.
>
> Perhaps the crucial qualitative difference is to be found in the extent to which, in one country or another, the male can still dominate <u>without</u> a definite effort to do so. It may be this which distinguishes the present period from fifty years ago, and on this point we do not believe that data are available (1973, p. 70).

This latter point is consistent with conclusions drawn by many researchers who have based their analysis on a social exchange model (see Bahr 1974). It has been argued that through employment outside the home a woman (1) increases her economic contribution to the family; (2) is exposed to alternative activities and social relationships that may both increase her social skills and lessen her dependence on her husband; and (3) may experience a change in perceived needs that lead her to be less satisfied with the resources her husband provides (Bahr 1974, pp. 169-70). Thus, employment alters the exchange between husband and wife in such a way as to increase the "power" of the wife: it reduces her "interest in the continuation of the affair" and thereby enables her to more effectively "dictate the conditions of association" (Waller and Hill 1951, p. 191, quoted in Bahr 1974, p. 169).

Engels came to a similar conclusion (though based on a different model of change) regarding the relationship between employment and domestic roles. Scott and Tilly (1975, p. 42) argue that Engel's position is the "antithesis of Goode's argument," for it asserts "that material changes in economic, political or social structures led directly and immediately to changes in value and behavior. It, too, is based on a model that assumes that change in one realm necessarily and directly leads to change in another"—a view which, as will be discussed below, Scott and Tilly consider untenable. In a passage written in the 1890s regarding female employment in Russia, Lenin (1964, pp. 545-46) illustrates clearly the Marxist conceptualization of change. Because of its direct relevance and obvious importance the paragraph is worth quoting at length:

> Large-scale machine industry, which concentrates masses of workers who often come from various parts of the country,

> absolutely refuses to tolerate survivals of patriarchalism and personal dependence, and is marked by a truly "contemptuous attitude to the past." . . . In particular, speaking of the transformation brought about by the factory in the conditions of life of the population, it must be stated that the drawing of women and juveniles into production is, at bottom, progressive. It is undisputable that the capitalist factory places these categories of the working population in particularly hard conditions, and that for them it is particularly necessary to regulate and shorten the working day, to guarantee hygienic conditions of labor, etc.; but endeavors completely to ban the work of women and juveniles in industry, or to maintain the patriarchal manner of life that ruled out such work, would be reactionary and utopian. By destroying the patriarchal isolation of these categories of the population who formerly never emerged from the narrow circle of domestic, family relationships, by drawing them into direct participation in social production, large-scale machine industry stimulates their development and increases their independence, in other words, creates conditions of life that are incomparably superior to the patriarchal immobility of precapitalist relations.

There is reason to question the foregoing arguments. The research of Safilos-Rothschild suggests that female employment alone may not be sufficient to alter behavior or values in other social contexts. What is crucial is how the women view their work activities. In a study conducted in urban Greece she found that employed wives with low work commitment "tended to give in to their husbands to an even greater extent than the nonemployed wives did" (Bahr 1974, p. 177). She also found that "the level of fertility of fecund working women with low work commitment is the same as the level of fertility of fecund nonworking women" (Safilos-Rothschild 1972, pp. 69-70).

Rodman's (1967) research stresses that the effect of a change of status cannot be understood without examining the culture of the particular population. Noting the contradictory finding that while in Greece the greater education of the husband increased the power of the wife in decision making, in the United States this change reduced the wife's power, he proposes a "theory of resources in a cultural context." In the United States there already exists an "emphasis upon the egalitarian ethic" and "a high degree of flexibility about the distribution of marital power." Thus, more education increases the husband's power by increasing his social status without significantly changing his beliefs about the proper distribution of power. In Greece, where patriarchal beliefs prevail, higher education exposes the husband to egalitarian ideals, the effect of which is stronger than that which results from an increase in social status (1967, p. 322).

Scott and Tilly, as already noted, seriously question whether work outside the home necessarily had a meaning different from that of the traditional labor of lower-class women. The peasant beliefs about the obligation of all family members to contribute to the household were perfectly consistent with new industrial employment:

> Traditional families . . . , operating on long-held values, sent their daughters to take advantage of increased opportunities generated by industrialization and urbanization . . . . No change in values was necessary to permit lower class women to work outside the home during the nineteenth century. Neither did industrialization "emancipate" these women by permitting more of them to work outside the home (1975, pp. 44-45).

With industrial development and the emergence of the middle class there was a stress on the unique capabilities and mission of women to fulfill their roles as wives and mothers, not equality between the sexes. Even Goode (1963, pp. 21-22) concedes that the greater exposure to egalitarian ideals which comes with increased education may change the domestic behavior of men only slightly:

> Lower-class men concede fewer rights _ideologically_ than their women in fact _obtain_, and the more educated men are likely to concede _more_ rights ideologically than they in fact grant. One partial resolution of the latter tension is to be found in the frequent assertion from families of professional men that they should not make demands which would interfere with his _work_: He takes precedence as _professional_, _not_ as family head or as male; nevertheless, the precedence is his. By contrast, lower-class men demand deference as _men_, as heads of families. [Emphasis in original.]

Backwardness as a Hindrance

Russia's industrial development at the beginning of the twentieth century was far behind that of Western Europe and the United States. Industrialization at a relatively late time meant that the nation had special problems and, perhaps, unique potential which may partly explain the distinct position of women in contemporary Soviet society.

Many decades passed after the Revolution before Russia began to lose its overwhelmingly rural character dominated by peasant institutions and traditions. Geiger (1968) has emphasized that in the 1930s Stalin's return to a more conservative policy with regard to marriage and the family found widespread support in a population that had been shocked by many of the postrevolutionary legal innovations (this is discussed further in Chapter 3). Barrington Moore (1966) has in part explained the development of totalitarian and fascist regimes by the presence of a large peasant class—a powerful conservative force subject to elite manipulation—at the time at which a nation industrializes. Soviet Russia's closeness to its peasant heritage would suggest that it could not escape the imprint of traditional values regarding women. It may be particularly important to examine the change and nature of socialization within the family—an institution that profoundly affects the transmission of culture and that also seems most sheltered from the influence of the political institutions.[1] As far as the data permit, this is considered in the chapters ahead.

The work of Gershchenkron (1965) and Habakkuk (1968) indicates that late industrialization makes for severe problems in achieving adequate capital accumulation. Competition with already developed nations necessitates the early use of large plants and enterprises, the adoption of a costly and complex technology, and a stress on producer as opposed to consumer goods. Adapting a peasant population to such change requires substantial investments in training and often considerable coercion. Capital formation is more likely to require a reduction in consumption levels. As later chapters will show, this experience was made far worse for the Soviet Union by internal and international conflicts. An important question to consider is how scarcity of capital impedes change in the status of women. Such change may be dependent on the ability of a society to create and sustain a network of new institutions particularly in efforts to alter the functioning of the family. Goode, as noted above (p. 2), did recognize that value change must be supported by structural change. Late industrialization may impede such structural change. However, Hochschild's (1973, p. 1023) review of the literature suggests that we cannot assume that the changes brought about by industrialization will normally foster equality:

> As measured by income, education, and occupation, we know women's status (relative to men's) [in the United States] has declined in the last 25 years. But even before that, the picture is unclear. Smith notes a decline from the Puritan era to the 19th century, especially at the end of the 18th century. And in an excellent study of women in the underdeveloped world, Boserup shows that as industrialization rises, the position of women declines.

Backwardness as an Asset

There is a more sanguine conclusion that can be drawn from the work of Habukkuk (1968) and Gershchenkron (1965). Lateness in development means that a nation must draw upon the most recent social and material technologies available to survive the competition on the world market. Such a challenge offers the nation the potential to surpass its predecessors. This argument is more explicit in the writings of Stinchcombe (1965) and Sahlins and Service (1960).

Stinchcombe (1965, p. 153) has noted that "the organizational inventions that can be made at a particular time in history depend on the social technology available at the time." Once formed, such organizations tend to perpetuate their original structure "both because they can function effectively with those organizational forms, and because the forms tend to become institutionalized." Thus the structure of an organization is directly related to the time at which it developed:

> The explanation is that organizations which are founded at a particular time must construct their social systems with the social resources available. Particularly, they have to build their elites so that they can recruit necessary resources from the society and to build the structure of the organization so that in the historically given labor market they can recruit skill and motivation of workers (1965, p. 168).

Service and Sahlin's (1960) evolutionary theory is on a different level of analysis. Their premise is that societies tend to organize themselves around the technology available. Certain groups in the society become dependent upon the continued use of that technology to preserve their dominant social position. They promote stable conditions through their control over the social institution and the accepted ideology (cf. Stinchcombe, 1968, pp. 108-18). Change that does occur constitutes adaptation to new conditions but not real innovation. The latter must come from the backward areas unimpeded by such a social structure (cf. Pirenne, 1966). Such regions can choose from the most efficient social and material technologies.

If recent developments have made it possible to alter the use of female labor, it follows from these evolutionary theories that the timing of industrialization should be directly related to the place of women in the social structure of the society. Thus, despite the obvious economic virtues, Goode contends that in the past women were excluded from many aspects of production: "In all great civilizations, women could have discharged most jobs adequately, had they been trained for them, and all civilizations would have been wealthier had they done so. However, those tasks were culturally defined as impossible for women" (1963, p. 56). Perhaps even more to the point, Melvin Reder (1957, p. 166) has noted the difficulties of introducing women into American industrial enterprise:

> . . . the camaraderie of men (especially manual workers) on the job simply cannot include women. In addition, attractive women can create rivalry among male workers

> which plays hot with discipline. These problems make it difficult to introduce women into a masculine environment. . . . Related to this is the fact that the initial hiring of women involves the employer in additional expenditures on lavatory facilities, etc.

Scott and Tilly (1974; 1975), as already noted, have argued that in Western European nations traditional values and the labor-force participation by married women eventually were replaced by middle-class notions of femininity. This was in part a product of a relatively early rise in prosperity and a decline in the demand for female labor that Soviet Russia has yet to fully experience (perhaps in part due to the lateness of industrialization). This type of "stability" in the social structure would appear to be an impediment to the improvement in the status of women. Goode (1963, p. 62) hints at this very point:

> One might hypothesize that where women have been in a socially and economically underprivileged position, and where men are unable to provide for them at a level viewed as adequate they are willing, like the men with few opportunities in tribal life, to seize new career opportunities. Women in Communist China, for example, have had less to lose and relatively more to gain from work than Western middle-class women who expect to be provided for. Western women receive support and encouragement for _not_ assuming a career and have a substantial investment in the _status quo_; the women in Communist nations receive propagandistic encouragement at the least, and often material benefits in addition.

The extent to which backwardness is an impediment or a catalyst in promoting change in the status of women is a question that can be very profitably explored from empirical study of Soviet Russia. However, full investigation of the issues raised here clearly requires a cross-cultural study design which is beyond the scope of this book.

MEASURING EQUALITY

It is important to recognize that most of the studies of "power" in the family suffer from very serious conceptual and methodological flaws well demonstrated and discussed by Turk and Bell (1972), Sprey (1972), Olson and Rabunsky (1972), and Safilos-Rothschild (1970-71). Measuring change over time has been extremely hampered by the absence of comparable research done in the past. Both these methodological problems and the preceding discussion suggest that further empirical study is warranted as well as a more careful specification of terms such as "improvement" and "equality."

My examination of change in the status of women has focused on the following dimensions: (1) educational achievement, (2) familial burdens, (3) occupational roles, and (4) control over the distribution of goods and services.

The measurement of improvement in women's position, in part a subjective evaluation of change in the above dimensions, must always be considered in terms of the status of men. Failure to do so, as Knudsen (1969) shows, can make for serious distortions.

Educational attainment is thus measured in terms of sex differences in the number of years of schooling and type of education. The latter is considered primarily in terms of the occupational opportunities made available by such training.

Familial burdens are measured by the relative expenditure of time and effort on household chores, including most aspects of child care. Again, it is not the absolute time spent on housework that is at issue, but the difference between the time spent by males and females of comparable familial status.

The study of occupational roles entails examining (1) the relative possibility of advancing to more prestigious and high paying positions; (2) the range of occupations open to females as compared to males; (3) the economic reward of those occupations; and (4) the level of responsibility and skill exercised in the positions.

Finally, control over goods and services is measured in terms of organizational participation, influence over decision making in the family, and the probability of being in a leading or managerial position in the labor force or government.

I define equality between males and females as the absence of sex differences in the physical and emotional effort necessary to acquire goods and services and to influence the sexual division of labor within the primary institutions of the society. The spheres of work, family, and politics are of central concern in this respect. Sexual equality may not absolutely require males and females to play identical social roles. However, it seems quite clear that equality is not achieved without a considerable increase for women in the quality and quantity of their education, a broadening of their occupational opportunities, a decrease in their familial burdens, and greater input into decisions regarding the distribution of goods and services.

SOVIET RUSSIA AS A SUBJECT OF INQUIRY

The radical political and economic transformation of Russia during the twentieth century makes the study of change in the status of Soviet women an inherently fascinating subject that is also theoretically significant. Soviet development is unique in many respects. This is a product of the timing of its economic development, the nature of its cultural heritage, the influence of a communist leadership, etc. However, the nation has also experienced large-scale social changes that are comparable to those of other countries. This combination of a historically distinct social setting and more universal social processes and related problems makes the study of Soviet Russia a particularly important test of theories of convergence: that is, those arguing that industrialization or modernization gives rise to uniform structural and ideological outcomes.

In general, the study of cultures at variance with those of Western industrial societies has the potential of revealing viable alternative social structures and solutions to existential dilemmas. Through comparative research we may avoid what Berger and Luckmann (1966, pp. 88-89) call the "reification of social reality":

> Reification is the apprehension of human phenomena as if they were things, that is, in non-human or possibly suprahuman terms. Another way of saying this is that reification is the apprehension of the products of human activity _as if_ they were something else than human products—such as facts of nature, results of cosmic laws, or manifestations of divine will. Reification implies that man is capable of forgetting his own authorship of the human world, and further, that the dialectic between man, the producer, and his products is lost to consciousness. The reified world is, by definition, a dehumanized world. It is experienced by man as a strange facticity, an _opus alienum_ over which he has no control rather than the _opus proprium_ of his own productive activity.

Hough's (1965) study of the lower levels of the Soviet Party and industrial bureaucracies is an important illustration of the value of comparative research. His finding that Soviet organizational efficiency is achieved with a dual hierarchy directly contradicts "conventional American assumptions about administrative structure and practices." Soviet lines of authority should produce chaos, according to classical theories of bureaucracy and of the organizational prerequisites of a complex society; yet they have sustained "great strides in public health, education and defense technology" (1969, pp. 7, 203). Cole (1973) found through his study of Japan that permanent employment—a phenomenon foreign to Western capitalism—was very much compatible with the demands of modern economic development. This was a viable "functional alternative" to labor practices that existed elsewhere. More to the point, Goode (1963) has been criticized for failing to examine the Soviet Union in a work in which he argues that family structures throughout the world are converging to the conjugal family type (Cuisinier and Raguin 1967, p. 522).

Fortunately, Soviet interest in researching the problems and position of women has been very strong. Much recent sociological research has been devoted to this subject and there has been considerable discussion of related issues in the Soviet press. The latter takes the form of experts answering questions or discussing recent research as well as many letters to the editor by both male and female readers.

Soviet researchers have conducted an enormous number of time-budget studies which can be used to measure differences in the everyday life of men and women. These studies were first conducted in the 1920s, making possible unique comparisons over time (Szalai 1972a, pp. 6-7). Trends in employment and population composition are especially revealed in the 1926, 1939, 1959, and 1970 Soviet censuses as well as in the prerevolutionary surveys and censuses. Unfortunately, there is a significant gap in the data as a result of the absence of sociological research between the late 1930s and the late 1950s. Also, only selected results have been published from the Soviet censuses (with the important exception of that conducted in 1926). In all, there is an abundance of material that has not been analyzed and adequately evaluated in Western studies of Soviet women.

As in much of the previous work on the subject, I have not focused upon the Soviet Union as a whole, but rather upon the Russian Republic. This is but one of fifteen Soviet Socialist republics, though it constitutes three-quarters of the land mass of the Union of Soviet Socialist Republics (USSR) and 57 percent of its population in 1940, 56 percent in 1959, and 54 percent in 1970 (Ts. S. U. 1971a, p. 12). (The decline is due primarily to the very high birth rates in the Central Asian republics and the declining birth rate in the RSFSR.) This geographical delimitation was in part based on the fact that data were available primarily from regions located within the Russian Soviet Federated Socialist Republic (RSFSR). I also sought to reduce the degree of cultural diversity within the population under study. There are a substantial number of different cultural groups within the Russian Republic. However, they do not compare to the variety that exist within the boundaries of the Soviet Union as a whole. The contrasts between, say, peoples of the Baltic republics and those in Central Asia are profound and obviously rooted in centuries of political, religious, and economic differences.

Both in 1959 and 1970, about 83 percent of the population of the RSFSR was of Russian nationality (Ts. S. U. 1971, p. 18). I also expect that the degree of cultural homogeneity is greater among the urban industrial labor force—a population of central interest here. However, within the population under study there remain distinct geographic, demographic, climatic, and other variations which must be left for others to consider more fully.

THE CHAPTERS AHEAD

The following chapter deals with the period prior to the 1917 Revolution, to delineate the continuities and discontinuities involved in subsequent developments affecting the female population. In Chapter 3 I explain why there were changes in women's labor force participation during the Soviet period, and in Chapter 4, trace and evaluate this and other changes in the extrafamilial status of women. The impact of such developments on the family life of urban workers is analyzed in Chapter 5. This is based largely on a comprehensive review of Soviet time-budget research. Chapter 6 deals with both the family life and occupational participation of women in rural Soviet Russia. Besides further illustrating the consequences of technological change, it serves to support contentions in prior chapters regarding the significance of the population shift to urban areas. In the concluding chapter I aim primarily at explaining why there were continuities during the Soviet period and suggest sources of future change. What is largely at issue here is the contrast between the change discussed in Chapter 4 and that in Chapter 5.

NOTE

1. What I am suggesting here is some form of historicist explanation: "One in which an effect created by causes at some previous period becomes a cause of that same effect in succeeding periods (Stinchcombe 1968, p. 103; emphasis in original).

CHAPTER

2 WORK AND FAMILY PRIOR TO THE 1917 REVOLUTION

THE PEASANT HOUSEHOLD

> In the pre-industrial Europe described by Peter Laslett and in the contemporary pre-modern societies studied by anthropologists, the household or the family is the crucial economic unit. Whether or not all work is done at home, all family members are expected to work, for their contribution is valued as necessary for the survival of the family unit. The poor, the illiterate, the economically and politically powerless of the past operated according to values which fully justified the employment of women outside the home (Scott and Tilly 1975, p. 41).

Family obligations combined with legal restrictions to impede Russian women employed outside their home from attaining economic independence. In tsarist times ownership of land and property was solely a male prerogative (Kharchev 1964, p. 128). Women earned wages primarily from work related to domestic chores; that is, as agrarian laborers, servants, and charwomen—work that could not command a price close to that paid to men. As early as 1798 a law was passed that established a man's earnings at between 50 and 80 rubles and a woman's at between 18 and 20 (Kharchev 1964, p. 18). A woman's earnings generally were not to be used at her own discretion but rather contributed to the economy of the household—an ancient institution in which a male as head of the family possessed ultimate authority. Brute force was often used to support the tradition of male dominance:

> The basic social unit was the dvor . . . , in other words "the family and its farm." There were often large peasant families, which still retained much of the patriarchal character they had had in the middle ages, ruled over by the father, who as head of the family and organizer of the

> farmwork, arbiter and final authority, was all-powerful. He was accustomed to a blind obedience which left no scope for individual initiative. Any infraction of paternal discipline was severely punished, usually by physical cruelty in the shape of beatings of sometimes maniacal violence. This element of cruelty, which was a normal feature in the process of upbringing, was also a general feature of peasant life (Lewin 1966, p. 25).

Conflicts involving the rights of a woman were as a rule resolved in favor of the man. Kharchev (1964, p. 129), a well-known Soviet social scientist, states that "the tsarist government stubbornly opposed the extension to the female population of even those scanty citizen's rights that had been established by the land reform of 1864 and the manifesto of Oct. 17, 1905."

In their families of origin women were subject to the rule of their fathers. With marriage the husband dominated, but the female's position may have initially deteriorated as a result of her having to work in the often hostile domocile of her in-laws. "Among the masses of the people, most of whom were held in serfdom from the late sixteenth until the nineteenth century, women became slaves and chattels, both to their male relatives and to their masters" (Kingsbury and Fairchild 1935, p. xix). In later life, however, she could hope to have somewhat increased status in the family (Kharchev 1964; Kosven 1963).

NINETEENTH-CENTURY EMPLOYMENT

Large numbers of women had traditionally earned a wage by doing weaving in their own homes. With the decline of cottage industry during the late nineteenth century it became more difficult to combine industrial and domestic labor. However, women did respond to the growing opportunities in the burgeoning textile mills, and by 1887 they constituted 38 percent of the textile workers in factories of the Russian Empire. Eighty-four percent of the 192,000 female factory workers were in this industry. It is noteworthy, though, that women constituted 27 percent of the chemical workers and 11 percent of those employed in the manufacture of lime, brick and glass. There were also about 3,000 females in metallurgy (about 2.6 percent of the workers in this area; Rashin 1940, p. 185).

As was the case elsewhere (cf. Cooney 1975) and also at a later time in Russia, there is evidence that during the last quarter of the nineteenth century female employment was more closely tied to economic vicissitudes than was male employment. One study shows that the percent of women among those in the Petersburg metalworking enterprises had reached 0.5 percent in 1881. Economic decline caused this figure to shrink to 0.1. The subsequent economic recovery had an equally marked effect in the opposite direction: While there were only 156 women in the industry in 1881, there were 1,048 (1.4 percent of all metalworkers) by 1900 (Rashin 1940, p. 188).

Other evidence of female responsiveness to market conditions comes from the cotton industry where the introduction of machines created the potential for employing women. Between 1881 and 1900 the number of women in the textile industries of Petersburg Province grew from 7,281 to 16,526 or from 43 to 56 percent of the workers in this area. Though not initially defined as "women's work," this type of employment was rapidly becoming an exclusively female domain (Rashin 1940, p. 189).

Detailed data on employment cross-classified by such variables as sex, age, family status, and literacy were available in the 1897 census (Troinitskii 1906). In the following discussion of this material I consider only the data from European Russia, for this area of the empire is of central interest here. However, 82 percent of the labor force of the Russian Empire in industry, transportation, communications, and service enterprises worked in European Russia.

Table 2.1 clearly shows the contrast between male and female employment. Almost half of all female wage earners were servants and only about one in every five was employed in industry. ("Industrial workers" in the 1897 census also includes those who are employed in transportation, communications, and trade and service enterprises.) Among males these figures were just about reversed. Overall, females constituted a third of the 68 million wage earners, though two-thirds of all servants.

The literacy rate is an important measure of the difference in male and female status and, probably to an increasing degree as industrialization progresses, their employment opportunities. (The exact definition of literacy is not specified. It may refer to either or both the ability to read and to write [see Bogdanov 1964]). In 1897, while almost half the male hired workers were literate, this was true of only a quarter of the females (see columns 6 and 7, Table 2.1). In the total population the literacy of both males and females was far lower, though the gap between them remained about the same: 17 percent of the females and 39 percent of the males were literate (Bogdanov 1964, p. 59).

Lenin (1964, p. 59) states that during this period "literacy [spread] among women factory workers with remarkable rapidity." One cannot dismiss the possibility, however, that this higher level of literacy was not a product of selective urban migration rather than the factory environment. The literate were more likely to know of industrial opportunitites as a result of their ability to read newspapers or letters from those who already migrated. Indeed, the trend in the sex ratio of the cities during the nineteenth century shows the increasing urban migration of females. In the cities of European Russia in 1838 there were only 75 females per 100 males. Shortly after emancipation this figure had risen to 86; by 1897 it had reached 90 and on the eve of the

TABLE 2.1

The Occupations and Literacy of Hired Workers in European Russia, by Sex, 1897

Occupation	Males	Females	Percent Females	Proportion Males	Proportion Females	Percent literate	
						Males	Females
Industrial workers	2,254,099	384,079	14.6	.49	.18	57.8	28.4
Agricultural workers	1,281,626	554,376	30.2	.29	.25	32.0	14.5
Day laborers and unskilled workers	479,307	206,558	30.1	.10	.09	35.2	13.7
Servants	593,434	1,054,304	64.0	.13	.48	49.1	23.2
Total	4,608,466	2,199,317	32.3	1.01	1.00	47.2	25.8

Source: Based on figures in Troinitskii (1906, Table 2, p. 2).

First World War there were just over 93 females per 100 males (Rashin 1956, p. 283). Some not wholly dependable and rather limited data show that literacy was rising throughout this period (Bogdanov 1964).

In 1897 female industrial workers tended to be younger than their male counterparts. The largest proportion of both sexes was between the ages 17 and 39; almost 8 percent of the females and 5 percent of the males were under age 15. Most significant is the fact that 39 percent of the female workers over age 15 were married (Troinitskii 1906, Table 2, pp. 2-5). (Fifty-six percent of the male workers were married. Sixty-three percent of all women in European Russia at that time were married [Rashin 1956, p. 180]).

Only 6 percent of the female industrial workers were "heads of family." Almost a quarter of the men were heads of family. Though no definition of the term was given, I assume that such women had families to support and did not have husbands to depend upon. The female would not have been the head of the family if a male were present. Females were primarily heads of small households. Fifty-seven percent were heads of households containing two or three members, whereas the figure for males was only 35 percent. A person living alone was not defined as a head of a family (Troinitskii 1906, Table 2, pp. 1-2).

Forty-three percent of the females and 17 percent of the males were classified as family members (other than the head of the family) living with their family. Thus, half the females returned to their families at the end of each day. The remaining women lived apart from their families, while this was true of about 60 percent of the males (Troinitskii 1906, Table 2, pp. 2-5). The data available do not make it possible to specify the ties of these workers to their families. It is probable, however, that many migrated temporarily during periods when their labor on the farm could be spared. They also may have had relatives living in the vicinity or, as is suggested by some evidence discussed below, working in the same factory.

Table 2.2 shows that female industrial workers—14.6 percent of all such workers—were represented in all the areas listed with the single exception of construction. The percent female among the workers was relatively high in the textile, chemical, tobacco, and clothing industries and work in bathing establishments. Again, these entailed types of work closely related to that which women had been accustomed to doing within the home. More than eight out of every ten female workers were in the five aforementioned areas. If women had been randomly distributed in all the occupations, this would have been true of only 18 percent of the female workers.

Males had a far more diverse employment pattern. The highest concentration of males was in metal processing, but this comprised only 14 percent of the male workers. Employment in the textile and clothing industries accounted for 65 percent of the female workers. The probability that two randomly chosen male workers would have different occupations was .93; the corresponding figure for females was .72.

TABLE 2. 2

Number and Distribution of European Russian Workers in 28 Occupational Categories, by Sex, 1897

Occupational Category	Males	Females	Percent Females	Proportion Males	Proportion Females	Difference[a]
Extracting of ores and mining	100, 751	7, 395	6. 8	.0447	.0193	-.0254
Smelting of metals	36, 944	1, 570	4. 1	.0164	.0041	-.0123
Processing of textiles	256, 932	188, 895	42. 4	.1140	.4918	.3778
Processing of animal products	57, 387	2, 535	4. 2	.0255	.0066	-.0189
Processing of wood	139, 187	5, 586	3. 9	.0617	.0145	-.0472
Processing of metals	311, 123	5, 242	1. 7	.1380	.0136	-.1244
Ceramic production	58, 272	7, 079	10. 8	.0259	.0184	-.0075
Production of chemicals	39, 640	14, 511	26. 8	.0176	.0378	-.0202
Distilling, and production of _piva_ and _myod_	31, 054	1, 545	4. 7	.0138	.0040	-.0098
Production of other drinks and fermented products	3, 443	160	4. 4	.0015	.0004	-.0011
Processing of vegetable and animal food products	149, 622	8, 781	5. 5	.0664	.0229	-.0435
Tobacco industry	8, 929	16, 512	64. 9	.0040	.0430	.0390
Printing	41, 321	5, 150	3. 6	.0183	.0134	-.0049
Production of physical, optical and surgical instruments, musical instruments, clocks, toys, etc.	6, 705	252	11. 1	.0030	.0007	.0023
Jewelry production, painting, production of religious articles, luxuries, etc.	22, 563	427	1. 9	.0100	.0011	-.0089
Clothing industry	203, 480	62, 338	23. 5	.0903	.1623	.0720
Construction	268, 808	0	0. 0	.1193	—	-.1193
Production of carriages	7, 959	20	0. 3	.0035	.0001	-.0034

(continued)

TABLE 2.2 (Continued)

Occupational Category	Males	Females	Percent Females	Proportion Males	Proportion Females	Difference[a]
Other production, not included in former groups or uncertain	41,017	7,095	14.8	.0182	.0185	.0003
Post office, telegraph, and telephone (office workers, guards)	4,244	21	0.5	.0019	.0001	-.0018
Water transport	36,532	204	0.6	.0162	.0005	-.0157
Railroads (workers and office workers, weighers, station servants, etc.)	128,223	11,402	0.8	.0569	.0297	-.0272
Carriers' trade	99,307	531	0.5	.0441	.0014	-.0427
Remaining land transport	17,902	285	1.6	.0079	.0007	-.0072
Trade in general	94,431	4,445	4.5	.0419	.0116	-.0303
Taverns, hotels, furnished rooms, and clubs	66,227	3,917	5.6	.0294	.0102	-.0192
Public house trade	12,813	1,847	12.6	.0057	.0048	-.0009
Establishments relating to the cleansing and hygiene of the body[b]	9,283	26,334	73.9	.0041	.0686	.0645
Total	2,254,099	384,079	14.6	1.0002	1.0001	1.1477[c]

[a]Column 5 minus column 4.
[b]Hereafter referred to as "bathing establishments."
[c]Sum of absolute figures.
Source: Based on figures in Troinitskii (1906, Table 3, pp. 10-11).

Thus, despite the diversity of female employment, there were very distinct differences in the work of males and females. About 57 percent of either the males or the females would have had to change occupations to eliminate the sex differences in the occupational distributions (see Appendix A for a discussion of this measure). This is largely accounted for by construction, metal processing, and textiles where either males or females show a distinct concentration (see column 6, Table 2.3).[1]

Family responsibilities appear to limit the range of women's employment opportunities. Had two married women been randomly chosen from among the industrial workers, the probability that they would have had different occupations was equal to .54, while the comparable figure for unmarried women was .74. (Another possible interpretation of these findings is that married women were discriminated against. See Lieberson [1969] for a discussion of the measure of diversity.) Married women were far more concentrated in the more traditional areas such as the textile and clothing industries. The similarity between the distribution of the very young and the married female workers suggests that mothers and children may have worked together. The clothing industry, for example, was composed of almost a quarter of all those aged 15-19 and 15 percent of all married workers, but of only 6 percent of all females aged 20-39 and 5 percent of those 40-59 (Troinitskii 1906, Table 2, pp. 2-5). Obviously, far more dramatic figures would have resulted if data were available showing employment by age group of unmarried women.

In general, young females were to a very large extent concentrated in those occupations in which there was a very high proportion of women. This, again, suggests the possibility that many young women were under the supervision of other female family members. Among those 15-19, 20-39, and 40-49, the proportion of female workers in occupations in which the percentage female exceeded 40 was, respectively, .56, .67, and .21. The proportion in occupations in which over 20 percent of the workers were females was, correspondingly, .84, .71, and .70 (calculated from Troinitskii 1906, Table 2, pp. 10-11). The contrast here is somewhat exaggerated by the fact that females constituted 19 percent of those workers aged 15-19, 13 percent of those 20-39, and 12 percent of those 40-59.

It is also interesting to note that women in the older age groups, not unlike what is true today, are far more concentrated in the service and transportation occupations (the last eight listed in Table 2.2) than were their younger counterparts. The proportion of the women in these occupations was .044, .143 and .262 respectively for the age groups 15-19, 20-39 and 40-59. While over 17 percent of the women 40-59 worked in bathing establishments and about 5 percent were employed by the railroads, the corresponding figures for those women aged 15 to 19 were only 2.3 and 0.3 percent (calculated from Troinitskii 1906, Table 3, pp. 10-11).

TABLE 2.3

Number and Frequency Distribution of Male and Female Workers in Industries of the Russian Empire in 1913, and Percentage of Females in 1900 and 1913

Industry	Workers (1000s)		Percent Females		1913		
	Males	Females	1913	1900	Proportion Males	Proportion Females	Difference[a]
Processing of textiles	417.3	478.8	53.4	44.3	.216	.679	+.463
Cotton	249.6	309.5	55.4	46.0			
Wool	94.4	63.8	40.3	36.4			
Silk	11.8	23.7	66.8	50.0			
Hemp, flax	42.9	52.8	55.2	49.7			
Combined textiles	18.6	29.0	60.9	49.7			
Paper production and printing	72.6	24.5	25.2	34.8	.038	.035	-.003
Mechanical processing of wood	120.1	14.9	11.0	10.3	.062	.021	-.041
Processing of metals, production of machines and tools	326.5	20.8	6.0	2.7	.169	.030	-.139
Processing of mineral products	170.2	37.6	18.1	12.7	.088	.053	-.035
Preparation of animal products	43.9	7.9	15.3	25.7	.023	.011	-.012
Food processing	287.3	73.7	20.4	9.7	.149	.105	+.044
Chemical production	51.5	30.4	37.1	20.3	.027	.043	-.016
Extracting industries	28.8	0.0	0.0	—	.015	.000	-.015
Other production[b]	5.5	0.1	1.8	—	.003	.000	-.003
Factory production connected with mining	105.2	3.5	3.2	—	.054	.005	-.049
Extraction of mineral resources	268.2	11.9	4.2	—	.139	.017	-.122
Processing mineral resources	34.8	0.7	2.0	—	.018	.001	-.017
Total	1,931.9	704.8	26.7	—	1.001	1.000	.959

[a]Column 6 minus column 5.

[b]This includes production not included in the groups above, which are under the jurisdiction of factory inspectors. The industries below are under the jurisdiction of mining inspectors.

Source: Based on figures in Rashin (1940, pp. 191-92, 200).

FROM 1900 TO WORLD WAR I

According to reports of factory inspectors, during the first 13 years of this century the percentage of women among those in the hired labor force of the Russian Empire increased from 26.1 in 1901 to 31.7 in 1914. The actual number of female workers increased by 164 percent (from 441,000 to 723,900). Even the percentage of women among those in metal and coal industries was rising. Between 1904 and 1913 the figure for the latter grew from 2.8 to 4.5 percent in the south of Russia. The percentage of women in the empire in metalworking and machine construction grew from 2.9 to 5.9 between 1901 and 1914 (Rashin 1940, pp. 194, 198).

By 1913 many factory inspectors were commenting on the increased use of female labor in areas where in the past there had been an insignificant number of women. For example, in machine construction plants in Petersburg Province women were beginning to work on several drilling machines of small size. In Ekaterinoslavskii Province women constituted 18 percent of all workers in metal processing industries, though they were restricted to work primarily on machinemade loops and spikes. Rashin (1940, p. 195) a Soviet historian, contends that there was a general tendency to expand the use of female labor in every area in which great physical strength was not required. However, Kingsbury and Fairchild (1935) give the impression that women's work was indeed physically demanding:

> The trades that employed women obviously were those producing consumption goods. The great metal plants, employing over 500,000 workers in 1913, used less than 1 percent of women and these in completely unskilled work, either as charwomen or to load and carry. They were in no respect an integral part of the industry. In construction, transportation and mining likewise, they had only a small part. Apparently where they were used at all, it was mostly to fetch and carry, to load and unload. If bricks were to come to the bricklayers or bags of sand and cement to the cement mixer, the women often brought them on their backs or in wheelbarrows. If lumber must come from the sawmill or to the carpenters they might load or unload it (pp. 7-8).

The expanded use of women in the textile industry that began in the 1880s and 1890s continued during the period between 1901 and 1913. Of the 83,000 workers who entered the industry between 1908 and 1913 over 75 percent were women. Between 1902 and January of 1914 the percentage of females among these workers increased from 47.8 to 56.2, and their numbers grew from 194,700 to 318,100 (Rashin 1940, p. 196).

A factory inspector in 1907 explained that the reason why women were being used in the textile industry was that they were more industrious, attentive, and "abstaining": they didn't drink, smoke, or complain. This distinct preference for females was by no means restricted to the textile industry. As early as 1904 a factory inspector noted that "as a result of the recent workers' movement factory owners are everywhere substituting men for women wherever they can. This is true not only among adults, but also among minors. They consider women factory workers to be more peaceful and stable" (cited in Rashin 1940, p. 195).

Especially after 1905 the increased employment of women was directly associated with the employer's concern about the political activities of male workers. There was a distinct preference for the sex raised to be obedient: "In an attempt to check the revolutionary movement in plants and factories, manufacturers found it convenient to augment the number of women." Thus, in 1906 the factory inspectors' reports indicate an increase of 22,808 women workers (5.5 percent of the adult workers in the country) and a simultaneous decrease of 1,423 men (Kingsbury and Fairchild 1935, p. 8). Factory employment did not lead directly to a change in political awareness.

Women's lower wages were an additional incentive to hire them. A study in June 1914 of 1,058,400 workers showed that adult females earned half as much as adult males. Rashin (1940, p. 404) explains that this was to some extent a result of the fact that females were restricted to semiskilled and unskilled jobs in many industries. Other data presented by Kingsbury and Fairchild (1935, pp. 12, 34) indicate that women in the cotton industry in Moscow prior to 1912 were earning an average of 90 percent of the wages of males: the least skilled women earned about 70 percent as much as men. Figures, apparently from the 1914 study mentioned above, show that the wages of women varied from as much as 72.1 percent of that of men in the textile industry to a low of 41.1 percent in metalworking.

Table 2.3 shows the distribution of women in industries of the Russian Empire in 1913 and data for approximately comparable categories in 1900. Rashin (1940, pp. 192, 199) states that the data for 1913 in Table 2.3 are based on workers in 19,292 enterprises and that the study accurately reflects the sexual division of labor in Russian industry. The data were collected by both factory and mining inspectors. Rashin considered the data for 1900 to be the most accurate for the period, presumably superior to the 1897 census.

Women constituted over a quarter of all the workers in these occupations—a sizable increase over the 18 or 19 percent estimated for 1900 (Rashin 1940, pp. 192-93). A considerable increase is shown in the percent female among the workers in all the categories except for paper production and printing and the processing of animal products. It may be that these exceptions are the result of differences in the 1900 and the 1913 classifications. However, the decrease in the proportion of women among those who processed animal products was also evident in earlier data (1885-1900) from Petersburg Province (Rashin 1940, p. 188).

Despite some change in the frequency distribution of female workers, the sex differences remained exceedingly pronounced. In 1913, 68 percent of the females were in textiles—a decline from 79 percent in 1900. The proportion of the women in the food industry had grown from .05 to .10 over this period, and the percentage of women among the workers doubled as well. The last column of Table 2.3 shows that it was in textiles that the largest difference existed between the male and female distributions. The proportion of the males in the processing of metals (.17) far surpassed the comparable figure for females (.03). This same contrast also existed in industries involved in the extraction of mineral resources: the figure for males was .14, while that for females was .02.

Furthermore, distinct differences between the work of males and females also prevailed within the industries (Kingsbury and Fairchild 1935, p. 17):

> Illiterate, as pre-war Russian women so predominantly were, unused to machinery or tools, they filled the places often of unskilled persons only. When they went to the machines, they worked on simple, repetitive processes, such as stamping and pressing. Few of them became skilled machinists or high-grade machine operators.

THE CONSEQUENCES OF WORLD WAR I

The First World War fostered a great increase in the number of women in the labor force. "While millions of soldiers were pouring across the country toward the western boundaries, their women were drawn into the mills and foundries, into tram cars and into offices. . . ." Factory inspection reports showed that in January 1917, women constituted 40 percent of the workers. Women and children entered the labor force in especially large numbers in areas like Moscow and Petrograd where large factories predominated. Between 1914 and 1917 the percentage of women among the textile workers in Moscow increased from 49.5 to 60.6 and in the metal industry of the city it grew from 7.4 to 19.6.

> The number in the entire metal trades of Moscow swelled from 65,000 to 110,000 persons, a growth of 68 percent. The change in Petrograd was even greater in the same group; women in the metal trades made up 20.3 percent of those employed in 1917 as against 3.2 percent in 1913.

> In the wood-working industries the women increased seven times. In papermaking and printing, in the preparation of animal products and in foodstuffs their proportion in the Petrograd district approximately doubled between 1914 and 1917 (Kingsbury and Fairchild 1935, p. 16).

Thus, on the eve of the Revolution, women were entering even those occupations that had up until that time contained only a very small and even declining percentage of females among the workers. The diversity of occupations opened to them had clearly increased very markedly, though the precedent for employing females of all ages, both married and unmarried, in a variety of industrial occupations clearly preceded this influx during World War I. It was probably still true, however, that women's status in industry remained far inferior to that of men and the sudden increase in their employment may have been only a temporary consequence of emergency conditions. The war, of course, did not end with a simple return to conditions that had preceded it.

NOTE

1. The measure to which I am referring is

> the basic index of dissimilarity generally accepted in sociological research as a representative indicator of segregation, and only recently of any form of social differentiation between two groups. With reference to the [occupational] differentiation by sex, the index is computed by calculating the proportional distribution of males and females in the [given] occupations, obtaining the difference between the proportions of males and females in each of the occupations, and dividing the sum by two (Poston and Johnson 1971, pp. 337-38).

CHAPTER

3

FEMALE LABOR DURING THE SOVIET PERIOD: SUPPLY AND DEMAND

The preceding chapter shows that female employment in industry was a culturally available response to social conditions in Russia. Such conditions included (1) an increase in occupational opportunities that was generated both by economic growth and by crisis, resulting in a scarcity or political undesirability of male workers; and (2) changes in the supply of women seeking employment (for example, as a result of the decline of cottage industry). During the Soviet period, the family's financial needs were to be sustained or enhanced and opportunities for nonagrarian employment were to continue to grow; it was not surprising to find that women's response was very much the same as it had been in the prerevolutionary period, especially when it now had great ideological support:

> The transformation of the woman from a private person burdened with household chores into a social person involved equally with the man in the building of the socialist society—and at the same time the transformation of the family, a unit traditionally bound by the economic dependence of women, into a social union of equal partners—was and is one of the cornerstones of socialist thought (Ofer 1973, p. 150).

To delineate the influence of changing conditions on female employment, I have used a supply-and-demand conceptual framework as defined and applied by Oppenheimer (1970, pp. 19, 23):

> A. Supply: Factors (independent of demand) that determine or influence the supply of women available for work. . . .
>
> B. Demand: Factors (independent of supply) that determine or influence the demand for workers—in terms of the number and types of workers—in jobs that women might fill.

C. Interaction of Supply-and-Demand Factors
  (1) Changes in supply that affect the number of workers demanded. . . .
  (2) Changes in demand that affect the amount or type of workers supplied. . . .

In the sections that follow, the most significant factors are discussed in relation to their influence upon supply and demand.

POPULATION SIZE AND THE SEX RATIO

Around 1910 the population within the territory of what is now Soviet Russia was equal to that of the United States. (The United States had a population of 92 million in 1910; the territory of present-day RSFSR encompassed 90 million in 1913 [Bogue 1969, p. 131; Ts. S. U. 1972a, p. 7].) Sixty years later, the United States comprised a population of 205 million, whereas Soviet Russia had reached only 130 million (Bogue 1969, p. 131; Ts. S. U., 1972a, p. 7). This far smaller growth rate in the Russian Republic is attributable to the decimation of the population in the course of severe internal and international conflict. In the USSR as a whole, it has been estimated that there were perhaps as many as 2. 8 million more deaths than births each year during the period of the Revolution and the Civil War (1917-21). The net population loss during collectivization (1929-35) was probably about 5. 5 million, while "the absolute decline in population during World War II, between 1941 and 1946, is estimated to have been twenty-five million" (Dodge 1966, p. 20). Severe famines and the Great Purge (1936-39) during this period also left their mark (Matthews 1972, Chapter 1).

Because of the difference in their social role, males experienced a far higher mortality rate. Table 3.1 shows the sex ratio for the population of the USSR and, where possible, for the Russian Republic.[1] It can be seen that the deficit of males in the population over age 16 was quite severe as early as 1926; it soon became far worse. In the RSFSR in 1959, there were just 58 males per 100 females in the age group 35 to 59—a group that would normally consist of administrators, skilled workers, professionals, etc., at the peak of their careers. It has been estimated that by 1990 the sex ratio of the population of the USSR will reach about 91 (U. S. Department of Commerce 1970, p. 3). Both in 1959 and in 1970, the sex ratio was even lower in the Russian Republic than in the Soviet Union as a whole.

Given the pace of industrial growth, the precedents of tsarist Russia, the small population growth rate, and the imbalance of the sexes, the employment of females clearly represented a necessary and viable solution to the profound shortage of labor. With regard to patterns in the United States, Oppenheimer notes:

TABLE 3.1

Sex Ratios of the USSR and RSFSR, 1897-1970, Selected Years

	All Ages	Under 16	16-34	35-39	60 and over
1897[a]	98.9	100.1	96.9	100.7	95.5
1926[a]	93.5	101.2	89.8	90.4	78.8
1939[a]	91.9	101.3	96.1	80.1	66.1
1946[a]	74.3	99.5	72.0	59.1	49.7
1950[a]	76.2	100.2	79.5	59.1	49.7
1959[a]	81.9	103.6	93.8	69.6	50.8
1959[b]	80.5	103.4	95.3	57.8	44.3
1970[a]	85.5	103.8	101.1	74.1	47.7
1970[b]	83.8	103.7	102.4	72.9	41.6

[a]USSR; for 1897 this refers to the Russian Empire.
[b]RSFSR.

Source: Based on figures in Dodge 1966, p. 6; Sovetskaya rossiya, April 17, 1971, p. 1; Ts. S. U., 1972b, pp. 16-17.

> an important question . . . is whether there has been a general rise in the demand for labor that could have been met by either male or female labor, or whether there has been a rising demand for female labor in particular [emphasis in original]. Although men and women are used interchangeably in some jobs, most demand for labor has usually been sex specific (1973, p. 949).

The demographic conditions of Soviet Russia were for many decades to produce an acute demand for labor of a very general nature (though, as will be shown in Chapter 4, sex labelling of occupations would not disappear).

FINANCIAL NEEDS OF THE SOVIET FAMILY

The state of the population also influenced the supply of women. As opportunities arose, more women may have sought nonagrarian occupations (a case of demand influencing supply). However, of far greater significance were the increasing numbers of families deprived of male breadwinners and the many women unable to marry or remarry. Women were thus forced to assume greater economic burdens.

TABLE 3.2

Number Married Per Thousand Population in the Russian Republic, by Age and Sex, 1926, 1939, 1959, and 1970[a]

Age	Males				Females			
	1926	1939	1959	1970	1926	1939	1959	1970
16 and over	688	702	692	716	606	597	505	563
16-17	9	5	4	4	45	34	24	20
18-19	138	63	38	40	280	222	143	159
20-24	509	361	269	297	682	599	479	536
25-29	827	757	802	771	843	783	752	819
30-34	914	904	921	878	840	815	768	848
35-39	939	937	953	926	807	794	711	834
40-44	943	945	963	942	756	751	606	783
45-49	935	940	965	949	696	676	525	708
50-54	912	925	958	952	614	589	452	588
55-59	883	898	946	949	545	488	392	478
60-69	785	817	908	925	408	363	332	342
70 and over	532	581	718	771	200	162	158	176

[a]The term "married" means presently married. Unmarried refers to those single, divorced, or widowed.

Source: Ts. S. U. RSFSR 1963, p. 98; Ts. S. U. 1972b, p. 263; Gosplan SSSR, 1931, p. 4.

TABLE 3.3

Indexed Number of Females Married Per Thousand in the Russian Republic, 1926, 1939, 1959, and 1970
(1926 = 100)

Age	1926	1939	1959	1970
16 and over	100	99	83	93
16-17	100	76	53	44
18-19	100	79	51	57
20-24	100	88	70	79
25-29	100	93	89	97
30-34	100	97	91	101
35-39	100	98	88	103
40-44	100	99	80	104
45-49	100	97	75	102
50-54	100	96	74	96
55-59	100	90	72	88
60-69	100	89	81	84
70 and over	100	81	79	88

Source: Table 3.2.

The Female Marriage Rate

Table 3.2 shows the proportion of females married by age group over the period between 1926 and 1970; the indexed figures in Table 3.3 show more clearly the changes over this period. The most severe decline in the proportion married occurred between 1939 and 1959 as a consequence of the war losses. The acute declines in those groups over 35 particularly indicates the loss of male heads of family. The decline in the youngest age groups was paralleled by a similar trend among the males—a sign of the increasing age at marriage over the period. And finally, the declining proportion married among those 20-34 is in large part indicative of the increased number of women who had never married.

Unfortunately, any cross-classification of marital and employment status is currently lacking,[2] though an ecological analysis of results of the 1959 census by Mazur (1973) indicates a strong relationship between these variables. He found that, in most regions of the Russian Republic, between 28 and 54 percent of the variance in the percentage of women active in the labor force could be explained by the relative proportion of women who were married:

> "The implication is that the limited opportunity for women to marry, often due to unfavorable age-specific sex ratios, determines their prerogative to remain in the labor force" (p. 43).

Mazur (1973, pp. 39-46) found that in the "thirty administrative areas in the most highly industrialized Moscow-Kiev-Tallinn part of Eastern Europe," as much as 54 percent of the variation in the proportion of economically inactive women was attributable to the "ratio of the proportion of married women aged 16 and over." In the rest of the Russian Republic, with the exception of 10 autonomous republics containing ethnic groups with a high birth rate and other regions of the USSR having a crude birth rate between 21 and 31, 28 percent of the variance was explained by this factor. Other potent factors that compelled women to respond to the demands of the labor market are not revealed by figures on the proportion of women married: (1) a very considerable number of male invalids were incapable of fully supporting their families; (2) Those women who did have their husbands present could not feel certain that these circumstances would not abruptly change; (3) According to Geiger (1968), many men were delinquent in their familial responsibilities; (4) As was true in the traditional household, throughout most of the Soviet period the contribution of male breadwinners alone was not sufficient to support a family. Each of the three latter points is elaborated upon in the sections below.

Decades of Uncertainty

Shortly after the Revolution, measures were initiated which, in the course of granting women full political and legal equality, also made divorce extremely simple:

> While women have gained much from the new ease in dissolving an unhappy relationship, many faced the necessity of self-support and, possibly, of furnishing whole or partial support for minor children. Even if married women did not need or wish to work, it was good insurance for her to have a working skill in reserve or to acquire one (Dodge 1966, p. 55).

Carr (1970, p. 40) emphasizes that the heritage of tsarist Russia left the overwhelming majority of the women illiterate and living in abject poverty characterized by "its subjection and maltreatment of women." The extreme conservatism of the family was well recognized at the time and, during at least the first decade following the Revolution, much effort was directed toward weakening the influence of the older generation. The backwardness of the Russian countryside was hardly conducive to the realization of women's rights. New freedoms too often simply meant new insecurities. "Peasant women, for example, rarely sought alimony in the event of divorce. In urban families the right to work, if it existed in the form of a concrete opportunity, was more often seen as a financial necessity. . . ." Although women had the option of not taking their husbands' names, by 1928 90 percent of the women were still doing so. New sexual freedoms may more often have led to the exploitation of females (Geiger 1968, Chapter 3).[3] If we are to believe Trotsky's account written in 1937, men benefited far more under these changing conditions and largely at the expense of the economic and psychological security of their wives:

> One of the very dramatic chapters of the great book of the Soviets will be the tale of the disintegration and breaking up of these Soviet families where the husband as a party member, trade unionist, military commander or administrator, grew and developed and acquired new tastes in life, and the wife, crushed by the family, remained on the old level. The road of the two generations of the Soviet bureaucracy is sown thick with the tragedies of wives rejected and left behind (quoted in Geiger 1968, p. 60).

As part of Stalin's broader program designed to strengthen the institution of the family and return to a more traditional morality, divorce was made "more difficult and more expensive and has doubtless reduced the precautionary motive for acquiring a marketable labor skill." (After much debate, divorce procedures were simplified considerably on December 10, 1965. In 1968 further changes made mutual consent sufficient grounds for granting a divorce "provided there are no minor children" [Mazur 1969, pp. 282-83].) However, the Great Purge (1936-39) created new fears: "In an atmosphere of sudden disappearance and secret trials, husbands and wives were concerned with the problem of the family's economic survival if the husband should be arrested" (Geiger 1968, p. 55). The extreme and surely far greater hardships and uncertainties of World War II soon followed.

In 1944, legislation was enacted that probably encouraged women to seek the security of an independent income. The law freed men from responsibility for children born out of wedlock and again made illegitimacy an identifiable and thus stigmatized status.

> The children of mothers who were literally without husbands as well as those who had husbands but had to live with them in de facto or unregistered marriage were identified in their personal documents with a dash in the place of their father's name. Moreover, they had neither the right nor the opportunity to take their father's names. The man on the street, it seems, considered both

> categories as illegitimate, and school children were to be heard addressing certain of their peers as, "Hey you, fatherless" (Geiger 1968, p. 108).

There is evidence that the population is still extremely critical of illegitimate children (see Kuznetsova 1973, p. 12).

This measure was apparently designed to raise birth rate in the face of an extremely depleted male population. A Soviet investigator has noted rather bitterly that this law has

> encouraged a frivolous attitude toward women and has not promoted the strengthening of the family. The irresponsible attitude of men toward their extramarital progeny has degraded their feelings of responsibility in relation to their "legal" children as well (Danilova 1968, p. 64).

The law did provide a state allowance to support a child born to the unmarried mother and permitted her to place the child in a state institution: "Thus the child born out of wedlock was no longer to be treated as his father's child; instead the state stepped in to assume a large part of paternal obligation" (Berman 1963, p. 339). However, as will be discussed below, the ability of the state to take over such responsibility has been far from adequate.

The 1944 law concerning paternity gave rise to substantial criticism. Change did not come until the mid-and late 1960s. At present the law emphasizes that the responsibilities and rights of the father are the same whether the parents are married or not. Paternity is established either on a voluntary basis or by a judge, and in no case do the child's documents have a blank in the place where the father's name is supposed to appear (Vorozheikin 1973, pp. 22-23). A Soviet commentator has noted that "it would seem that first priority has been given to the interests of mother and child" (Kuznetsova 1973, p. 12). However, it is significant to note that a Soviet demographer in research conducted as late as 1968 and 1969 in Belorussia found that in cases in which there was a premarital birth or pregnancy some women would use any means available, including threatening suicide, in order to conclude a marriage. "She does this not only to protect her reputation, but, at times with the sole purpose of avoiding the notorious mark on the birth certificate" (Yurkevich 1970, p. 100).

Male Irresponsibility

Geiger (1968) has contended that irresponsibility on the part of Soviet men has been promoted by a whole range of policy decisions.

The 1944 law, in fact, is probably an excellent example of what he is referring to. The passage summarizing Geiger's argument is worth quoting at length:

> . . . the Soviet man, just emerging from a patriarchal family tradition, has tended to retain his rights but to allow his duties to go by the board. The post-revolutionary family policy of the party and central government unwittingly reinforced the tendency. The promise of legal, economic, and other features of equality for women and assertions of the state's willingness and desire to take over household maintenance and child-rearing, in line with classic Marxism, if at first taken by the Soviet man as an unwelcome intrusion into his family relations, have later been interpreted as an invitation to forsake his own responsibilities toward his wife and children. At the same time, his other difficulties and status losses and scanty bonding force of his marital ties have made him want desperately to hold on to the traditional prerogative that most forcefully set him off as a man—namely, the right to behave in a free and self-serving way in sexual life, drinking, and other matters. Two additional factors—the great amount of moving about inside the USSR and the man scarcity—have underscored the ability of the man to behave, if he wishes, according to his instincts rather than the requirements of a stable marriage. The theme of the deserted and helpless peasant or working-class wife has been a constant one for decades (pp. 244-45).

Geiger is probably exaggerating the extent to which developments during the Soviet period lead men to relinquish their familial responsibilities. For example, there is evidence that alcoholism among males, a serious problem in the Soviet Union and a frequent cause of divorce, can to a large extent be explained by long-extant cultural factors (see Connor 1972). Also, the prevalence of irresponsible behavior on the part of men is very difficult to establish from the highly inadequate crime statistics (containing mainly frequency distributions rather than rates) and the lack of relevant surveys of public opinion. The surveys that do exist are too often plagued by serious sampling problems.

However, Geiger (1968), on the basis of the interviews of Russian emigres in the Harvard Project (see Inteles and Bauer 1968, Part I), too easily makes statements such as the following: (1968, p. 241): "Among that *half or more of the population of men* that has felt no improvement as the years have passed, disappointment and desperate need have sometimes led to antisocial, often criminal, activities" [emphasis added]. Or, after quoting the story of a 40-year-old truck driver from Vologda, Geiger (1968, p. 246) tells us that

> such marriages are reported with enough frequency and seem likely on theoretical grounds that they probably make up a major type of Soviet marriage. The most prominent features are the primitivized, self-oriented, often cynical personality of the husband and a helpless wife who usually must silently accept the husband's activities [emphasis added].

It would seem that, in making such conclusions, far more caution is warranted. I also sense that underlying this "theory" are assumptions concerning the "normality" of the nuclear family, and the necessity of females fulfilling expressive functions in order to maintain its stability.

Dean Knudsen, in an article describing the declining socio-economic status of women, has been critical of these kinds of assumptions which he feels are pervasive in the literature on the family:

> As a result of the preconceptions regarding appropriate sex roles, sociologists have asserted the value and necessity of certain family structures, which, if changed, would precipitate dysfunctional consequences for the total society. The traditional family is thus justified by appeals to a normative order which defines females as complementary to males. Fulfilling maternal roles is therefore the primary and highest order if not the only appropriate behavior (1969, p. 191).

The Economics of Family Life

The presence of a working husband did not assure the family of an adequate income. This is true even today with much improved wages and living conditions. A recent Soviet study showed that the "normative budget for a minimum material comfort level for a family of four (husband, wife, thirteen-year-old boy and seven- to eight-year-old girl)" can be maintained only if there were two workers per family earning the average monthly wage of workers and employees in the USSR;". . . a third child in the family could cause certain material difficulties." In 1967, a study of 250,000 families of workers and employees (thus excluding collective farm workers) with at least one child under age 16 showed that, in the RSFSR, 34.9 percent of the families had two children and 12.3 percent had three or more children. A study of newlyweds in Kiev in 1970 showed that the average number of children desired was two. The first nationwide study of fertility was reported in 1971. Based on interviews with 33,602 women from families of workers and employees, it showed that in the Russian Republic the average ideal number of children reported by the women was 2.67 and the average intended number was 2.21 (A Demographic Problem 1969, p. 77; Ts.S.U. 1969b, p. 112; Chuiko 1972, p. 112; Heer 1972, pp. 260-61).

Recent survey data support the notion that economic necessity is still a potent force motivating women to engage in the labor force. In a study of 427 female workers in factories in Moscow, Penza, and Leningrad, 53 percent of the women stated that they worked because of the necessity to supplement the income of the family (Slesarev and Yankova 1969, p. 421). Kharchev and Golod (1969, p. 448) obtained the same results in a study of female workers in Leningrad. In a study of 595 families in Leningrad, all the women stated that, along with other factors, the need for additional income motivated them to work. The investigator concluded:

> The participation of women in social production is, under the conditions of socialism, dictated to a significant extent by economic necessity. . . .
>
> In an overwhelming majority of cases the participation of women in social production is connected with strivings to raise the family income in conjunction with the growth of the cultural and material needs of family members (Mikhailyuk 1970, p. 24).

FAMILY STRUCTURE AND THE SUPPLY OF WOMEN

For married women, and especially those with children, family structure can have a profound influence on their ability to enter the nonagrarian labor force. If the care of young children can be left to older siblings or to a grandparent, and the husband or other relatives share housework, the supply of women available for employment increases. The family structure takes on added importance in the absence of an extensive network of child-care centers or other services, or of modern appliances to facilitate such time-consuming tasks as cooking and laundering. As will be discussed below, the deficiency of such services was acute during most of the Soviet period.

Fewer Births, Not Fewer Children

The decline of fertility in Soviet Russia was especially rapid and contributed greatly to the shortage of labor. This has created a formidable dilemma in that Soviet demographers attribute the declining birth rate to the employment of females. A significant withdrawal of women from the labor force is not presently feasible, and yet the declining birth rate augurs a more extreme shortage of labor. Dodge (1966, p. 24) has demonstrated that the cost of a realistic program aimed at encouraging women to have more children would be exorbitant and that its efficacy could not be guaranteed.

However, the overall effect on family size (and, thereby, the domestic responsibilities of married women) was actually quite limited. This was true because, as is characteristic of demographic transitions, high levels of fertility were associated with high mortality, and the slow evolution to low mortality paralleled the decline in fertility. As can be seen from Table 3. 4, the rate of natural increase remained quite stable. Not until the 1960s did it show a sharp change, and this was

TABLE 3.4

Crude Birth and Death Rate, Natural Increase, and Infant Mortality in the RSFSR, 1913-71, Selected Years

	Crude Birth Rate	Crude Death Rate	Natural Increase	Infant Mortality
1913	47.8	32.4	15.4	273
1940	33.0	20.6	12.4	205
1950	26.9	10.1	16.8	88
1960	23.2	7.4	15.8	37
1965	15.7	7.6	8.1	27
1969	14.2	8.5	5.7	25
1970	14.6	8.7	5.9	23
1971	15.1	8.7	6.4	21

Source: Ts.S.U. RSFSR 1971, p. 25; 1972, p. 12.

a decline. As late as 1940, the infant mortality rate was about four times as high as it was in the United States at that time (Bogue 1969, p. 586); these deaths substantially negated the consequences of high fertility.

Detailed fertility rates for the USSR, estimated by Mazur (1967), give a very plausible picture of the trends that took place in Soviet Russia (Table 3.5). His figures show a very rapid decline in the number of births per woman up until the mid-1930s. In june 1936, the 1920 law permitting abortion was nullified. The new legislation followed "a nationwide discussion in which many expressed opposition [to abortion on demand]" (Carr 1970, p. 39). However, it was probably not public opinion that was foremost in the minds of Soviet leaders, but rather the growing threat of Germany and fears that the declining birth rate would mean acute shortages of workers and soldiers. Other measures were also enacted to encourage larger families:

> Provisions were added to grant material aid allowances to mothers of large families and provide more maternity services, and the people were promised that within eighteen months the number of nursery beds for children would double and the number of permanent kindergartens increase threefold. The exposed position of the Soviet mother was further recognized by raising to two years' imprisonment the penalty for divorced fathers' refusal to pay alimony in judgments awarded for the maintenance of their children (Geiger 1968, p. 96).

A Soviet study of abortions by Sadovokasova (1968) indicates that in the first year following the legislation the number of registered abortions dropped more than threefold—more than fourfold in rural areas.

TABLE 3.5

Annual Total Fertility Rate of the USSR, 1926-66

Year	Total Fertility Rate	Year	Total Fertility Rate	Year	Total Fertility Rate
1926	5,566.0	1940	3,752.1	1954	2,974.4
1927	5,418.3	1941	3,742.6	1955	2,909.1
1928	5,318.1	1942	2,933.1	1956	2,859.2
1929	4,985.8	1943	2,366.2	1957	2,903.9
1930	4,826.1	1944	1,942.0	1958	2,899.3
1931	4,255.0	1945	1,762.1	1959	2,903.8
1932	3,573.6	1946	2,868.3	1960	2,940.0
1933	3,621.6	1947	3,232.9	1961	2,879.6
1934	2,904.9	1948	3,079.4	1962	2,755.0
1935	3,263.3	1949	3,007.5	1963	2,688.1
1936	3,652.7	1950	2,851.1	1964	2,564.4
1937	4,308.6	1951	2,914.7	1965	2,487.7
1938	4,351.3	1952	2,898.8	1966	2,452.4
1939	3,964.4	1953	2,762.9		

Source: Mazur 1967, p. 38.

> However, in the following years, the initial effects of the prohibition subsided, and the number of abortions increased rapidly up until 1940. In 1939, the number of abortions per thousand women aged fifteen to forty-nine amounted to 26.5 according to our calculations (Sadovokasova 1968, p. 209).

The increase in abortions was probably also fostered by the "general tendency [during the 1930s] for maternity leaves to be shortened and benefits reduced" despite the promising legislative enactments. This culminated in December 1938, with very large curtailments in maternity benefits as the nation prepared for war (Dodge 1966, pp. 64-65).

Abortion was not made legal until November 1955, though it was apparently a widely accepted practice for women impregnated during the German occupation. A Soviet source also shows that the number of registered abortions increased following the return of the Russian army beginning in 1946:

> Thus, the 1936 resolution forbidding abortion in point of fact did not and could not be any serious stimulant to raise the birth rate . . .; it merely led many women with unwanted pregnancies to have illegal abortions, risking their health and sometimes their lives (Sadavokasova 1968, p. 210).

Looking again at Mazur's figures in Table 3.5, it can be seen that fertility plummeted during World War II. The Soviet Union never experienced a baby boom of any consequence. The postwar fertility rate reached its apex in 1947—about 81 percent of the level in 1939. Even this was not achieved without the aforementioned 1944 legislation that relieved males of their responsibility for illegitimate progeny, gave increased benefits to large families, and taxed single persons and small families. This, the Soviet demographer Vostrikova (1964, p. 209) contends, "undoubtedly . . . was of great importance in reaching the high level of fertility in the post-war period." (Dodge [1966, pp. 23, 68-69], on the other hand, indicates that there was very little change in the level of benefits provided to pregnant women during the 1930s and that these "measures appear to be a doubtful incentive to larger families.") However, these increased benefits were substantially curtailed three years later. David Heer has characterized the family allowance system in the Soviet Union as having "anti-natalist effects in the post World-War II period":

> In 1947 the size of grant [established in 1944] was cut in half and after that date the value relative to the average wage steadily declined. As a result the allowance for families giving birth to a fifth child while their fourth child was eligible for monthly payments, was reduced from around 51 percent of the average wages in 1944 to around 12 percent by 1964 (1972, p. 258).

Thus, the overall effect of changing demographic rates in Soviet Russia has been not so much to decrease the number of children in a family as to change the number of children dying and the timing of a woman's childbearing:

> Increases in family size due to increased life expectancy in all age groups for both men and women, including infants, have enabled women by the age of thirty to have approximately the same number of live children as their mothers and grandmothers managed to save in the course of higher reproduction by the age of forty (Mazur 1967, pp. 44-46).

A woman may now spend less time bearing children. The desired family size can be achieved early in her life cycle. However, the care of children may become difficult, for now the mother does not have the help of older children. In 1968, for example, 40 percent of all births in the USSR were first births (Urlanis 1971, p. 11).

Grandparents, Husbands, and Child Care

Though grandparents and other female relatives may in the past have been an important source of help for the working mother, this does not appear to be the case in most families today. A female Soviet investigator has noted that, while at present the two-generation family is the rule, in the 1930s three-generation families were not uncommon. Furthermore, the modern family has brought with it an increased number of domestic chores that the mother must now assume:

> In the past, the responsibilities of women in the house were primarily limited to the preparation of the food, cleaning the residence, washing clothes, etc., whereas today the chief activities have become the upbringing of children, checking to see that they have done their homework, visiting children's institutions, making all the purchases for the house (including even large expenditures), organizing the leisure time of the family, etc., i.e., responsibilities not specifically relegated to women in the old patriarchal family (Yankova 1970, p. 70).

Note the particular emphasis on tasks associated with children that now have greater importance. The investment of time per child would appear to have increased (cf. Aries 1962; Scott and Tilly 1975). Along similar lines, a Soviet commentator has remarked that "the public organizations have shifted the main burden of upbringing to the school, the school has shifted it to the family, and in the family it is the woman who must assume this burden" (Libedenskaya 1967, p. 14).

Dodge's (1966, p. 28) analysis of data from the 1959 census supports the contention that families with children are not choosing to live with the parents of the couple. In the USSR "most older persons live in small families," whereas most children and adolescents live in larger size families. Urlanis (1971), a well-known Soviet demographer, has complained that, despite the evident benefits to the woman and to society, young married couples prefer to live apart from their parents.

In a study of female workers in industrial enterprises in Moscow, Leningrad, and Penza, it was found that grandparents resided in only 15 percent of the families and in only 8.4 percent did they do the housework (Yankova 1970, p. 78). Another study of female workers in Leningrad showed that parents of the married couples did housework in 15.2 percent of the cases and "other family members" besides the wife did so in only 3.3 percent (Kharchev and Golod 1969, p. 444).

Perhaps most convincing is a study of 250,000 families of industrial and office workers conducted in 1967. It revealed that, per 100 families in urban areas, there were 136 females over age 16. Seventy-four percent of these were employed in the labor force. Pensioners and grant-aided students are grouped together, but, when we add to this those over 65 without a pension, the total number of such women per 100 families was only equal to 22 (Ts. S. U. 1969a, p. 111).

There is also evidence in recent decades that the employment of women over age 50 has been increasing rapidly in the expanding service sector and in light industry (see Chapter 4). Many have apparently been motivated to return to work in order to complete the necessary number of years of employment to receive a pension. In the 1960s, both the level of pensions and the minimum wage rose (Litvyakov 1969). This will mean that even fewer grandparents will be available to help young mothers.

As will be quite evident from the time-budget data presented in Chapter 5, men do very little housework. This also holds true for child care: "Fatherlessness exists even when the fathers are alive" (Libedenskaya 1967, p. 14). Kon (1973, p. 11), an author of several Soviet studies on youth, has recently stated that "researchers . . . have agreed that the role of the father in the upbringing of his children does not at all compare to that of the mother: Fathers spend less time with them, and children rarely relate their secrets to their fathers." Kon attributes this primarily to the inability of the fathers to deal with such relations, rather than their lack of interest in them: "For contemporary men, emotional contacts in the family are more important than they were several generations ago." But it appears that wives must take the responsibility for creating the family cohesiveness and intimacy that the men desire.

Note that I am referring here to male irresponsibility of a different sort from that discussed above and referred to by Geiger. In this case I am suggesting that males fail to fulfill domestic functions such as housework and child care. The prior discussion referred much more to instrumental functions; that is, supporting the family economically.

THE PROVISION OF SERVICES

To foster the labor-force participation especially of married women, the development of service enterprises to relieve the burdens of housework is essential. The lack of help from other family members makes this all the more important. In addition, the Revolution brought with it opposition to housework on ideological grounds. Lenin stresses the need "to include the woman in social productive work, to tear her away from domestice slavery, to free her from the depressing and forced subordination under the eternal and exclusive world of kitchen and child care" (quoted in Liegle 1975, p. 5). However, for a number of reasons to be discussed later, the level of services available to the population has been exceedingly inadequate. This is well illustrated by the institutional arrangements for child care.

Child-Care Facilities

What Geiger (1968, pp. 57-58) has called the "extensive" communal dining facilities, children's institutions, and laundries that were developed during the war, did not continue. Communism "could not be continued for financial reasons, and owners and managers of private enterprises during the NEP period were reluctant to invest in such uneconomic ventures as creches and public restaurants." It was estimated that, in 1925, about 3 percent of the children were attending creches (institutions for the care of children up to age three). There was considerable dissatisfaction with the quality of these early child-care facilities as well as with the other communal institutions.

During the late 1920s and early 1930s there was a large growth in the number of creches, as well as of kindergartens caring for children between ages three and six. Enrollment in kindergartens in the USSR, for example, grew from 107,500 to 1,061,700 between 1927 and 1932. World War II abruptly halted this progress despite the fact that, during the decade following the outbreak of the war, 92 percent of those entering the labor force were women—the largest proportion in any period before or since. Between 1940 and 1960, the number of women in the labor force rose by more than 30 million, whereas the already inadequate number of places in children's institutions increased by only 7 million. It has been estimated that the number of places actually needed per 100 women in the fertile age groups is between 70 and 80 (Dodge 1966, pp. 76-87; Litvyakov 1969, p. 111; Mikhailyuk 1970, p. 26).

According to a Soviet statistical handbook, the number of children in preschool institutions in the Russian Republic in 1960 had reached 3,038,000. This increased 177 percent by 1966, and 189 percent by 1972. In the Soviet Union as a whole in 1960, 13 percent of the children aged one through six could be accomodated in preschool institutions. By 1965, 22.5 percent of such children reportedly were in preschool institutions throughout the USSR, and 31.7 percent were accommodated in year-round facilities in 1971. By 1973, the number of children in these institutions increased an additional 11 percent (Ts. S.U. 1968a, p. 127; 1974, p. 708; Ts.S.U. RSFSR 1972, p. 377; Kharchev 1964, p. 275; *Literaturnaya gazeta*, February 27, 1971, p. 12).[4] These figures are still relatively low, but they are beginning, for the first time in Soviet history, to reach levels more in line with the needs of the country. (Dodge [1966, p. 31] estimates that in the USSR in 1959 30 percent of the women in the labor force were likely to have children residing at home. The more recent increase in female employment surely raised this figure, although the decrease in the birth rate probably had a somewhat compensating effect.)

At present, one still finds complaints that there are not a sufficient number of places for all women who desire child care, that the facilities are acutely understaffed, and that working conditions create a serious problem of labor turnover. A manager of a kindergarten-day nursery elaborates upon these shortcomings:

> Previously kindergartens and nurseries were crowded into tiny rooms. Now they have spacious game rooms, sleeping quarters of 40 to 60 square meters each, cloakrooms and washrooms. Is it conceivable that a single attendant can cope with this amount of work, feed the children four times a day, and wash the dishes?! . . .
>
> In the kindergarten, specialists with a degree in teacher training receive from 80-100 rubles. But in day nurseries medical personnel, who have diplomas, receive 65 rubles. This is what causes high turnover. Children barely grow attached to auntie Lyuda when a new auntie Valya appears. And so it goes, ad infinitum. In addition, if teachers serve in day nursery groups, the time they work there is not counted toward their length of teaching service (Razina 1975, p. 24).

Care of young children of school age has also been a serious difficulty. Boarding schools are generally not viewed very favorably, though there has been greater demand for them than space available. They accomodated about 5 percent of the pupils in grades 5 through 10 in the RSFSR in 1954. The figure increased only slightly by 1961. There is a lack of exact figures on the expansion of enrollment in recent years, though some evidence indicates that it has been seriously lagging behind goals set by the government (Dodge 1966, pp. 87-89). The high cost plus the tendency to send "problem" children to them appears to be making boarding schools even less desirable for parents (Kosarev 1973, p. 15).

Another form of care for school-age children has been to extend the time they are under the supervision of the school. The longer day school programs have been expanding rapidly since 1960, when enrollment in the USSR was about 525,000. It was reported that in 1968-69, 3.9 million students, 10 percent of the children between the ages 7 and 14 attended schools having this program (Dodge 1966, pp. 89-91; Mikhailyuk 1970, p. 142; U. S. Department of Commerce 1973, p. 14). A 1973 source indicates that almost 6 million children were involved, though there is growing dissatisfaction with the way the program is being conducted (Kozhevnikova 1973, p. 16).

Women have thus been compelled to take time off from work to bear children and nurture infants and may find it very difficult to remain in the labor force while the children are young. For example, in

Novosibirsk Oblast and Krasnoyarsk Krai, it was found that 75 percent of the women age 16 to 35 were not working in social production because of difficulties in placing children in preschool institutions (Sonin 1965, p. 205). In a study of women in Lithuania, 46.1 percent of the women who wished to work only part time said that this desire arose from their need to care for their children (Panova 1970, p. 90). Many reluctant working women have undoubtedly found it necessary to leave their school-age children unattended:

> It is fortunate if there is a grandmother at home or an extended-day program at the school. Someone will be keeping an eye on the child. But what if there is neither? Then you hang the key to the apartment around the child's neck, give him hundreds of instructions about gas, electricity, matches and strange voices outside the door, and send him off! The key is a two-ton weight on the mother's heart (Kuznetsova 1968, p. 19).

A study of 70,000 women working in the Ukraine showed that "approximately 70 percent of those giving birth do not return to their jobs for one year" (A Demographic Problem 1969, p. 78). A more recent source indicates that "as a rule, women return to work without waiting for the end of the year allotted to them by law. Seven or eight months—that is the length of time they are willing to spend in the role of 'just a mother'" (Ovchinnikova 1973, p. 11).

It is interesting to note that the increase in availability of places in preschool institutions comes at a time when there is growing support for care at home of children below age two:

> Although even people with impeccable grandmas seek to enroll their children in kindergartens, young parents who send their offspring to nurseries are sometimes viewed with condemnation, and not only by their neighbors. In children's consultation offices, physicians sometimes remark: "A fine child, very healthy—it's a pity he's in a nursery" (Ovchinnikova 1973, p. 11).

A survey of female workers in large cities showed that 80 percent of the women advocated keeping their children of nursery age at home because they get sick too frequently (Yankova 1970, p. 80). It is the mother who is then forced to take time off to care for them. In a Lithuanian study, women expressed similar sentiments. In Moscow, nurseries have actually refused to care for children under age one (Litvinenko 1970, p. 41; Andrushkyavichenye 1970, p. 80; Mikhailyuk 1970, p. 141). In 1973, only 10 percent of all children under age one, and 30 percent between age two and three, were reportedly attending nurseries (Ovchinnikova 1973, p. 11). A Soviet writer indicates that those in nurseries "are mainly from the least prosperous families and from families where only the mother is present." He contends that the great increase in personnel needed to improve nurseries is not economically feasible, and also that "it is necessary not to forget the moral-ethical significance of the spontaneous participation of mothers in the care and upbringing of their own children" (Litvyakov 1969, pp. 96, 97). Urlanis (1971), a prominent demographer, concurs: "Nurseries were a necessity in their own time, but now we are wealthy enough not to deprive a child of its mother's affection." This is again evidence of the growing emphasis on women's tasks associated with children.

Housing

Housing conditions influence the time needed to complete housework. In the Soviet Union, the deficiencies in this area have been inordinate. They were, however, clearly inherited from tsarist times during which dwelling units for the swelling urban population were abysmal. In European Russia the population in cities grew from 6.1 to 18.6 million as a result of the industrial growth between 1860 and 1917 (Smith 1973, p. 406). The housing shortage appears to have worsened with the tremendous influx into Soviet cities after approximately 1926.

Furthermore, the investments in heavy industry left insufficient resources to meet the needs of the population. During World War II, there was immense destruction of housing in the European part of the USSR.

Intensive construction efforts initiated during the mid-1950s resulted in the building of more housing units in the USSR between 1959 and 1968 than in any other nation and "enabled 87.7 million citizens (37 percent of the population) to move into newly built dwellings." Despite this, there is still considerable overcrowding. Using Soviet standards and adjusted statistical data, it was found that the number of per-capita square meters of living space in the RSFSR in 1968 was below the sanitary norm. Only in Moscow did it surpass this level (Morton 1973, pp. 119-20). The average space per person in the Russian Republic in 1971 was 11.2 cubic meters (13.9 in Moscow), as compared to 8.1 in 1958. But, in the same year (1971), the figure for East Germany was 20.8; it averaged 20 or more in most of Western Europe and was at least 25 in the United States (Morton 1973, p. 123; Smith 1973, pp. 406, 422).

Dodge has noted that

> hot water is practically unavailable even in the cities, where it is estimated that less than 3 percent of the urban population is supplied with hot water. This means that almost every drop of hot water in the Soviet Union must

be heated in a pot on the stove, and the family laundry alone can take the equivalent of two strenuous days a week (1966, p. 97).

TABLE 3.6

Municipal Utilities in Urban Areas of the USSR

	Percentage of the Population Supplied with Utilities			Percentage of State Housing with the Utilities		
Type of Utility	1927	1939	1956	1959	1971	Plan for 1975
Electric lighting	40.7	84.8	89.3	n.a.	n.a.	n.a.
Running water	25.9	38.7	34.0	56.0	73.0	80.0
Plumbing	17.5	28.1	31.4	n.a.	n.a.	n.a.
Central heating	n.a.	11.1	22.4	44.0	n.a.	78.0
Bath	n.a.	7.5	8.9	30.0[a]	65.0[a]	70.0[a]
Hot water	n.a.	0.7	2.2	n.a.	n.a.	50.0
Sewerage	n.a.	n.a.	n.a.	53.0	78.0	80.0

n.a.: data not available.
[a]This includes showers.
Source: Dodge 1966, p. 47; Smith 1973, p. 417.

Yet a 1964 study of workers' families in Leningrad showed that, among the 584 "randomly selected" families, 94.1 percent regularly washed clothing at home (Pimenova 1970, p. 142)!

The provision of other utilities does not appear to be as limited. Table 3.6 shows two sets of data which together reveal the considerable progress that has been made. The figures for 1927, 1939, and 1956 show the provision of services to all urban residents, while those for the later years and the plan for 1975 pertain only to the more modern and better equipped state housing. Private dwellings have constituted about a third of all city housing space since 1940 (Morton 1973, p. 122). Note that there is an absence of data on the provision of hot water, although a very high level is planned for 1975. Rural housing constitutes about 40 percent of the total housing stock in the USSR. It has been estimated that including this would decrease the most recent figures by about half (Smith 1973, p. 416).

One area in which there has been a very impressive achievement is in the provision of gas to the population: "In 1960 there were 3,300,000 gas-equipped apartments in the [USSR], in 1965 there were 10,300,000, in 1970 the figure was 23,400,000, and in 1973 the total was 33,900,000" (Perevedentsev 1974, p. 4). Data from the Russian Republic indicate that the use of gas has been growing at an accelerating rate since the 1950s (Ts.S.U. RSFSR 1971, p. 393).

TABLE 3.7

Household Stocks of Selected Durables in the USSR, 1955, 1960, 1965, and 1970
(units per 1,000 persons)

Commodity	1955	1960	1965	1970
Sewing machines	31	107	144	161
Refrigerators	4	10	29	87
Washing machines	1	13	59	139
Radios	66	129	165	199
Televisions	4	22	68	143
Automobiles	2	3	n.a.	n.a.
Vacuum cleaners	1.5	8	18	31

n.a.: data not available
Source: Dodge 1966, p. 97; Ts.S.U. 1971, p. 562.

Household Appliances and Service Enterprises

The availability and quality of services and appliances is another factor influencing the time and effort that need be devoted to housework. Again, this was an area with relatively low priority and has thus been severely neglected during most of the Soviet period. In recent years, the production of household appliances has been increasing rapidly (see Table 3.7). One source shows that by the end of 1973, per every 100 families in the USSR, there were 67 television sets, 59 sewing machines, 49 refrigerators, and 60 washing machines. Furthermore, "the number of washing machines belonging to families would be far greater if so many modern self-service laundries, in which all the work is done by automatic machinery, had not appeared recently" (Perevedentsev 1974, p. 4).

It is difficult to believe these figures. If they are true, it would mean that remarkable progress has been made in a very short period. In a 1970 Soviet publication, it is reported that 21 percent of the families in the Soviet Union had washing machines and about 11 percent had refrigerators. Public dining establishments served on the average about 20 percent of the population. The laundries were handling 3 percent of the nation's needs, while everyday services in general reduced the amount of time spent on housework by only about 5 percent. This had been achieved only with a 17.6 percent growth in these services between 1966 and 1970 (Mikhailyuk 1970, pp. 129, 130, 138).

A 1964 study of workers' families in Leningrad showed that only 1.8 percent ate primarily at cafeterias. About 60 percent ate at a cafeteria only when they were at work; 95 percent ate primarily at home, manifesting their strong aversion to the quality of both the service and the food in the communal institutions. A more recent study of workers also conducted in Leningrad produced similar results: 3.3 percent of the women used the cafeteria and 13 percent used the laundry (Piminova 1970, p. 142; Danilova 1968, pp. 53-54).

Endless complaints about the poor services and bad quality of appliances can be found in the press.

> In 1965 the All Union Science Research Institute of Technical Aesthetics distributed a questionnaire among purchasers to tap their opinion about the quality of household appliances. The research showed that the people were very interested in useful appliances, but that the majority of them were not satisfied with the existing ones. Since then seven years have passed and yet not one of the suggestions of the purchasers have been reflected in the quality of appliances (Baskina 1972, p. 12).

Even so, there has been a very great increase in the use of service enterprises. Between 1960 and 1965, for example, the number of everyday service enterprises (repair shops, laundries, dry cleaning and dying shops, barbers, etc.) increased by only 66 percent while the volume of work completed grew by 197 percent (Ts. S. U. 1969a, p. 664). A large proportion of the workers in the service industry and food industry are low-paid and not very highly motivated older women. Long lines combined with the rudeness of the insufficient personnel create a rather exasperating situation. A Soviet commentator has remarked, "Lost time can be calculated in hours, but what units can be used to measure the shattered nerves and soured dispositions?" (Rubinov 1967).

The Discrepancy between Income and Need

The widespread lack of appliances, the deficiencies in communal services, and the inadequate housing probably create a more difficult situation for younger couples than for old persons. During the stage in the life cycle of the married couple when housework is likely to be at its peak, that is, when small children are present, many couples are in a particularly adverse material position to carry out the burdens of housework efficiently. In a recent survey of couples in Kiev marrying for the first time, 40 percent of the brides reported that the primary condition that would have to be met before they had their desired number of children was improved living conditions or their own apartment (Chuiko 1972, p. 9). The younger couples may not be able to afford appliances or find an apartment that is adequate for their needs. In a study of working women in Vilnyus, Lithuania, it was found that those aged 31 to 40 were about twice as likely to have a sewing machine, twice as likely to have a washing machine, and ten times more likely to have a refrigerator as were younger women (Andrushkyavichenye 1970, p. 418). In the study of 427 women in factories of Penza, Leningrad, and Moscow, the average number of household appliances was 1.45 among women 31 to 40 years old, while those aged 26 to 30 averaged only 1.03 (Slesarev and Yankova 1969, p. 429). Women aged 20 to 24, however, averaged 1.5 appliances. This might have been due to the fact that these women were still living in the home of their parents, though women over age 50 in the same sample averaged only 0.9 such appliances. Note also that there were only 23 women aged 20 to 24 in the sample, while there were about 7 times as many in each of the two older groups (Slesarev and Yankova 1969, p. 418).

It has been reported that time spent on housework in housing having the basic modern conveniences (running water, gas stoves, central heating, etc.) is 1.5 times less than the time expended in old housing (Mikhailyuk 1970, pp. 125-26). In the latter study cited above, it was found that only 30 percent of women under age 30 had housing with the basic modern conveniences. Seventy to 80 percent of the older women had such housing (Slesarev and Yankova 1969, p. 427):

> Thus, the analysis of actual data has revealed a truly fundamental contradiction which needs to be resolved by means of all the measures of social regulation. Young married women with small children recently beginning their working career are frequently unable to obtain a separate dwelling unit. A difficult period lies ahead for the family lacking their own home. This coincides with the not less difficult and complicated period of the female worker's adaptation to her profession and to her work group.

In a recent large survey of couples getting married in Kiev, half the respondents said that they would be living with their parents; this was largely out of financial necessity (Chuiko 1972, p. 13).[5]

Values, Sexism, and Services

To some degree, the spread of modern appliances and the use of service enterprises has been impeded by the values held by some women. Of course, compared to other factors affecting availability and quality of services, this is probably of only limited significance. However, it is very revealing of the way women view their domestic role and how this may be changing in the younger generation.

A study of 427 women factory workers in Leningrad, Penza, and Moscow showed that those with only an elementary education were far less likely to have household appliances than women who had more

TABLE 3.8

Appliances in the Households of Female Workers, by Educational Level (percent of total families)

Type of Appliance	Female's Educational Level	
	Elementary	Higher Than Elementary
Washing machine	0	13
Sewing machine	15	50
Vacuum machine	1	19
Refrigerator	4	34
Radio	14	62
Television	19	65

Source: Slesarev and Yankova 1966, p. 428.

schooling (see Table 3.8). Undoubtedly, a large part of this difference is attributable to the higher income earned by the latter. However, the researchers stressed that a difference in values is also of significance here. Women with an elementary education are likely to be older and, as is evidenced by the absence of televisions and radios, they are less exposed to modern ideas. Many of the unskilled workers with lower education do have sufficient income to afford modern appliances, but they object to their use:

> The old women consider the use of everyday machines superfluous, grounding this on the conviction that "the true housewife should rely on her own hands, on her skills; she must not dread tiring herself in her work for the family" (Slesarev and Yankova 1969, p. 429).

The same study showed that all the women placed great importance on the prestige they received from being good housekeepers. Many women gave the following kinds of responses in the interviews: "A good housekeeper always finds time, strength and the means to put the house in order"; "A good housekeeper does not need special help"; A good housekeeper is not too lazy to once more do the washing and clean up the apartment." Ten percent of the women refused to use the service shops on these grounds. Many more showed a strong preference for the "mechanization of everyday life," that is, the use of modern appliances in the home, as opposed to the "industrialization" of housework through the use of communal dining facilities and other service enterprises. Besides finding meals at home "tastier, cheaper and more convenient", they noted that "dinner gathers all the members of the family around the table"; "At dinner it is possible to talk over all the news of the day, to discuss current goings-on" (Slesarev and Yankova 1969, p. 429).

Younger women seem more inclined to favor the "industrialization" of everyday life. "Thet conceive of their prestige as a housekeeper as not connected to the traditional role of fulfilling all household tasks but rather as associated with the role of organizer of the home." They also advocate the equal division of the household tasks between husband and wife, but these women still do not see this equality as extending to some of the more recent functions such as "organizer" (Slesarev and Yankova 1969, p. 433).

The advocacy of an equal division of labor in the home and the extensive use of service enterprises may not be a sign of a change in the beliefs of contemporary Soviet women. It is possible that this may be a product of being in a specific stage in the life cycle when women are particularly burdened with housework and child care. If a women feels that her prestige is connected with fulfilling household tasks, then she appears to have a surplus of support for that prestige at this early stage. However, as the children grow older and she has fewer child-rearing tasks, she might be less inclined to reduce further this source of her prestige; that is, she may become more traditional in her attitudes with regard to the role of men in the house. Unfortunately, there is as yet a lack of data tracing life-cycle changes in the beliefs of women.

There is evidence that the fulfillment of domestic chores contributes to the positive self-image of both young and older women. In a recent article, Yankova (1972, p. 12) states that 92 percent of the female workers in a sample drawn from industrial enterprises in Moscow felt that their "production, social-political and family-everyday roles" were <u>equally important</u>. All these roles, she cautions, can foster and hinder the development of the personality. Thus, it is necessary to eliminate the purely mechanical and uncreative housework, but certain functions should remain: "For women it is necessary to maintain only those functions which in their essence are creative and, therefore, which shape the personality of women—the upbringing of children, the organization of leisure and such" (1972, p. 12).

The significance of these functions is well illustrated by a rather unusual study of 595 families of workers in Leningrad (Piminova 1971, pp. 44-45). Forty-three percent of the families acknowledged that a "head of the family" did exist. In 20 percent of these families, the wife was considered head of the family. The interesting point here is the distinction in the reasons why a male was considered head and why the wife was considered to be the head: "If the man is the head of the family the most decisive factor is his role as breadwinner, whereas for women the primary factor is her role as the organizer of the daily life of the family." A woman's "prestige" appears to be largely derived from her familial and not from her occupational role. (Since only 7 percent of the women in the sample were not employed and many of these were probably grandmothers, it can be assumed that the great majority of the wives who were heads of families were employed.)

It is no surprise that these conceptions of the distinct roles of males and females are learned very early in life. They clearly have a profound effect on the relative ease with which domestic and occupational roles can be combined:

> Little girls are given the preparation for doing housework, but boys frequently are freed from household responsibilities. In this way the young generation of men come to look upon housework as "women's work"; this strengthens the survivals of the past. . . . Unfortunately, it is necessary to note, this prejudice is not only not eliminated by the schools but is actually encouraged. Thus, household knowledge and skills are part of the study program. However, this instruction is given only to girls. . . .
>
> Neither the family nor the school raise the young generation of men to take on family responsibilities.[6] (Danilova 1968, p. 62).

After having argued against this early socialization, the female Soviet writer still contends that women, far more than men, have inherent qualities as well as "centuries of experience" which enable them to raise children (Danilova 1968, pp. 39-40). This belief seems very widespread. It has already been noted, for example, that there is a growing feeling that children should not be kept in nurseries away from their mothers (see "Child Care Facilities" above). Suggestions for relieving the burdens of women usually entail finding ways for women to combine the functions of being a mother to her child with employment outside the home, rather than having the husband take a more equal role in the upbringing of the child. Danilova (1968, p. 47) maintains that mothers should have longer paid vacation time to be able to care for sick children. B. Sukharevskii (1972, p. 10), the Deputy Chairman of the State Committee of the Soviet Ministry of the USSR on Questions of Work and Wages, argues that women should be allowed to work part time to care for their children. This would prevent them from losing their work skill level during long leaves of absence which they are presently forced to take. A female economist expresses succinctly the sexist belief that appears to be held by a great many: "It is high time we stopped regarding women as the same kind of labor force as men. Administrators should not forget that people are divided into men and women. Women have household chores to do in addition to their jobs" (quoted by Baskina 1968, p. 14).

Thus far, two contradictory forces were shown to be influencing female labor-force participation. On the one hand, the demand for labor was extreme and women were compelled to earn an income to support themselves or their families. On the other hand, the nature of domestic responsibilities did not change in such a way as to free more married women for labor force participation. This was resolved by women's assuming the "double burden" of housework and employment. Time-budget data in Chapter 5 will provide ample evidence of this. Before considering the actual trends in female participation in the nonagrarian labor force, it is important to consider two other factors which shaped the nature of supply and demand: urbanization and the actions and policies of the Soviet government.

THE IMPACT OF URBANIZATION

The forced collectivization of agriculture under Stalin began in 1929 and provided the "push" for a mass migration to the cities. The rapid development of industry during the same period created the "pull" through growing employment opportunities. If the pace of industrialization is not sufficiently rapid, the lack of employment opportunities in agriculture for the urban population may create a growing pool of unemployed workers. It is possible that increased efforts to foster industrialization may in part have been a consequence of this sort of urban condition; that is, supply may have stimulated changes in demand. This is suggested by the expressed concerns of the government with regard to female workers (see Chapter 4) and the magnitude of migration. In any case, if women were to adapt to changing employment opportunities, urbanization meant that they would have to enter the nonagrarian labor force.

Soviet sources indicate only an 8 percent growth in the urban population between 1913 and 1926 (see Table 3.9). The Civil War, famine, and disease had a particularly marked effect on the cities. "By 1920 or 1921, between one-third to one-half of the previously urban population had left the cities and retired to the countryside" (Ofer 1973, p. 144). Between 1926 and 1939 there was a dramatic change: the urban population far more than doubled. The proportion of the total population in urban areas increased from 18 to 34 percent. This massive population movement continued during subsequent decades as the size of the rural population finally began to show a substantial decline. The change between 1939 and 1959 in part reflects the altered boundaries of the RSFSR.

The magnitude of the population movements, especially between 1926 and 1939, cannot be fully appreciated without also considering the change in the distribution of the urban population. In 1926 about a third of the urban residents lived in cities with a population of 20,000 or less, while just under 40 percent were in cities exceeding 100,000. By 1939, only 22 percent lived in the small cities and more than half the urban population was located in cities of over 100,000 people. The movement into cities paralleled an increased concentration of the population in large cities—cities in which it was even less likely that substantial segments of the population could be supported

TABLE 3.9

Indexed Urban and Rural Population of the Russian Republic and Percent Urban, 1913, 1926, 1939, 1959, and 1970 (1913 = 100)

Year	Urban	Rural	Percent Urban
1913	100	100	17
1926[a]	108	104	18
1939[a]	239	99	34
1959[b]	393	75	52
1970[b]	517	66	62

[a]The population referred to is that within the territory of the Russian Republic before September 17, 1938.

[b]The population referred to is that within the territory of the Russian Republic at present. The shifts in territorial base have an inconsequential influence on the figures in the table.

Source: Based on figures in Ts. S. U. 1963, p. 11; Ts. S. U. 1972a, p. 7.

by agricultural employment. The number of Soviet Russian workers in agriculture declined from about 46 million in 1926, to 20 million in 1939, and to only 14 million by 1959 (Ts. S. U. 1963, pp. 39, 280, 290; 1972a, p. 77). These figures exclude the number of workers in forestry, unavailable for 1926, as well as those safely engaged in private agriculture. I am uncertain of the definition of agricultural workers used in the 1926 census, as collectivization did not seriously begin until October 1929. In September 1929 only 7.4 percent of the peasant households were collectivized (Lewin 1967, p. 514).

THE ACTIONS OF THE PARTY AND GOVERNMENT

The government and Party had an influence upon the supply of, and demand for, female labor (1) by directly recruiting women and promoting an ideology which advocated female labor-force participation; (2) by greatly expanding educational facilities; (3) through laws and and quotas affecting female employment; and (4) by shaping the process of industrial development.

Recruiting and the Work Ideology

Considerable direct action was carried out to get women involved in the political movement and the labor force. Massell (1968) has shown that in Soviet Central Asia in the first decade following the Revolution there was extensive and intense agitation among the women. Elsewhere, in order to persuade women to exercise the rights they had been granted by new legal codes of the Revolution, a special section of the party, Zhenotdel, was formed and "occupied itself mainly with the task of drawing women into broader public activities" (Geiger 1968, p. 57). Early efforts, however, were directed at women almost exclusively in urban areas: "Prior to the 1930s, peasant women, who made up four-fifths of the population, remained a largely neglected group." Collectivization apparently elicited the support of many peasant women, for, along with many other new rights and obligations, they had the prospect of keeping the wages they earned rather than having to turn them over to the family patriarch (Dodge 1966, p. 65). The government's actions at this time were probably accompanied by considerable efforts to indoctrinate the women or at least to expose them to the ideas of the Revolution (Dodge 1966, p. 66):

> The collective farm system was generally implemented by loyal party members from the cities, sent out by the central government for the purpose of forcible persuasion. Also, in the early days of collectivization, most farm officials were not of peasant origin and did not share the prejudices of the peasant class. Hence, it is probable that women did have a more equal opportunity for promotion and that the traditional subordination was resisted.

The movement to involve women in the "socialized" labor force had strong ideological justification. Assessing how much urban women accepted this ideology and to what degree this had an independent effect on their labor-force participation is quite difficult. However, compared to the motivation that arose from sheer financial necessity, this surely was of far less significance.

The close connection between the nature of an individual and his relation to the means of production is a key tenet of classical Marxism, and we find this strongly stated in Lenin's writings with regard to women. He recognized how demeaning and stulifying housework was and strongly advocated women's involvement in social production (Geiger 1968, p. 45):

> Lenin saw in the liberation of women, the weaker sex, a symbol of the general liberation, though he placed more

> stress on the psychological factor of participation in social production as a source of personality development, which would then serve to put women on equal footing with men.

This theme, the development of women's personality and equality with men, is closely associated with the belief that women must work to be good upbringers of their children. Thus, a female Soviet investigator who appears to be stating the accepted ideological stance argues that women who do not work will not be respected by their children and will not have sufficiently developed their own personalities to properly raise their children and teach the value of work (Danilova 1968, pp. 38-40). Similarly, another commentator argues that "in families in which women do not work, the youngsters are inculcated with a scornful attitude towards women and their work" (Labzin 1965, p. 102). Field and Flynn (1970, p. 270) have noted the widespread evidence of the work ideology:

> There is little doubt, from a perusal of the Soviet sources, that the woman who deliberately chooses to become a housewife and mother and to restrict her activities to husband, children and hearth is not considered a "complete" Soviet woman because she is not participating fully in the building of a new society and because her position and 'dependence' are too strongly reminiscent of the bourgeois housewife of a former stigmatized past.

In addition to these sex-specific ideological themes there also were more general appeals for citizens to enter the labor force as a patriotic duty. Women were certainly also influenced by this.

In his private interviews with East European women, Mazur found no support for the commonly held view that "the extensive utilization of female labor [is] a result of state intervention through newspaper exhortations, etc., as if the mass persuasion were the most important factor in women's decision-making concerning gainful employment" (1973, pp. 47, 49). Survey data regarding the degree to which women have internalized these work values may be subject to serious biases. In general, it is difficult to judge the representativeness of Soviet samples, but in this case we have the added problem of dealing with a subject of central ideological significance. The particular reaction of a Soviet citizen to a native interviewer or researcher cannot adequately be assessed.

Nevertheless, the bias found in self-reporting by subjects in the United States is surely not unlike that in the Soviet Union. In a study designed specifically to explore the problem, Phillips and Clancy concluded that

> people's assessment of the desirability of various characteristics strongly influence their reports of the presence

> or absence of such characteristics in themselves. Furthermore, by including measures of need for approval in our interviews, we have ascertained that this factor, too, affects people's reports on various questions. Finally, we have shown that including trait desirability as a "test factor" has the result of specifying both the direction and magnitude between people's sexual status and their responses to various measures (1972, p. 938).

(Questions dealt with general happiness, religiosity, number of friends, marital happiness, and prejudice).

It is also very difficult to judge the extent to which women's attitudes are a product of the work experience itself. The evidence in Chapter 2 indicates no need for women to change their value system to participate in the labor force. Work outside the home may have assumed a new meaning as a result of the ideology promulgated by the Party and conditions in which the family and other institutions were disrupted and changing. Of especial importance was the deficit of males. Compared to tsarist times, women may have been geographically further separated from their families as well. Labor-force participation was no longer simply a way to fulfill one's traditional obligations, but now represented a means of obtaining greater respect, of contributing to the welfare of the nation, and even of being a more capable mother. (However, in Chapter 7 I will argue that there appear to be definite limitations to the change in the meaning of work. It may have inspired women's labor-force participation, but may not have symbolized independence and equality with men—a basis for insisting that men devote equal time to domestic chores.) Employment may have made women more receptive to the ideology. For those already doing work outside the home, the ideology may have been a catalyst in getting them to adapt to the changing labor market and do work to which they were not accustomed (cf. Ulam 1960, Chapter 3).

The influence of these new meanings and also of the continuing low regard for housework is illustrated by the following comments of a Soviet woman (Libedinskaya 1967, p. 12):

> During the war, in my student years, I had to dig ditches at Moscow's defense lines; gather firewood; serve at a hospital, work at a radio center for dispatching transport; climb power transmission line poles; and trudge along railroad tracks for many kilometers in freezing weather. But each of these jobs, and some were very hard, had meaning and purpose; this is probably why I remember them now without horror. But the kitchen sink endlessly filling with sticky cups and greasy plates makes my flesh crawl.

She also notes that heavy bags of groceries can often exceed weight limitations on women's work in industry and, perhaps more importantly, "in production . . . a woman retires at the age of fifty-five, while a housewife has no pension." The most convincing propaganda for many may have been the paycheck:

> Women who have devoted themselves entirely to housework in families where fathers can afford everything needed often complain that their husbands reproach them for their inability to save money. Any woman who has any self-respect at all would not only dig ditches but do the dirtiest work, if only to avoid hearing humiliating reproaches and to have the right to spend the money she has earned as she sees fit.
>
> How many wives would no longer have to put up with the perpetual female humiliations if each were materially independent and unafraid of the possibility of being left alone and losing benefits of her husband's position! (Libedinskaya 1967, p. 12).

Again, it is necessary to stress the problems with assessing the extent to which women have accepted these beliefs or derived real satisfaction from work outside the home. Field and Flynn (1970, pp. 272-74), though, present evidence that there are types of women that they classify as "comrade reluctant" and "comrade parasitic" who, to varying degrees, reject the importance of participating in the labor force.

One further measure of the effect of the ideology is the extent to which men's views reflect the stress on female employment. The limited data available on this subject indicate that they may be far more inclined to have a wife waiting at home to serve them. For example, a study of female workers in Leningrad showed that 73 percent of the sample of women felt that, as opposed to expressing complete approval, their husbands had "reconciled themselves" to their spouses' outside employment as being a necessity (Kharchev and Golod 1969, p. 442). *Literaturnaya gazeta* (July 1, 1970, p. 11) reports that, in a survey of 1,000 husbands, 61 percent expressed this feeling about their wives' employment. Kuznetsova (1967) found that, in the letters she received in response to an article published earlier, there was a definite difference in the emphasis men and women put on the relative importance of housework and work in social production. Men conceived of the former as the key role of women, and one too often neglected. In an apparently typical response sent to *Literaturnaya gazeta*, a husband from Moscow wrote the following:

> A woman earns almost as much as a man. She considers herself independent and equal. The man's prestige in the family has been thoroughly shaken and is determined

> only by his prestige on the job. The woman has already stopped thinking of how to surprise her husband with a tasty dinner, and more often she surprises him by cooking nothing at all (p. 7).

The females do not fail to recognize the anxiety of the men:

> Here is what Yadrentseva, a reader from Odessa, has to say: "Through the force of circumstances, our men are losing prestige in the eyes of women. In spite of the men themselves, whether they like it or not, they are becoming less respected." A note of loss concerning the former "masculine ideal" could be heard in a great many letters.
>
> I. Selvinsky (Literaturnaya gazeta, No. 15, 1967), told us brilliantly of the loss of the feminine ideal. As we see, the process is double-edged. This too is a break with the traditions that gave the male a halo of authority, power and strength and garbed women in flounces of lovely, submissive weakness (p. 8).

Though social class is surely an important variable (cf. Komarovsky 1967), there is, unfortunately, no information on the background of the men.

Education

An industrializing economy demands a skilled labor force. The schools' providing this may have been of even greater importance than their inculcating a particular ideology. Ofer argues that

> the Soviet government has throughout clearly recognized the economic importance of investment in human capital. As a socialist central government, it has been in a position to evaluate better and earlier than other governments the considerable external effects—external to individual users—or "public good" elements of education and health services and the potential contribution of investment in them toward the main goal—the drive for faster economic growth (1973, p. 151).

Treiman (1970) and Matras (1975) have noted that, as is the case of urbanization, the increase in supply can influence demand. A larger pool of individuals with specialized training will increase the demand for positions in which they can exercise their skill and receive the status and monetary compensation to which they had been aspiring.

However, the very increase in supply can lead to a decrease in the price offered for such labor:

> This is particularly true because of the reluctance of educated persons in newly industrializing countries to accept jobs which are not commensurate with their level of training. The falling price of white collar labor should, all else equal, provide an incentive for employers to expand the number of such positions. Also, the prospect of large numbers of unemployed educated persons may induce governments to expand the number of positions in the public bureaucracy as a way of gaining the support of such individuals and of reducing the potential for social unrest which is inherent in the existence of a discontented, educated population (Treiman 1970, p. 223).

The structure of the labor force is also influenced by the demand for manual labor which proceeds from this same population transformation:

> As the educational level of the labor force increases, the supply of persons willing to do tedious and routine work tends to decrease. . . . The reduction in the supply of manual labor should force wages up. Or, to find individuals willing to work for low wages, the employer must accept inferior personnel who may not be able to perform even routine tasks competently. Both alternatives provide incentives to reduce dependence upon labor by automating production as much as possible (Treiman 1970, p. 223).

Such market mechanisms must surely have had a profound effect on the Soviet economy, despite the political controls over the labor force.

Tables 3.10 and 3.11 show the dramatic changes in educational attainment.[7] Note the extremely low level of literacy of females as compared to males in 1897 and even 1926. This contrasts markedly with 1959 and 1970, when the proportion of the employed female population with a secondary education had exceeded that of the males; males had only a slight edge with regard to higher education. As can be seen in Table 3.11, between 1939 and 1970 there was an almost six fold increase in the proportion of the employed female population with at least some secondary education.

The tremendous investment in education by the government made female labor very much in demand. The growing pool of women with higher education may also have created pressure to provide appropriate employment. Thus, as will be shown in the next chapter, in recent decades the number of women in professional and semiprofessional occupations grew at a very rapid rate.

TABLE 3.10

Percentage Literate in the Russian Republic, by Sex, 1897[a], 1926, 1939, 1959, and 1970

	Total Population	Males	Females
1897	29.6	44.4	15.4
1926	60.9	77.1	46.4
1939	89.7	96.0	83.9
1959	98.5	99.3	97.7
1970	99.7	99.7	99.6

[a]Area comparable to that of the Russian Republic.
Sources: Ts. S. U. 1963, p. 143; Ts. S. U. RSFSR 1971, p. 24.

Quotas and Legal Restrictions

Demand for women was "artificially" increased in the early 1930s by the setting of minimum quotas for the employment of women (see Chapter 4). The growing need for labor soon made these measures unnecessary, but they may have been an important initial stimulant for hiring women and changing employers' beliefs regarding the suitability of females for certain work. However, legislation enacted soon after the Revolution to protect women from injurious occupations restricted their early employment. These laws were violated especially prior to World War II, though there is evidence that the restrictions did make managers reluctant to hire women during at least the 1920s. Both the strong ideological commitment to employing women in industry and the government's concern that restricted work of women may have forced many into prostitution led to the issuance in 1925 of instructions to relax restrictions on the use of women in night work and of pregnant women on day shifts. At this time, however, there were no formal changes in the law. Such changes did occur just prior to World War II, when the list of occupations forbidden to women was reduced. After the war, large numbers of women continued to engage in heavy labor "for a decade or more," particularly in coal mining and construction (Dodge 1966, Chapter 4; Carr 1970, pp. 392-94). There is evidence that women at present continue to do this type of work.

A Soviet source reports that in 1957 there were more than 150,000 women working underground. The same source also reveals that regulations concerning the weight women are allowed to lift are frequently violated (Mikhailyuk 1970, pp. 83. 95). Further evidence that women are engaged in extremely heavy labor comes from the Soviet weekly *Literaturnaya gazeta* (Shim 1967, p. 12):

TABLE 3.11

Educational Achievement of Employed Persons in the RSFSR, by Sex, 1939, 1959, and 1970 (per 1,000 persons)

	Higher Education		Secondary, Complete and Incomplete	
	Males	Females	Males	Females
1939	16	10	119	99
1959	36	35	392	417
1970	68	65	578	602

Source: Ts.S.U. RSFSR, 1971, p. 25.

> Communication lines are being laid on a noisy Leningrad street. In the trench are two dozen women's backs, bent over. Women's hands in canvas gloves are tugging at an unyielding cable in sticky wrapping. . . .
>
> There is no need to multiply such present-day pictures, for they are familiar to anyone who has seen a construction site, a peak bank, or a highway under repair. . . .

The author later argues (1967, p. 13):

> It is necessary for women to be able to insist on their legal rights and to implement them, or else wishes will remain wishes and we shall start wondering and complaining all over again about how long women will haul rocks around while the muscular bartender pours out beer at his counter.

Legislation regarding the use of female labor that had been developed in the late 1930s changed little up until 1956. After that date, "legislation in the rights field continued to repeat, reinforce, and slightly expand earlier provisions for pregnant and nursing mothers." However, a significant decree was issued by the Presidium of the USSR Supreme Soviet on May 19, 1949. It "was designed to protect the working mother's right to support herself and her child and . . . forbade managers to refuse pregnant and nursing mothers employment on pain of punishment . . . (Dodge 1966, pp. 68, 70). Dodge (1966, p. 75) contends that protective legislation has been more strictly enforced in recent times, though women displaced by such legislation have "for the most part, been absorbed elsewhere in the economy with no loss of income."

The Soviet Strategy of Economic Growth

Soviet industrial development involved only a limited expansion of the service sector, a low level of private consumption, and very high labor-force participation rates for the entire population. It has already been suggested that lateness of development makes for severe problems of accumulating capital—problems that often cannot be resolved without coercion and reduced consumption levels (see Chapter 1).

The Soviet development pattern can thus be explained in part by the timing of industrialization. Historical conditions specific to the Soviet Union also were of profound significance. The heavy drain of resources for military purposes and some of the difficulties in procuring foreign trade and capital are attributable to hostile international relations. And, finally, the cultural prerequisites for utilizing female labor were inherited from tsarist times, as was the extreme poverty that necessitated women's financial contributions to the peasant household.

However, Soviet development was also a product of a strategy of economic growth to some degree independent of these preceding factors. Gur Ofer (1973), using comparative data, shows that the Soviet service sector is far smaller than one would expect given the level of economic development of the USSR. He argues that this would have been true even if historical circumstances had not produced an extreme pressure on resources, for

> the authorities would tend to devote the resources released to increasing the growth rate and they would keep the allocation between investment and consumption virtually unchanged. . . .
>
> What is specific to the socialist countries is that they, more than any other countries, are willing and able to achieve growth for growth's sake—to tolerate a longer waiting period between investment and the consumption of its fruits, to invest in producers goods designed to produce more producers goods (1973, p. 159).

By simultaneously participating in the labor force and providing necessary domestic services, women contributed doubly to the capital formation of the nation. Ofer is inclined to see this as, in large part, a product of deliberate policy which led to a very

> low proportion of current production going to private consumption. The effects of this allocation policy are considerable pressure on the population to work (the income effect) and a lower demand for services not supplied by the government, since disposable income per capita is low and services are assumed to have positive income

> elasticities. This policy also reduces the proportion of GNP consisting of goods sold to households, thus reducing the need for commercial services at both the wholesale and retail levels (1973, p. 151).

The more recent rise in the standard of living—a product of a change in the system—makes it necessary to stimulate female labor-force participation through the provision of household services "to compensate for the declining inducement of the need for income to send women to work" (1973, p. 165).*

Given the unique events which shaped Soviet history, I believe that it is very difficult to judge the influence that a different strategy of economic growth might have had. Also, Ofer's assumptions about the goals and criteria for decision making by the Soviet leadership are debatable. In this context, I wish to merely raise these issues; their resolution is clearly beyond the scope of this book.

---

*There is some evidence that the higher the income and education of a woman the more she will desire to work. Soviet writers attribute this to the new and more expensive tastes that are acquired by the women and their families. It is certainly also attributable to the fact that women receiving higher wages and having a better education are more likely to have desirable jobs. To support their argument Soviet writers also point to data indicating that the higher the education of nonworking women the more likely they will desire to be employed (Litvyakov 1969, p. 12; Mikhailyuk 1970, p. 25). But, again, these women obviously have better job prospects (Slesarev and Yankova 1969, p. 412).

Mazur's (1973) finding that there is a strong negative relationship between the percent of the population in the urban part of an administrative region and the percentage of the female labor force working in social production does not square well with the rising-needs argument. Mazur explains his findings by an indifference curve:

> . . . as the degree of urbanization increases, so does the desire by the married women for work outside the home, but only to a certain point. As the rate of increase slows down and eventually levels off at the point of a very high degree of urbanization, the motivation to be gainfully employed to satisfy the need for additional good and services tends to decline (p. 49).

However, evidence shows that there is far higher female employment in large cities than in small cities (Mikhailyuk 1970, p. 344; Ivanchenko 1965, p. 174). This suggests that Mazur's (1973) work may contain an ecological fallacy. On the other hand, it was found that among those in Krasnoyarsk Krai and Novosibirsk Oblast having an

CONCLUSION

A Soviet investigator has criticized Dodge (1966) for implying that financial need alone motivated women to work. He cites a Moldavian study showing that 70 percent of the women would continue to work even if their income were no longer needed (Mikhailyuk 1970, p. 24). A study of female workers in the large cities showed that 85 percent of the women preferred to continue working, even if they could receive the same income by staying at home (Slesarev and Yankova 1969, p. 425):

> The work of women plays an important role in the growth of their personalities, fosters the growth of their prestige in social life . . . and in the family, and is an important step towards her achievement of actual equality with men. This, incidentally, is understood and favorably viewed by the female workers themselves.

The researchers report that they received responses such as the following from the women: "Women workers have a broader mental outlook than those not working"; "Women having skills absolutely should work"; "Working women command more respect" (1969, p. 425).

In spite of this, throughout most of the Soviet period, financial need certainly appears to have been the primary factor motivating women to work outside the home. In this respect, there was great continuity with the peasant household of prerevolutionary Russia. In the Soviet period, there was a change in the nature and quantity of labor demanded as well as a substantial increase in the level of skill and ability of female workers. The outcome was an inordinate growth in the number of women in the nonagrarian labor force.

Though the lack of data on the family status of the employed population makes it difficult to determine the change over time in the domestic burdens of female workers, there is little evidence that, until the last few decades, the change in such responsibilities had any substantial influence on the supply of women seeking employment. Housework does not appear to have been eased by changes in family composition, the division of labor within the family, or the provision of appliances, service enterprises, housing, etc.

---

incomplete higher or secondary specialized education the percentage occupied solely in the private subsidiary economy (growing produce and raising livestock on a private plot of land) and in housework was 5.9 in large cities and only 2.7 in small cities (Mikhailyuk 1970, p. 40).

In sum, the major factor that might have been expected to increase the supply of female labor—namely, the transformation of women's traditional role in the household and the family—was not found to be present. Instead, what did transpire to a large extent was an interaction whereby the demand-increasing factors (the multiple effects of the shortage of males, the rapid expansion of industry, etc.) also increased the supply of female labor. In addition, the changes in supply resulting from urbanization and women's rising educational attainment may have fostered and shaped the demand for female labor.

NOTES

1. It is important to emphasize that the data for the USSR are very much representative of the Russian Republic. This is apparent from a comparison of sex ratios, birth rates, etc., which show a marked similarity, although the population losses seem to have been more severe in the latter at least during the Second World War. The decline in the birth rate was also somewhat more extreme in the Russian Republic. This was due to the high rates sustained in the Central Asian Republics.

In several other instances in this and the following chapter, I have been forced to rely on figures from the Soviet Union as a whole in the absence of appropriate material for the Russian Republic. Though this is obviously imprecise, the examination of a very wide range of data for the Russian Republic and the USSR leads me to feel confident that this does not introduce any serious distortions.

2. The published results of the 1939, 1959, and 1970 censuses do not show employment by marital status. The 1926 census contains data of this sort which have yet to be analyzed.

3. In general Geiger (1968) views the changes promulgated by the government as being rather negative (this is discussed at greater length below). This contrasts with, for example, Carr's (1970, pp. 41-42) interpretation, which is somewhat more sympathetic: "The Revolutionary attitude to the family can be understood only as a reaction to pre-revolutionary conditions; and the achievement of the revolution in inculcating acceptance of the equality of the sexes and in promoting a higher regard for women was real and indubitable."

Carr does recognize, however, as is illustrated by the continuation of this passage, that there was considerable disruption in social relations: "Apart, however, from these conscious strivings to remove the abuses of the old order, the sequence of war, revolution and civil war had produced many of the same unpremeditated and disintegrating effects on family and sex relations as on other aspects of social life" (p. 42).

4. It should be noted that between 1965 and 1970 the number of of children aged three to six in the Soviet Union decreased by 15.5 percent (U. S. Department of Commerce 1969, p. 14).

5. Questionnaires were given to 10,000 couples marrying for the first time. Twenty percent were returned and considered sufficiently complete to be used in the study (Chuiko 1972).

6. Medlin (1960, pp. 131, 143) noted that in 1960 curriculum changes in the schools of the Soviet Union increased the training girls received in domestic science, whereas boys were to be spending more time on such activities as woodworking. Furthermore, in an effort to coordinate the activities of the schools and industrial and agricultural enterprises in the expanded polytechnical program, girls were to be given the opportunity to get their production training in restaurants and accounting houses.

7. During the nineteenth and early twentieth centuries women had been making substantial progress in entering the tsarist school system. By 1900 girls constituted 25 percent of the enrollment in secondary schools. This figure reached 55 percent by 1914. Since 1870 women have been admitted to Russian universities, and by 1916 they accounted for almost a quarter of the 125,000 students in higher education. Unlike female workers during these years, university women were extremely active politically, and both in 1886 and 1910 repressive measures were instituted against them to combat their agitation (Dodge 1966, pp. 101-2).

CHAPTER

4

WOMEN IN THE NONAGRARIAN LABOR FORCE, 1917 TO THE PRESENT

After the discussion in the previous chapter, the reader should not be surprised by the figures in Table 4.1. There has been a very great change in the occupational structure of the female labor force, but the rate of participation has remained at a very high level. This is true even in the age groups in which women are bearing children. Since 1926, however, there have been substantial reductions in the school-age groups and among the elderly.

In the United States, 23.3 percent of the women aged 14 and older were in the labor force in 1920. The figure had reached 34.5 percent by 1960 and 42.6 percent by 1970. However, the peak employment of women prior to 1940 was among those aged 20 to 24, prior to childbearing and marriage for most women. By 1960 peak employment had clearly shifted to the period <u>after</u> childrearing: 47.4 percent of the women aged 45 to 49 were in the labor force as compared to 35.3 percent in the age group 25 to 34. This pattern has begun to change in more recent years: "In early 1974, some 13.5 million mothers of children under age 18 were either working or looking for work, 12 percent more than in 1970 and 69 percent more than in 1960" (Oppenheimer 1970, pp. 3-8; Nye and Berardo 1973, p. 271; Waldman 1975, p. 64). It is important, however, to note that unlike their American counterparts, Soviet women have been engaged almost exclusively in full-time employment.

In the USSR between 1959 and 1970 the labor force participation of women aged 14-19 has declined sharply, reflecting the continued increase in school attendance. However, with the exception, perhaps, of the most elderly, in all other groups rates have clearly risen to levels surpassing even those of 1926. It has been suggested that "current rates of participation are close to the demographic maximum and will remain almost constant through the seventies" (Lapidus 1975, p. 182).

TABLE 4.1

Percentage of the Population Participating in the Labor Force[a], by Sex and Age, in the USSR in 1926 and 1959, and in the RSFSR in 1959

	Males			Females			
	1926[b]	1959[b]	1959[c]	1926[b]	1959[b]	1959[c]	1970[b]
10 to 14	58	—	—	53	—	—	7[d]
15 to 19	88	63	64	80	63	62	21[e]
20 to 24	98	88	89	93	81	83	88
25 to 29	99	94	94	75	80	81	
30 to 34	99	95	95	75	78	79	86
35 to 39	99	97	96	77	77	78	
40 to 44	99	94	94	77	76	76	83
45 to 49	99	92	91	77	75	73	
50 to 54	98	90	86	72	69	68	75
55 to 59	97	82	78	68	55	47	53
60 to 64	92	79	67	55	48	39	37
65 to 69	84	54	45	47	35	30	
All ages	64	56	56	52	49	43	n. a.

[a]n. a.: data not available.
[b]USSR
[c]RSFSR
[d]Age group 14-15.
[e]Age group 16-19.

<u>Source:</u> Dodge 1966, pp. 35, 37, 262; Lapidus 1975, p. 182.

THE CHANGE IN LABOR FORCE PARTICIPATION

Opportunities for female employment have not been uniform throughout the Soviet period despite these continually high rates.[1] In the early decades following the Revolution women were to face particularly severe difficulties. With the depressed economy of the 1920s they were the first to suffer. The evolution of the labor force in construction illustrates quite well both the change and the problems experienced by women.

Construction had been an exclusively male domain prior to the Revolution (see Table 2. 2). The urban census of 1923 showed that in European Russia women had made their entrance into the occupation—0. 55 percent of the workers were females. By 1926 this figure rose to 1. 55 percent, although women constituted 6. 4 percent of the 22, 536 unemployed construction workers. Eighteen out of every 100 male construction workers were unemployed, while this was true of 82 out of every 100 female construction workers (Gol'tsman 1961, pp. 168-69, 171-72).

Dodge notes that efforts to increase the employment of women during the 1920s were

> motivated by the desire to relieve unemployment and to secure economic independence of women rather than to mobilize unused manpower reserves because of a labor shortage. The authors of the First Five-Year Plan were not moved by the pressure of labor shortages to plan a substantial increase in the proportion of unemployed women, but they were concerned that in the absence of countermeasures the rapid expansion of heavy industry, in which the proportion of women was relatively low, would lower the proportion of women employed in the economy as a whole (1966, p. 165).

However, by 1930 the labor shortage actually threatened the fulfillment of the plan, and efforts to effect an increase in the utilization of female labor were fully justified on economic grounds alone. The increase was planned for all areas of production as well as construction, trade, and education.

In the construction industry the efforts of the government were particularly evident during the First Five-Year Plan. In the first four years of the plan almost 340, 000 women entered the industry. By 1932 women constituted 12. 8 percent of the construction workers. A labor union census taken later in the year showed that outside the Central Asian Republics women constituted 15. 9 percent of the industrial and residential construction workers and 17. 3 percent of those in railroad construction (Gol'tsman 1961, pp. 174-75).

The percentage of women in the construction industry varied considerably from one region to another. The smallest percentage of females could be found in the Moscow and Leningrad Oblasts; the highest percentage was in the Urals, Western Siberia, and the lower and middle Volga regions. This was, apparently, attributable to both the recency of the industry in the region and the demand for labor. Moscow and Leningrad had historically attracted both migrant and permanent construction workers. The eastern regions were experiencing rapid growth in previously undeveloped areas. The construction of large-scale industry brought about an acute need for labor, and it was largely young people that responded to this demand; the percentage of females among them was sizable. It appears likely that new labor practices such as the hiring of women may more easily have been instituted in areas where industry had recently expanded as opposed to areas with deeply entrenched traditions of hiring only males. See the discussion of backwardness as an asset in Chapter 1.

A census conducted by the construction labor union on October 1, 1930 showed that women constituted 10.9 percent of the membership. However, among newly entering members in the second half of 1930, 31.9 percent were women. The women were on the average 4.5 years younger than the men. This rapid increase in the entrance of young workers was also evident in many other industries. Among ferrous metalworkers, for example, 59.9 percent of the men and 78.2 percent of the women were under 30. The figures among electrotechnical workers were, respectively, 64.9 percent and 75.2 percent (Gol'tsman 1961, p. 175-77).

In the construction industry there was evidence that women compared unfavorably to men in the average time they were continuously working at their jobs (the "stage of work") and in their level of work skills. Even among those workers who were the same age, the skill level of the men was higher than that of the women. This was not due to differences in qualifications alone. Gol'tsman (1961, pp. 174-75) states in no uncertain terms that employers showed a prejudice against women and underrated their ability.

Thus, at a very early stage, the combined effect of the lower age of women, their lesser work stage and skill relative to those of men, and employers' discrimination led to the inferior status of women on the job. There is no reason to believe that this situation was unique to the construction industry. This initial pattern may well have reinforced prejudices regarding the capabilities of women—prejudices that have yet to be eradicated.

Though the highest proportion of females could be found among construction workers doing mechanized work, the work in general still required considerable physical exertion (Gol'tsman 1961, p. 178). The definition of "women's work" may not have changed very greatly, although the setting of that work did.

TABLE 4.2

Percent Female and the Frequency Distribution of Women in Branches of the Economy of the USSR, 1929, 1933, and 1940

	Percent Female			Frequency Distribution		
	1929	1933	1940	1929	1933	1940
Industry	28	31	41	.36	.36	.38
Construction	7	16	23	.02	.04	.03
State farms and subsidiary agricultural enterprises	28	26	34	.13	.09	.05
MTS[a] and RTS[b]	—	7	11	—	.00	.00
Transportation	9	14	21	.04	.04	.06
Communication	28	38	48	.01	.01	.02
Trade, public dining, procurement, material-technical supply	19	41	44	.04	.13	.12
Public health	65	71	76	.09	.07	.10
Education, science and scientific services	54	56	58	.14	.13	.15
Government and social institutions, credit, and insturance	19	29	35	.08	.07	.06
Other branches[c]	31	14	18	.09	.04	.04
In the national economy	27	30	38	1.00	1.00	1.01

[a]Machine and tractor service stations.

[b]Tractor service stations.

[c]Residual (total female employment minus reported or estimated employment in the sub-branches of the national economy in each column).

Source: Dodge 1966, pp. 178-79.

The entrance of women into the industry was symbolic of the profound changes that were taking place in the economy as a whole (see Table 4. 2). Despite the fact that the percentage of women rose substantially among the workers in fields like industry and construction, note that even in this early period it is evident that the proportion of the female labor force in the tertiary sector, where women in many other industrialized nations are commonly concentrated (Sullerot 1971), was, in general, rising most rapidly. This was particularly true of trade and public dining.

The rapid economic development that began in the late 1920s expanded occupational opportunities as extensively as the previous decline had been depriving women of such openings. As already noted, the designers of the First Five-Year Plan were concerned with the lack of demand for female labor. However, the minimum quotas for females in vocational schools, training classes, and in certain professions and trades had become unnecessary by the end of the 1930s; it was clear that the demand for female labor no longer needed to be bolstered by the state. In the USSR as a whole, women constituted 82 percent of the 4, 047, 000 workers who entered the labor force between 1932 and 1937:

> The largest gains were made in industries in which few women workers had been employed. Nevertheless, although the number of female workers and employees increased threefold between 1927 and 1937, the overall increase in workers and employees was so great that the percentage of women increased only from 27. 0 to 39. 3 percent (Dodge 1966, p. 176).

As was the case during the First World War, during World War II women entered nonagrarian occupations in especially large numbers. Between 1941 and 1950 they constituted 92 percent of the workers and employees entering the labor force (Litvyakov 1969, p. 111).[2] By 1945 women constituted 55 percent of the workers and employees in the Soviet Union. There is evidence of a decline in the figure following the war. Data from the Russian Republic show that this trend was reversed in recent years and the percentage female rose from 50 to 53 between 1960 and 1971 (Dodge 1966, pp. 178-79; Ts. S. U. RSFSR 1972, p. 317).

As a concomitant of industrialization the proportion of the labor force in agriculture contracts (Treiman 1970). In Soviet Russia between 1939 and 1959 the proportion of all female workers engaged in private and socialized agriculture labor declined from . 64 to . 40; the decline for males was smaller but still substantial: from . 38 to . 30 (Ts. S. U. 1963, pp. 156-58, 176-80). (Beginning with 1939 it is possible to utilize census data to measure trends in employment and to examine data pertaining specifically to the RSFSR as opposed to the broader geographic unit, the USSR. However, as I have already stressed, the developments in the latter are very comparable to those in the former.

Elsewhere, in the absence of data on the Russian Republic, it will again be necessary to rely upon those for the Soviet Union.)

The 1939, 1959, and 1970 censuses provide detailed data on the structure of the labor force by sex. (The very detailed data in the 1926 census will require considerable analysis before they can be compared to the material from the other censuses. There are no published data on any other census taken between 1939 and 1959.) I have divided the occupations into the two major categories utilized in the Soviet census: (1) nonprofessional or manual occupations. (In the census this includes workers in agriculture. I have excluded such workers; they are treated separately in Chapter 6.) (2) Professional and semiprofessional occupations—those "requiring primarily mental exertion (*zanyatye preimushchestvenno umstvennyn trudom*)." The trends in these areas differed considerably.

As can be seen from Table 4.3, women constituted a third of all nonprofessional workers in 1939 and were well represented in all occupations.[3] Clearly, however, they were overrepresented in those fields in which there were traditionally large numbers of women. That the crisis of the Second World War did not have shortlived effects is evident from the 1959 figures. The percentage of women among the workers increased by seven points, and this was well distributed (this is analyzed in greater detail below). Between 1939 and 1959 the number of nonprofessional workers had grown by 7.9 million; women accounted for 64 percent of this increase.

Far more dramatic changes occurred in the professional and semiprofessional occupations (see Table 4.4). Whereas the percentage of women among the workers in the total labor force increased by five points (from 49.1 to 54.0) between 1939 and 1959, among this group of workers the increase was *four times as great*. The number of women in these occupations increased by over 3.5 million, but the number of males actually *declined* by 300,000. By 1959 women constituted the majority of professional and semiprofessional personnel.

Thus, overall, as the tertiary sector continued to expand, the difference between the male and female labor-force participation increased. A growing proportion of the males were in nonprofessional occupations, while the female labor force was far more rapidly shifting into the professional and semiprofessional occupations.

In the period since at least 1959, there has been an improvement in services, somewhat better housing, and increased production of consumer goods (see Chapter 3). Besides, perhaps, making it somewhat easier for women to enter the labor force, the growth of the service scetor and light industry also provided employment opportunities for women who had only limited skills and found other types of work too physically demanding. These also were kinds of occupations which may specifically have been deemed "women's work," thus making the demand for labor sex-specific.[4] If the jobs were close to their homes, this also may have made it easier for the women previously engaged

TABLE 4.3

The Nonprofessional Labor Force of the RSFSR, by Occupation and Sex, 1939 and 1959

	1939				1959			
	Percent	Frequency Distribution			Percent	Frequency Distribution		
Occupation	Female	Female	Male	Difference	Female	Female	Male	Difference
Employed at power installations and working with hoisting-transport machines	22.5	.0117	.0206	.0089	33.8	.0319	.0448	.0129
Metallurgical and metalworkers	13.9	.0519	.1876	.1285	17.9	.0942	.3101	.2159
Chemical workers	48.7	.0109	.0059	.0050	61.0	.0142	.0065	.0077
Employed in production of construction materials, glass and chinaware	44.9	.0099	.0062	.0037	59.3	.0161	.0080	.0081
Woodworkers	18.1	.0177	.0408	.0231	21.4	.0159	.0420	.0261
Paper workers	57.1	.0014	.0005	.0090	66.4	.0014	.0005	.0009
Printing workers	59.6	.0096	.0033	.0063	73.7	.0085	.0022	.0063
Textile workers	76.4	.0945	.0149	.0796	85.4	.0568	.0070	.0498
Garment workers	77.1	.0526	.0080	.0446	92.6	.0596	.0034	.0562
Leather workers	32.4	.0068	.0073	.0005	52.8	.0042	.0027	.0015
Shoe workers	21.2	.0096	.0182	.0086	46.3	.0078	.0065	.0013
Food workers	42.9	.0267	.0181	.0086	71.9	.0282	.0079	.0203
Construction workers	5.2	.0123	.1144	.1021	19.9	.0512	.1481	.0929
Fishing and fishbreeding workers	19.1	.0035	.0076	.0041	15.6	.0010	.0039	.0029
Railroad workers	21.4	.0189	.0353	.0164	35.1	.0313	.0416	.0103
Water transport workers	8.5	.0015	.0081	.0066	18.2	.0027	.0088	.0061
Automotive transport and urban electrical transport workers	9.7	.0071	.0339	.0268	6.5	.0105	.1091	.0986
Postal workers, letter carriers	49.9	.0842	.0178	.0664	80.5	.0907	.0064	.0843
Public dining workers[a]	70.7	.0087	.0045	.0042	91.0	.0098	.0017	.0081
Communal and household service personnel	52.7	.2306	.1056	.1250	72.3	.1853	.0511	.1342
Orderlies, nurses, nursemaids	96.1	.0391	.0080	.0383	97.7	.0435	.0007	.0428
Other nonprofessional workers[b]	29.9	.2837	.3406	.0569	47.4	.2352	.1870	.0428
Totals	33.8	1.0000	1.0000	.7782	41.8	1.0000	1.0000	.9394

[a]This category has been changed to conform with the 1970 reclassification of some subcategories.

[b]This is a residual category.

Source: Based on figures in Ts.S.U. 1963, pp. 228-43, 252-54, 278-81, 285-88.

TABLE 4.4

The Professional and Semiprofessional Labor Force of the RSFSR, by Occupation and Sex, 1939 and 1959

	1939				1959			
	Percent	Frequency Distribution			Percent	Frequency Distribution		
Occupation	Female	Female	Male	Difference	Female	Female	Male	Difference
Heads of state, etc.[a]	13.1	.0130	.0445	.0315	27.3	.0098	.0312	.0214
Heads of establishments[b]	6.4	.0112	.0845	.0733	13.4	.0125	.0960	.0835
Engineering-technical personnel	22.5	.0907	.1613	.0706	41.2	.1826	.3096	.1270
Agronomists, zootechnicians, veterinary personnel, and foresters	14.6	.0089	.0269	.0180	40.6	.0156	.0270	.0114
Medical personnel	82.3	.1195	.0133	.1062	91.6	.1405	.0154	.1251
Scientific personnel, teachers, and training personnel	57.8	.1905	.0717	.1188	71.3	.1773	.0850	.0923
Literary and press personnel	32.4	.0043	.0046	.0003	50.8	.0051	.0059	.0008
Cultural-enlightenment personnel	51.7	.0335	.0161	.0174	71.8	.0298	.0139	.0159
Art personnel	30.0	.0090	.0109	.0019	32.6	.0056	.0137	.0081
Juridical personnel	14.4	.0020	.0061	.0041	37.0	.0027	.0054	.0027
Communications personnel	68.4	.0430	.0102	.0328	80.2	.0379	.0111	.0268
Trade, public dining, procurement, and supply personnel[c]	12.0	.0244	.0928	.0684	38.4	.0375	.0716	.0341
Planning and record-keeping personnel	42.7	.3009	.2081	.0928	76.4	.2495	.0916	.1579
Clerical personnel	81.4	.0899	.0106	.0793	95.2	.0480	.0029	.0451
Communal establishment and everyday service personnel	39.7	.0169	.0133	.0036	62.4	.0157	.0112	.0045
Other professional and semiprofessional[d]	8.9	.0423	.2250	.1827	14.6	.0300	.2085	.1785
Total	34.0	1.0000	1.0000	.9017	54.3	1.0000	1.0000	.9351

[a]The full title of the category is "Heads of state, administrative, party, Young Communist League, trade union, co-operative organization, & other social organizations and their structural subdivisions."

[b]The full title of the category is "Heads of establishments (industrial, construction, agricultural, forestry, transport, communications, and their structural subdivisions)."

[c]This category has been changed to conform with the 1970 reclassification of some subcategories.

[d]This is a residual category.

Source: Based on figures in Ts.S.U. RSFSR 1963, pp. 244-51, 255-58, 282-84, 284-91.

solely in private agriculture or housework to combine family responsibilities with full-time employment. By their very nature, many service enterprises may be located near or in residential areas. Efforts were directed to getting more women into the work force, for they did constitute a large pool of very much needed labor. Among those aged 16 to 54 in Soviet Russia in 1959, there were 2.6 million women in private agriculture and an additional 3.7 million who were neither in school nor in the socialized sector of the labor force. Of the latter, 59 percent had children under the age of 14 (Ts. S. U. 1963, pp. 158-59).

The number of women not in school or the socialized labor force by 1970 is not available from the census, but it does show that the number of women engaged solely in private agricultural endeavors contracted to only 669,185 (Ts. S. U. 1973b, p. 164). I have already indicated that female labor-force participation rates have risen substantially between 1959 and 1970. Another source confirms this in noting that between 1961 and 1970 two-thirds of those entering the labor force were persons who had previously been engaged in housework and private subsidiary agriculture. This trend appears to have been particularly significant in the European regions. The rise in the minimum salary and in pension benefits constituted a significant incentive. Many older women returned to work to be able to qualify for a pension (Litvyakov 1969, pp. 92-93, 106-7).

In the latter part of the 1960s, apparently to further increase the use of housewives and the elderly, a major drive was initiated to provide part-time work and to even promote cottage industry:

> By October, 1969 the R. S. F. S. R. Ministry of Light Industry was employing about 7,000 persons at home, and it was expected to expand that number shortly thereafter. By 1972 there were some 100,000 part-time active workers in the R. S. F. S. R. (Feshbach and Rapawy 1973, p. 494).

Overall, between 1959 and 1970, trends established during the previous period continued (see Tables 4.5 and 4.6).[5] Females constituted 72 percent of the additional 6.8 million professional and semiprofessional workers and a considerably smaller percentage (55.1) of the additional 7.5 million nonprofessional workers (excluding agricultural workers).[6] Thus, in 1970 over 60 percent of the professional and semiprofessional workers were women as opposed to only 34 percent in 1939. Three-quarters of this increase had occurred between 1939 and 1959. While women had also comprised 34 percent of the nonprofessional workers in 1939, this figure moved upward at a very slow rate to reach 45 percent in 1970. (By "nonprofessional," let me remind the reader, I am referring only to occupations outside of agriculture. In 1939 most women doing manual work were in agriculture, and thus only 33 percent of all females not in private agriculture, as opposed to 51 percent of the comparable group of males, were in nonprofessional occupations. The figures for 1959 were, respectively, 45 and 59 percent.

The source for these figures is the same as that for Tables 4.3 and 4.6.) Based on the data for the census years only, in this case the annual rate of increase appears to be about the same over the whole period.

It is also significant that only in the period between 1959 and 1970 did the movement of women out of agricultural employment outstrip that of men: The percentage of women among these workers (excluding private agriculture) declined from 58 to 52. This is a particularly positive sign, for it is in the rural areas that the traditional subjugation of women in the spheres of work and family are most severe and intractable (see Chapter 6).

In 1939, 54 out of every 100 employed females worked in agriculture (excluding private agriculture), while 13 in every 100 were in professional and semiprofessional occupations. By 1970 the figures were about 15 and 35 respectively—almost the reverse of those in 1939. The proportion of the males in agriculture had been substantially below that of females in 1939, but it too fell considerably. However, the male labor force shifted primarily into nonprofessional occupations, and by 1970, 63 percent of the males, as opposed to 50 percent of the females, were in this area.

OCCUPATIONAL SEGREGATION

There are significant changes that are not revealed by an examination of only the broad differences in the evolution of the male and female labor force. It is necessary to consider the difference between the distribution of men and women within the nonprofessional and within the professional and semiprofessional occupations. If the rate of female participation in these areas is controlled, what is the overall extent to which women are under- or overrepresented within the occupations? How has this changed over time?

These questions have been raised before in research on other nations. A review of the basic findings will make the examination of the situation in Soviet Russia more meaningful.

Previous Research and the Measures of Segregation

Edward Gross's study of the occupational segregation by sex has drawn considerable attention. He found that in the United States between 1900 and 1960 the degree of such segregation had remained almost constant. Poston and Johnson (1971) argued that professional occupations should be considered apart from the others, for it was here that physical attributes and differences in educational attainment were least likely to interfere with the growing use of achievement criteria—a concomitant of industrialization. Using data from four southwestern states, they were able to show that five measures of industrialization could explain "better than 68 percent of the variation in professional differences by sex" (p. 333). They asserted that industrialization reduces segregation by sex in these occupations. However, the use of ecological analysis and of cross-sectional data seriously detract from the credibility of the conclusion.

Of greater significance is the recent cross-national study by Rosemary Cooney (1975). Her sample included nations from Eastern and Western Europe, as well as the United States, Canada, Australia, and New Zealand. Like Poston and Johnson, she included only professional occupations in her analysis. She concluded that "economic development does not diminish the importance of sex as an allocation mechanism affecting . . . professional employment opportunities" (1975, p. 114). Cooney found that the rate of female participation was unrelated to the degree of segregation. Her data support her hypothesis that, on the one hand, the participation rate of women is dependent upon two factors: (1) the growth of the professional sector and (2) the increase in female higher educational enrollment. Declining segregation, on the other hand, is contingent upon distinctly different factors: a deficiency in the number of working-age males and high economic growth. The longitudinal study of Soviet Russia constitutes an important test of this.

The degree of segregation by sex within the occupations is determined by the use of the unstandardized and standardized measures of dissimilarity—measures commonly employed in studies of this nature. The unstandardized measure "may be interpreted as the percentage of females (or males) who would have to change occupations in order that the distribution of sexes in occupations should be the same" (Poston and Johnson 1971, pp. 337-38). The influence of an occupation on this summary measure is determined by the proportion of the labor force in that occupation. The standardized measure gives equal weight to each occupation and is unaffected by changes in the distribution of the labor force. Both measures are independent of the rate of female participation, thus making it possible to determine the effect of this rate upon the extent of segregation (Cooney 1975, p. 113).

Occupational Segregation in Soviet Russia

On the basis of arguments in the research discussed above and the nature of changes in the rate of female participation, it seemed plausible that measures based on a grouping together of all nonagrarian occupations may have concealed conflicting trends. With the data from the 1939, 1959, and 1970 censuses, I have, therefore, analyzed occupational segregation separately within the nonprofessional grouping and the professional and semiprofessional grouping.

Both Poston and Johnson and Cooney stress the distinctness of professional occupations. Since Soviet Russia experienced rapid industrialization and economic growth (see Cohn 1962; 1970) as well as a severe deficit of males, their arguments would lead us to expect a reduction in segregation by sex over time.

With respect to the nonprofessional occupations, a similar trend might be predicted at least for the earlier period. The very extreme conditions that fostered supply and demand especially between the 1930s and well past World War II may have been sufficient to eliminate many sex barriers (see Chapter 3). This should, of course, also apply to the professional and semiprofessional occupations. The government and Party also appear to have been instrumental in this direction. Furthermore, the expansion of industry in new regions may have provided great potential for altering traditional patterns of female labor-force participation. As is illustrated by the discussion of the construction industry, the new enterprises developed in areas lacking established structures and the workers were often younger than their counterparts in already industrialized areas. The implementation of new beliefs about women's rights embodied in the ideology of the Revolution could thus find support more readily in the institutions first created during the Soviet period (see the discussion of backwardness as an asset in Chapter 1).

However, there are grounds for believing that this trend may have been reversed in recent years. Because of the subsequent growth of the tertiary sector providing alternative opportunities for women and the reduction in the deficit of males of working age, I predicted that there would be an increase in segregation in the nonprofessional occupations. Exigencies of the preceding years might give way to the cultural biases of the population. Men might be particularly prone to replace women in the more lucrative manual occupations and, as will be discussed below, the prejudices of employers may often have facilitated this.

Finally, recent Soviet policy appears not specifically aimed at providing men and women with the same type of work, but rather with recognizing sex difference in physical capacities (see Tatarinova 1973). Changed conditions may have permitted this to be stressed more than the idea of labor-force participation in general. Laws restricting female labor can be more strictly enforced and women can be encouraged to seek employment that does not require strenuous labor. Again, when these are high-paying jobs, men will certainly fill available openings. This orientation would also be expected to influence the occupational training of women.

Unfortunately, there is a lack of data for the earlier period to fully test these hypothesis. For the years 1929, 1933, and 1940, I have calculated the occupational segregation (the index of dissimilarity) for the branches of the economy listed in Table 4.2, excluding workers on state farms and Machine Tractor Stations and Tractor Service Stations. The fact that there were so few categories and my having to derive the number of males from the rough percentage of females and number of

TABLE 4.5

The Nonprofessional Labor Force of the RSFSR, by Occupation and Sex, 1959 and 1970[a]

Occupation	1959				1970			
	Percent Female	Frequency Distribution			Percent Female	Frequency Distribution		
		Female	Male	Difference		Female	Male	Difference
Employed in the production of construction materials, glass, and chinaware	59.3	.0160	.0080	.0080	59.5	.0119	.0065	.0054
Woodworkers	21.4	.0158	.0421	.0263	25.4	.0134	.0318	.0184
Textile workers	85.4	.0564	.0070	.0494	84.8	.0377	.0055	.0322
Garment workers	92.6	.0593	.0034	.0559	94.6	.0600	.0028	.0572
Leather workers	52.8	.0041	.0027	.0014	69.1	.0029	.0011	.0018
Shoe workers	46.3	.0077	.0065	.0012	59.2	.0065	.0036	.0029
Food workers	71.9	.0280	.0079	.0201	82.4	.0254	.0044	.0210
Construction workers	19.9	.0508	.1483	.0975	29.0	.0560	.1104	.0544
Railroad workers	35.1	.0311	.0417	.0106	37.7	.0198	.0264	.0066
Automotive and urban electrical transport workers	6.5	.0104	.1093	.0989	4.6	.0097	.1611	.1514
Postal workers, letter carriers	80.5	.0097	.0017	.0080	89.8	.0110	.0010	.0100
Public dining workers	91.0	.0901	.0064	.0837	94.6	.1209	.0056	.1153
Orderlies, nurses, nursemaids[a]	97.7	.0432	.0007	.0425	98.1	.0574	.0009	.0565

Machine-construction and metal workers	17.1	.0849	.2983	.2134	17.3	.1027	.3972	.2945
Chemical workers	61.6	.0139	.0063	.0076	60.2	.0171	.0090	.0080
Paper and cardboard workers	68.5	.0026	.0009	.0017	67.2	.0025	.0010	.0015
Printing workers	74.2	.0072	.0018	.0054	74.6	.0060	.0016	.0044
Communal, household and everyday service personnel	73.2	.2007	.0532	.1475	82.6	.1623	.0276	.1347
Laboratory assistants (workers)	92.4	.0038	.0002	.0036	90.7	.0122	.0010	.0112
Inspectors and sorters	83.5	.0265	.0038	.0227	89.1	.0322	.0032	.0290
Warehouse workers, weighers, receivers and distributors	65.3	.0323	.0124	.0199	80.2	.0385	.0077	.0308
Other nonprofessional workers	38.5	.2052	.2374	.0322	45.1	.1940	.1907	.0033
Total	42.0	1.000	1.000	.9575	44.7	1.000	1.000	1.0505

[a]Occupations listed below "orderlies" are different from those listed in the 1959 census.

Source: Based on figures in Ts.S.U. 1973, pp. 24-30, 170-71.

females within each branch makes the measure quite crude. However, it is interesting to note that the predicted decline does take place. (The unstandardized measure is 27, 21, and 22 for the years 1929, 1933, and 1940 respectively; the standardized measure for these years equalled 33, 34, and 29. There is also evidence of a slight further decline by 1950.).

As already indicated, the censuses conducted since 1939 make it possible to distinguish between types of occupations. The general nature of the differences between the male and female distributions within the professional and semiprofessional occupations and within the nonprofessional occupations can be seen from columns 4 and 8 of Tables 4.3 through 4.6.

The major differences in the nonprofessional occupational distribution occur in four areas (see Tables 4.3 and 4.5). Females have been far more concentrated than males in communal and household services,[7] whereas the reverse has been true in construction. The proportion of women in the former occupational category has increased considerably (the percentage female rose by about 30 points) as did the proportion of males. A similar trend is evident in construction, though since 1959 the proportion of the males declined and the proportion of the females remained stable. The percentage of females among the construction workers rose by 10 points. This occupation contributed slightly to an increase in the difference between male and female frequency distributions.

Far more significant have been the changes in the remaining two areas: automotive and electrical transport and metallurgy. These are closely tied to industrial growth (Treiman 1970). These highly segregated areas (male-dominated) came to have a much higher proportion of the labor force and thus increased the difference between the occupational distributions. For example, while about 5 percent of the females and 19 percent of the males were in metallurgy in 1939, the corresponding figures for 1959 were 9 and 31. The percentage of females declined among the transportation workers, but it increased somewhat among the metalworkers. Thus, the most important change was not in the degree to which women were under- or overrepresented in the occupations, but rather in the distribution of the *total* labor force.

Within the professional and semiprofessional occupations there are many large and changing differences between the distributions of males and females. Females have been far more concentrated in the areas of medicine, science, planning and record keeping, and clerical or secretarial work. In contrast, the proportion of males is especially high in engineering-technology, the residual category entitled "other professional and semiprofessional occupations" and, rather significantly, in the category "heads of establishments" (see Tables 4.4 and 4.6).

There is an inordinately large proportion of professional as well as semiprofessional and nonprofessional workers in occupations that are not specified in the census. This, of course, hinders the assessment of

TABLE 4.6

The Professional and Semiprofessional Labor Force of the RSFSR, by Occupation and Sex, 1959 and 1970

Occupation	1959				1970			
	Percent	Frequency Distribution			Percent	Frequency Distribution		
	Female	Female	Male	Difference	Female	Female	Male	Difference
Heads of state, etc.[a]	27.3	.0099	.0314	.0215	34.1	.0073	.0217	.0144
Heads of establishments[b]	13.4	.0126	.0966	.0840	17.1	.0138	.1038	.0900
Agronomists, zootechnicians, veterinary personnel and foresters	40.6	.0157	.0272	.0115	41.8	.0116	.0250	.0134
Medical personnel	91.6	.1419	.0154	.1265	91.0	.1243	.0190	.1053
Scientific personnel, teachers and training personnel	71.3	.1791	.0856	.0935	72.1	.1730	.1036	.0694
Literary and press personnel	50.8	.0052	.0060	.0008	57.8	.0046	.0052	.0006
Art personnel	32.6	.0056	.0138	.0082	33.7	.0048	.0146	.0098
Juridical personnel	37.0	.0027	.0055	.0028	42.0	.0023	.0050	.0027
Communications personnel	80.2	.0383	.0112	.0271	85.1	.0272	.0074	.0198
Planning and record-keeping personnel[c]	76.4	.2520	.0922	.1598	87.1	.2286	.0523	.1763
Engineering-technical personnel	42.1	.1820	.2959	.1139	46.4	.2236	.3993	.1757
Cultural-enlightenment personnel	56.6	.0326	.0296	.0030	67.9	.0278	.0203	.0075
Trade, public dining, procurement, and supply personnel	40.0	.0395	.0702	.0307	62.2	.0420	.0394	.0026
Communal establishment and everyday service personnel	57.3	.0057	.0051	.0006	68.4	.0058	.0042	.0016
Typists and stenographers	99.6	.0128	.0001	.0127	99.4	.0128	.0001	.0127
Secretaries, clerks, and other office personnel	94.4	.0343	.0024	.0319	96.5	.0302	.0017	.0285
Agents and expeditors	43.6	.0060	.0093	.0033	61.3	.0057	.0056	.0010
Other professional and semiprofessional personnel	12.3	.0241	.2028	.1787	32.9	.0546	.1719	.1173
Total	54.2	1.0000	1.0000	.9105	60.7	1.0000	1.0000	.8477

[a]The full title of the category is: "Heads of state, administrative, party, Young Communist League, trade union, cooperative organization, and other social organizations and their structural subdivisions."

[b]The full title of the category is: "Heads of establishments (industrial, construction, agricultural, forestry, transport, communications and their structural subdivisions)."

[c]Occupations listed below "planning and record-keeping personnel" are different from those listed in the 1959 census.

Source: Based on figures in Ts.S.U. 1973b, pp. 30-33, 172-74.

the full extent to which males and females are segregated. There is somewhat more detail in the listing of the total number of workers in occupations as opposed to the list of female workers. Thus, from the 1959 census one can discover the total number of workers, but not the number of females, in such nonprofessional occupations as hunting, mining, lumbering, and truck loading.

As already indicated, the best means of summarizing the difference between the patterns of male and female labor-force participation is by calculating the index of dissimilarity. To fully assess the extent of occupational segregation, I have, however, utilized the detailed census listing of occupations rather than just the main occupational categories shown in Tables 4.3 through 4.6. (In 1959, including residuals, there were 57 professional and semiprofessional categories and 53 nonprofessional categories. In 1970 the figures were 64 and 51 respectively.)

Table 4.7 shows that there has been a significant change within the nonprofessional occupations, but as the analysis above suggested, this was due to a shift in the structure of the labor force. When this is controlled for through standardization, the change disappears entirely for the early period and is only very slight since 1959. Detailed analysis also confirms the discussion above by revealing that the unstandardized measure is most influenced by the increase in the concentration of workers in a diversity of metalworking occupations (but mainly among fitters and assemblers of machinery) and one subcategory of transportation workers: chauffeurs or taxi drivers. Between 1939 and 1970, 97 to 99 percent of these particular transportation workers were men. Over the same period, the proportion of the nonprofessional male labor force in this occupation grew from 3 to almost 16 percent!

Change within the professional and semiprofessional occupations is very slight and varies over the period. The shifts within the occupations appear to have largely cancelled out one another.

Given the very substantial increase in the labor-force participation of Soviet women, especially in the professional and semiprofessional grouping, these findings provide significant support for Cooney's (1975) assertion that such an increase is not necessarily associated with a decline in segregation. However, the notion that professional segregation declines with a deficit of males and growing educational attainment must be rejected. Poston and Johnson's (1971) assertion about the expected shift from the use of ascribed to achieved criteria appears overly simplistic. (It is important, though, to note that a more strictly defined grouping of professional occupations might have altered these findings.) Overall, the pattern in Soviet Russia corresponds to that found by Gross (1968) for the United States. Industrialization does not result in reduced occupational segregation by sex.

By 1939 female labor force participation was already extremely diverse. Women had entered many occupations from which they had previously been either completely or almost completely excluded.

TABLE 4.7

Unstandardized and Standardized Measures of Occupational Segregation, 1939-1970

Year	Professional and Semiprofessional		Nonprofessional[a]	
	Unstandardized	Standardized	Unstandardized	Standardized
Using detailed categories from the 1959 census:				
1939	49.5	55.3	40.2	56.3
1959	53.1	51.8	50.2	56.3
Using detailed categories from the 1970 census:				
1959	53.1	48.7	51.7	51.3
1970	50.9	49.8	56.8	53.1

[a]This does not include workers in agriculture and forestry.

Source: Based on data in Ts.S.U. 1963, pp. 228-58, 278-88; 1973b, pp. 24-33, 170-74.

Many nonprofessional occupations that were destined to grow substantially contained a relatively small contingent of females. In the course of the next 31 years, the concentration of the female labor force in these areas would grow rapidly, but the same would hold true for the males. Overall, the extent to which women were under- or overrepresented in occupations (relative to their numbers in the occupational grouping) remained stable.

However, this continuity should not be interpreted as a lack of very significant changes in other respects. Two such changes already discussed have been the massive shift of the female labor force out of agriculture and women's growing dominance in the professional and semiprofessional occupations. Remember that the rate of participation is controlled for in the measure of segregation, but one must not lose sight of the changes taking place.

Furthermore, there were important advances in women's educational attainment (discussed at greater length below), which, combined with professional occupational segregation, may foster improvement in women's position. It has often been noted that the family unit may have isolated women in such a way as to impede collective action. Growing numbers of women with an increased level of education may find that their occupational ties constitute a critical organizational resource for bringing about change and awareness.

Women's Access to Top Positions: The Vertical Hierarchy

Certain types of segregation are far more significant than others. Clearly, for example, the exclusion of women from top positions is of a very different order from their constituting a small proportion of the taxi drivers. However, the weigting procedure commonly used in calculating the measures of segregation does not emphasize these distinctions. This is enhanced by the lack of detail in the census and by the small number of workers in leading positions.

I have selected the top professional occupations available in the census. Table 4.8 shows the percentage of women in the categories divided by the percentage of women in the total professional and semiprofessional labor force for the particular year. The figures show directly the extent to which women are underrepresented (under 100) or overrepresented (over 100) within the occupations and permit comparison over time. I have called this the "relative percentage."

As is the case in the overall pattern of professional and semiprofessional segregation, there is a mixture of increases and decreases that appear to counteract one another. The vertical structure of occupations, however, is far less ambiguous.

Tables A.1-A.4 show that in industry, construction, and teaching and among scientific workers the percentage female declines very rapidly the higher the prestige and responsibility of the position. Census data shows that this is also true in medicine (Ts. S. U. 1963, p. 287). Change in this pattern has been quite slow. Though women constitute about a third of the deputies in the various bodies of government and over 40 percent of local personnel, these are relatively unimportant political positions (Lennon 1971, p. 50). In the 1960s women constituted only about 20 percent of the Communist Party membership, and between 1950 and 1961 only between 3 and 4 percent of the membership of the Central Committee of the Party were women (Rigby 1968, p. 301; Dodge 1966, p. 214).

Other sources support these findings of vertical segregation. A Soviet investigator notes that despite the fact that women are highly capable of such work, very few are employed as equipment setters (naladchik oborudovaniya). In industries where the percentage of women varies between 52 and 80, the percentage of females among those doing this type of extremely skilled labor varied between only about 2 and 7 (Mikhailyuk 1970, p. 68).

A study of an instrument shop typical of those in large cities such as Volgograd and Moscow showed that the average skill level of female lathe operators was 35.5 percent below that of men with the same specialty. The skill level of female polishers and milling machine operators was found to be, respectively, 35.5 percent and 57.1 percent below that of men. The author attributed the difference to the familial

TABLE 4.8

The "Relative Percentage" Female in Selected Occupations in the RSFSR, 1939, 1959, and 1970

Occupational Category	1939	1959	1970
Heads of state, etc.[a]	38	50	56
Chiefs of production—technical departments, sectors, groups and bureaus	21	25	24
Heads of shops, sections, workshops, and divisions	28	30	27
Engineers (including chief specialists)	40	63	70
Designers, draftsmen	140	104	95
Chief physicians and other heads of public health institutions	123	108 (113)[b]	(100)[b]
Heads of scientific research institutions and organizations, scientific personnel, teachers in higher educational institutions	96	72	70
Judges	42	49	n. a.

n. a.: data not available.

[a]The full title of the category is "heads of state, administrative, party, Young Communist League, trade union, cooperative organization and other social organizations and their structural subdivisions."

[b]The figures in parentheses are for an occupational category listed in the 1970 census which differs slightly from that in the 1959 census.

Source: Based on figures in Ts. S. U. 1963, pp. 244-51, 255-58, 285-88; 1973b, pp. 30-33, 172-74.

responsibilities of women which prevent them from substantially raising their work qualifications (Labzin 1965, p. 100).

From his review of the data, Dodge (1966, pp. 214-15) concludes:

> Although the prospects for a woman entering and succeeding in a professional career in the Soviet Union appear to be much more favorable than in the United States or in other Western countries, the prospects for advancement are not equally favorable. The proportion of women in administrative and professional jobs, although much higher now than before World War II, tends to decrease with each successive increase in rank. . . . There appears to be an undeniable tendency for female specialists in all fields to congregate in the lower and middle echelons. Perhaps the most striking instance of this is the small number of women among the party professionals, but it holds to a lesser degree in all other areas of activity.

Developments since this was written do not appear to have substantially reversed this pattern.

In addition, women are overrepresented in those occupations requiring the least skill. This is also often unlikely to be detected with the use of summary measures or even from an examination of the disaggregated Soviet census data. A Soviet investigator has noted that men predominate among workers doing mechanized work, while in the majority of cases it is women who do the unmechanized work. Thus, in every industry, with the exception of coal, light, and food industries, a far higher proportion of the women than the men are doing unmechanized work. The difference between the proportions is often substantial, as can be seen from Table 4.9. Women constitute over 80 percent of the workers doing subsidiary and auxiliary jobs—work requiring little knowledge but "significant physical strength" (Mikhailyuk 1970, p. 67):

> The degree of mechanization of the auxiliary work is significantly lower than that of primary jobs. This has a detrimental influence on the working conditions of the women engaged here. According to the data of the Central Statistical Board the percentage of primary work that is mechanized in the machine-construction industry, for example, is about 60-70 percent, while this is true of only 25 to 30 percent of the auxiliary work,

The unfavorable position of women in the early decades of the Soviet period has in many respects clearly persisted into the present.

TABLE 4.9

Percentage of the Workers in Selected Industries Doing Unmechanized Labor, by Sex, n.d.

Industry	Males	Females
Construction materials	37	69
Wood	37	69
Peat	10	56
Light metals	13	23
Ferrous metal	19	23
Chemical	12	15

Source: Mikhailyuk 1970, p. 66.

WAGE DIFFERENCES

There are no published data on the differences in the wages of males and females overall or within specific occupations. However, there is occasional mention of wage differentials in the press and in some small studies (Lennon 1971, p. 54). Thus, for example, one study of families in Odessa shows that the salary of the husband was higher than that of the wife in 73 percent of the cases; the wife's salary was higher in only 7 percent of the cases (Mikhailyuk 1970, p. 69). A Soviet investigator was sufficiently impressed by the data on wage differentials to note the following:

> The elements of economic inequality of the sexes although of a temporary character, nevertheless at present not only promote the preservation of the well-known material dependence of women on men, but also in some way serve as a justification for the preservation of the bourgeois prejudice concerning the inferiority of women as productive workers (Labzin 1965, p. 106).

The wage differences appear to be the result of the concentration of women in occupations that pay less. Data on the wages by sector of the national economy can be compared with the percentage of women in the sector. From at least 1940 until the present the evidence available indicates that it is in those areas where women predominate that wages have been relatively low. It is particularly significant that the decreases in the proportion of women in transportation, construction, and industry since 1945 have paralleled faster increases in wages in these areas than in other sectors of the economy. Data specifically for the Russian Republic since 1960 (for preceding years it was necessary to rely on data from the USSR as a whole) show that the growth in the percentage of females particularly in the fields of science and government and administration paralleled slow increases in wages relative to other sectors (Sacks 1974, pp. 160-64).

This pattern may be interpreted in a number of ways. It is quite plausible that change in the type of tasks performed in a sector of the economy may lead to a decline in wages. Women may find the work easier to combine with family responsibilities, while men may be discouraged from seeking such employment by low wages or lack of prospects for advancement. It may also be the case that work in the sector may become defined as more approrpiate for women than men. Thus, for example, the expansion of clerical positions in government and administration may have created demand specifically for female labor. Defining an occupation as "women's work" may contribute to a lower evaluation of the job and the monetary reward that should be rendered. The definition may also emerge as women come to dominate the sector, thus reinforcing the trend toward lower wages (see Prather 1971).

An alternative explanation in terms of power must also be considered. As discussed in Chapter 2, during the prerevolutionary period women's wages were far lower than men's. An employer apparently could pay women less without great resistance. Women were far more passive than men. That wages have risen more rapidly in fields dominated by men may be a sign that they still are capable of exerting greater pressure. That men dominate top positions in almost all areas may also be in part attributable to this factor. If power or political pressure is significant, collective action or at least greater awareness on the part of women takes on particular importance. I have already suggested that this may be emerging as a consequence of both occupational segregation and higher educational attainment.

EDUCATIONAL ATTAINMENT

In Chapter 3 only a very general measure of education was considered. Since occupational attainment is closely tied to education, it is important to give further attention to this in evaluating change in the relative status of males and females.

Both in 1959 and 1970, in the urban population of the RSFSR,[8] a slightly larger proportion of females than males had an incomplete higher or a specialized secondary education. The proportion of males with a higher education exceeded that of females in both years. In 1959 in the age groups below 40 the proportion of women with a higher

TABLE 4.10

Percentage Increase in Proportion Having Higher Education and Incomplete Higher and Secondary Specialized Education in Three Age Groups, by Sex, between 1959 and 1970

Age in 1970	Higher Education		Incomplete Higher and Secondary Specialized	
	Males	Females	Males	Females
30-39	370	253	135	113
40-49	159	117	113	102
50-59	122	111	110	105

Source: Based on figures in Table A. 6.

education actually was greater than that of men; by 1970 the situation had placed women in a relatively less favorable position (see Table A. 6).

Table 4.10 shows that the educational achievement of men was growing at a far more rapid rate than that of women. This was true both with respect to higher education and incomplete and secondary specialized education. As time-budget data in Chapter 5 will show, women have far less time to continue their studies later in life.

In 1959, 4.7 percent of the urban females aged 20 to 29, as opposed to 3.3 percent of the comparable group of males, had a higher education. In 1970 the corresponding figures were 7.1 for females and 4.8 for males. This may be a sign that males are further delaying their education, recognizing the opportunities to continue their schooling while gaining work experience. It will be interesting to see whether women are able to sustain this initially larger edge as the cohort ages.

Many problems with the analysis of the above data make the conclusions tentative at best. In particular, the censuses are 11 years apart instead of 10 and thus the cohorts cannot be followed precisely. The 1970 figures include some persons from a younger cohort and exclude some of the oldest persons in the original cohort; that is, the age group in 1959 which I am using for comparison. This should inflate the estimates of the educational achievement of both sexes in the cohorts in 1970. A more serious problem, however, lies in the fact that while 52 percent of the population lived in urban areas of the RSFSR in 1959, the figure increased by 10 percentage points by 1970. Thus, the cohorts include a substantial number of rural migrants whose educational level is likely to be considerably lower than urban residents, particularly in the case of the women. It is not possible to adequately estimate the degree to which male-female differences are distorted by this addition to the urban population, though it almost certainly lowered the educational achievement of the age groups. It is also possible that the increase in the urban population is due to changes in the classification of regions. The influence of this is even more difficult to assess.

Such problems warrant the examination of other material dealing with educational attainment. To this end I have also considered the census data on the education of the urban population employed in the labor force (excluding private agriculture). The picture revealed by this somewhat contradicts that based on the urban population as a whole.

In 1959, 57 percent of the males and 55 percent of the females had either an elementary education or less. However, females were twice as likely as males to have less than an elementary education, while males were about 1.5 times as likely as females to have an elementary education only. The proportion of males and of females having a higher education or incomplete higher education was quite comparable. Females were somewhat more likely to have a secondary general and secondary specialized education, while males were slightly more likely to have an incomplete secondary education. Thus, the only substantial difference between males and females was in the lowest educational levels. In 1970 this difference decreased substantially and the educational achievement of both males and females increased at quite comparable rates (see Table A. 7).

The lack of data on specific age groups is a serious limitation, for important trends may be hidden. However, the exclusion of women from top positions and their predominance among workers in the least skilled occupations appears even more striking in light of the available data. The increase in the educational level of urban working women gives a far more sanguine picture than we found in the case of women in the urban population as a whole. Working women are likely to be younger and thus better educated than women not in the labor force. Again, it seems important to determine whether men may have greater opportunities to advance their education and thus create a larger gap between their educational achievement and that of females as the cohort ages. The overall figures do not show whether males have entered the labor force early and delayed the completion of their education. If this were true, since the younger age groups of men constitute a very substantial proportion of the depleted population, the average figures at this time would give a rather low estimate of the ultimate educational achievement of the men.

Norton Dodge (1966, pp. 112-19) has documented the decline since 1945 in the inordinately high proportion of women among those in higher educational and specialized secondary institutions. This has been the result of the gradual return to equal numbers of males and females in the student-age groups as well as direct efforts to increase the number of male students admitted. Dodge noted that there were 5.4 applicants per male acceptance, while there were 8.7 applicants per female acceptance in the science departments of Moscow State University. He has suggested, "There is the possibility that a quota system or other preferential treatment for men has been instituted in order to reduce the percentage of women in some fields" (1966, p. 113). An article in the Soviet press in 1970 verified that this indeed was the case, at least in the medical profession:

> . . . Medical Institutes' entrance reqiurements are lower for boys than for girls. Problems with women doctors arise because of marriage, relocation difficulties and temporary or permanent retirement when family considerations are placed above professional ones, especially when the family's material situation makes this possible. This is the rationale for higher requirements for girls (Doletsky 1970, p. 27).

This supports Dodge's (1966, pp. 136-39) explanation of three phenomena: (1) the decreasing percentage of women among students in higher education in recent decades, (2) the decreasing proportion of women in all fields "as the degree ladder is climbed," and (3) the greater attrition rate of female graduate students as compared to male graduate students. He contends that, on the one hand, household responsibilities make women less inclined than men to "want to undertake the rigors of advanced training." On the other hand, the government has recognized that it is economically more rational to increase the enrollment of males. Since men will have a longer productive life, the investment of the scarce educational resources in male advancement will therefore have a greater payoff.

However, since Dodge (1966) completed his research the percentage of women among students in higher educational institutions in the USSR has increased in virtually every field. In the USSR the percentage of women among students in higher education had reached 77 percent in 1945-46 and declined to 43 percent in 1960-61. But since that time it has again risen and in 1973-74 it reached 50 percent. The corresponding figures for the RSFSR for 1960-61 and 1970-71 were 45 percent and 51 percent respectively. Women in the USSR constituted as much as 69 percent (in 1945-46) of students in secondary specialized institutions. The figure declined to 47 percent in 1960-61 and has risen to 54 percent in 1970-71 paralleling the trend in higher education. The figures for the RSFSR were again very similar: 49 percent in 1960-61 and 56 percent in 1970-71 (Ts. S. U. RSFSR 1971b, p. 441; Ts. S. U. 1974, p. 723).

The differences that do remain are indicative of the persisting pattern of male and female occupational choices or opportunities. In 1973-74 women constituted 68 percent of the students in education, art, and cinematography; 61 percent in economics and law; 56 percent in public health, physical culture, and sports; 39 percent in industry, construction, transportation, and communications; and 32 percent in agriculture (Ts. S. U. 1974, p. 723).

Finally, it is important to stress that the same educational achievement does not necessarily provide men and women with the same job opportunities. Persisting sex-role segregation is certainly to a significant extent a product of discrimination.

This is well illustrated by a Soviet source which discusses the problems women face in gaining access to occupations not considered to be "women's work":

> Difficulties in the job placement of girls who do not enter higher education institutions or technicums are greater than for boys. This is explained by the production specialization of the city. . . . Here is a typical case. Four girls graduated from school No. 4. . . . Each received the specialty of electrical fitter at the electromechanical plant in the course of their production training. The plant conferred a skill rating on them, and it was there that they received their practical training. But in the fall the enterprise did not hire them, for their specialty was evidently not a female one (Podkorytova 1969, p. 55).

Another Soviet investigator states that "the housework burdens of women as well as the old prejudice that women are less capable of leading people and directing production create difficulties for them to move into leading posts" (Labzin 1965, p. 100). Women in such positions may often feel great pressure to prove that they are capable:

> Alexandra Nichipor, Minister of Light Industry for Byelorussia, discussed the problems of a women holding an important job. . . . "You ask how it is for a woman to be a minister? . . . It's much more complicated than it is for a man. A man can decide and then change his mind. He can make a mistake. And if I make a mistake . . . 'Well, is it possible to demand much from her? She's just a woman. . . .'" (Jacoby 1970, p. 17).

The next chapter shows that this prejudice in part stems from women's inability to fully devote themselves to their careers as a result of inordinate family responsibilities. However, it is clear that this discrimination has roots beyond the reality of the situation.

CONCLUSION

Conclusions regarding the achievement of Soviet women in the realms discussed in this chapter can often be predicted by the political persuasion of the writer. This is illustrated in the extreme by the writings of Lennon (1971) and Mandel (1975). Given the complexity of changes and continuities, it is not surprising to find such differing selections or interpretations of the available data. For example, how is one to evaluate the fact that in 1970 in the RSFSR 61 percent of chief doctors and other heads of medical institutions were women? This is certainly an outstanding achievement relative to other nations. Yet, since 91 percent of the medical personnel were women, the claim can be made that this is evidence that at higher levels women are vastly underrepresented. To emphasize this point one could note that among medical personnel the probability of a male having a top position is about 6.6 times greater than that of a female.

However, it cannot be denied that women are engaged in occupations from which they are often completely excluded in other countries. The change in this respect has been very drastic, especially when one looks at the restricted employment of tsarist times. In 1970, for example, women constituted 60 percent of the chemists, 42 percent of the engineers, 42 percent of all legal personnel, 18 percent of the lathe operators, and 45 percent of the teachers of higher education. But they also constituted 29 percent of the construction workers, 99 percent of the typists and stenographers, and 85 percent of the textile workers (Ts. S. U. 1973e, pp. 170-74). Soviet Russian women are in top positions, in traditionally female-dominated occupations, in jobs requiring heavy physical labor, and those requiring the very highest levels of education available. It is, in fact, in the area of education that one of the most impressive developments has taken place and undoubtedly this has contributed to women's growing dominance in professional and semiprofessional occupations.

But careful analysis shows that, at least since 1939, occupational sex-role segregation remains constant and at a high level. This segregation may help women to share their experiences, develop a greater awareness of their common dilemmas and possibly press for change. However, segregation has also meant limited access to top positions, overrepresentation in the least skilled work and a difference in the wages of men and women.

That persisting or growing occupational differences do not necessarily mean a lack of improvement is well illustrated by the broad changes in the labor force. Women's movement out of agriculture, an extremely propitious development (see Chapter 6), has been accompanied by, relative to men, a much larger shift into professional and semiprofessional occupations. The result has been a greater difference between the occupational participation of males and females. This suggests that women are benefiting from their growing educational achievement, although many of the semi-professional occupations may have low status and monetary reward. The recent ambiguous changes in education and in the top professions make it difficult to predict whether Soviet women in the future will sustain or increase this accomplishment. It should be remembered that this occurred during a period when there was an extreme deficit of males, which has been filled in recent decades.

Overall, the case of Soviet Russia illustrates the complexity of the analysis of change in the occupational status of women. It is evident that an adequate assessment cannot be based on the degree of change in the measure of occupational segregation alone. The distinct continuity revealed by this, however, suggests the need to revise theories regarding the impact of industrialization.

NOTES

1. The rate of female labor force participation has apparently not been as consistently high in urban areas. As discussed in Chapter 2, urbanization necessitates adapting to a different labor market. Men adjusted more rapidly. A 1931-32 time-budget study of families in Leningrad showed that 46 percent of the women over age 18 were engaged in the labor force (Lebedev-Patreiko 1933, p. 33). Dodge's (1966, p. 33) estimates for the urban labor-force participation rate (including private agriculture) for women aged 16 to 59 in the Soviet Union was 40.1 percent in 1926, 45.2 percent in 1939, and 67.0 percent in 1959.

2. "Workers and employees" includes state farm workers, but excludes those on collective farms. Also excluded are workers in what is called the "private subsidiary economy" or private agriculture. These are mostly persons who grow vegetables and raise farm animals on plots of land which they own privately. The number of such workers is not usually listed in Soviet statistics, as they are not part of the "socialized labor force." Census data shows that in 1939 and 1959 over 97 percent of those in private agriculture were women (Ts. S. U. 1963, pp. 156-58, 176-80).

3. The low figure for construction contrasts with that found in Table 4.2. This is due to the fact that the figures in Table 4.3 refer specifically to those involved in construction work, while those in 4.2 must refer to all workers (secretaries, accountants, etc.) in the construction field.

4. The poor distribution of industries in the country has often meant that there have been cities that offered primarily jobs in heavy industry suitable for men only, or areas where light industry was predominant and women were in the great majority. Many women not employed attributed this to their inability to find appropriate work. This was particularly true of small and medium size cities where industry is less diverse (cf. Sonin 1965, p. 204; Markov 1965, Chapter I; Mikhailyuk 1970, pp. 34-35). The spread of light industry to these areas of the country has undoubtedly provided jobs for these already motivated women.

5. The comparison of the recent shifts in the occupations of men and women with those that transpired between 1939 and 1959 is somewhat complicated by the different classification of occupations used

in the 1970 and 1959 censuses. Data for 1959 from the census of that year, however, are again presented in 1970 using the new classification. Comparisons between 1939 and 1970 often can only be made indirectly by first analyzing change between 1939 and 1959 according to the 1959 census and then comparing 1959 and 1970 as the data are presented in the 1970 census. Tables 4.5 and 4.6 show the material from the 1970 census. Only the first several occupations are precisely the same as those in Tables 4.4 and 4.5 (see footnote a in Tables 4.5 and 4.6).

6. Given the stage of economic development, it is not surprising that the professional and semiprofessional labor force was growing much faster in the period between 1959 and 1970 than during the previous 20 years (cf. Treiman 1970). Between 1939 and 1959 the number of professional and semiprofessional workers had increased by only 3.2 million and the number of nonprofessional workers grew by 7.9 million (the source of these figures is the same as that for Tables 4.3 and 4.6).

7. The difference in occupational categories used in the 1970 and the 1959 censuses again causes some problems here. Thus, in 1959 service personnel were classified as "communal and household service workers". In 1970 the category that was almost the same was listed as "communal, household and everyday service personnel." Similarly, in 1959 metalworkers were classified under "metallurgical and metalworkers", and the comparable category in 1970 was "machine-construction and metalworkers" (see Tables 4.3 and 4.5). This does not appear to distort the comparison between 1939 and 1970 (see footnote 5).

8. Figures are not available exclusively for workers in the nonagrarian sector. Given the choice between using data on the rural population, the total population, or the urban population, it seemed that the urban population most accurately reflected the educational level of males and females in families of workers in the nonagrarian labor force. The fact that almost all the nonagrarian workers in the time-budget studies lived in urban areas was also a strong consideration in making the selection.

CHAPTER

5

TIME-BUDGETS OF URBAN WORKERS

INTRODUCTION

To fully assess the relative status of males and females, it is necessary to consider the pattern and demands of daily living that result from their multiple but distinctive roles. These mundane aspects of life have a profound influence on occupational aspirations and opportunities as well as the possibility of obtaining further education and job training to realize one's ambitions.

Time usage reflects everyday life and can reveal the interrelationship between domestic and occupational roles. The time a worker has to rest, to engage in studies, to socialize with colleagues and superiors, etc., almost certainly influences both job satisfaction and an individual's ability to advance in a career. It seems apparent that large amounts of time that need be committed to tedious housework, or time usage that is constrained by scheduling of domestic chores such as shopping, cleaning, supervising children, etc., can seriously burden those having full-time employment. The two sets of activities—"free-time" pursuits as opposed to housework, as these are defined in Soviet studies—are clearly interdependent. Time is a "fixed sum resource" (Heirich 1964, p. 387). Given the time constraints which arise from physiological needs and the time that a worker is obligated to devote to his or her job, it is clear that there is limited flexibility. Time spent on housework must often come at the expense of one's "free time."

If the position of women progressively improves in the course of industrialization or as a result of changes associated with female employment, one would expect the free time of Soviet working women to increase during the twentieth century and the time they spend on housework to become more equivalent to the time men devote to this:

> Employment emancipates women from domination by their husbands and raises their daughters from inferiority to their brothers (echoing the rising status of their mother). The employment of women affects the power structure of the family by equalizing the resources of husband and wife. A working wife's husband listens to her more, and she listens to herself more. She expresses herself and has more opinions. . . .
>
> In the division of labor there is a similar parallel between what happens to parents and to children. Husbands get drafted into domestic service when their wives leave home. . . .
>
> The old asymmetry of male-dominated, female-serviced family life is being replaced by a new symmetry, both between husbands and wives and between brothers and sisters. To this emerging symmetry, the dual employment of mothers as well as fathers is a major contributor (Blood 1965, pp. 46-47).

Furthermore, if an egalitarian ideology is significant, its effects should be most profound among those groups more likely to be exposed or attuned to changing beliefs: young persons, those with higher education or higher occupational status, those living in large cities as opposed to small isolated areas. Sex differences in housework and free time should be less than average in such groups.

Scott and Tilly (1975) argue that female employment did not require a change of values and that industrial development eventually fostered greater emphasis on women's domestic role, not equality of the sexes. This suggests that little change will transpire in the relative time usage of males and females as industrialization progresses. Goode's (1963, pp. 15-16) observation with regard to the impact of advances in household technology supports this, although his overall perspective is certainly more consonant with the view expressed in the above quote by Blood (see Chapter 1):

> Most of these devices merely raise the standards for cleanliness and repairs, and allow the housewife to turn out more "domestic production" each day. Every study of the time allocation of mothers shows that housewives work extremely long hours. For those who have assumed otherwise, let me remind them that the washing machine brings back into the home a job that an earlier generation delegated to lower-class labor or the laundry; that the vacuum cleaner merely raises standards without substantially speeding up work; that the electric sewing machine is exactly analogous to the washing machine. On the other

> hand, the organized activities of children have become so complex, and the number of objects in the house so numerous, that even the middle-class housewife must spend much time in essentially administrative activities when she is not laboring with her hands.

SOVIET URBAN TIME-BUDGET RESEARCH

Soviet time-budget research has been very extensive, dating back to the 1920s. A recent Soviet review of the literature listed approximately 70 different studies conducted before 1970, and this was obviously incomplete. Another source indicates that:

> Between 1959 and 1965 alone, time-budget surveys involving well over 100,000 man-days of recorded human activities were carried out by the Institute for Economics of the Soviet Academy of Sciences in Novosibirsk and by some related research organizations—partly for general scholarly purposes, partly for supplying much needed data to authorities concerned with the planning of manpower resources, educational facilities, communal services, etc. (Szalai 1973, p. 8).

There is evidence of considerable recent research and efforts to coordinate these endeavors (Rapoport 1974), although the most recent study from which data have been published is from 1966.

In 1965 there was a study of time use that involved 12 nations. Some of the general findings from this research provide a basis for evaluating the accuracy of the Soviet work and the extent to which generalizations can be made from the available data.

Robinson (1967, p. 6) found that there were "characteristic national patterns of time expenditure" that were revealed by the results from only a single city: "The figures from the hardly typical city of Jackson, Michigan are almost identical to figures obtained from a nationwide American urban sample, but also differ noticeably from figures for any European survey site." This bolsters confidence in the Soviet research which reports findings from a great variety of sites.

There is a large gap in the research between the mid-1930s and about 1958, when these and other sociological investigations could not be conducted. The atrophy of the social sciences which resulted is very evident when one compares the detail and sophistication of the work of Strumilin (1957; 1964) in the 1920s with that done in the late 1950s and early 1960s. More recent work has clearly benefited from the gradual accumulation of knowledge and experience and probably also a greater exposure to the conduct of the discipline outside Eastern Europe.

This chapter is largely based on a secondary analysis of material in published Soviet studies. Considerable effort was necessary to reorganize the reported data into a uniform classification scheme. The standard classification employed in Soviet reports limits the changes that can be made. This is especially true of the many recent studies in which time use is divided into only a few major categories. I have focused on four main divisions of daily time usage: (1) formal work (including travel to and from the place of work, washing up, lunch breaks, etc. ; (2) housework, including aspects of child care and gardening; (3) sleep, eating, and other physiological needs; and (4) "free time", perhaps best described as time not engaged in any of the above activities. (The reader will find it valuable to refer to Appendix B for a detailed breakdown of the activities within any particular time-budget category referred to in the text which follows.)

The usual tests of significance are generally inappropriate or worthless because of the crude nature of the sampling procedures and the almost complete absence of data on the variance in time expenditures. The studies show only the average time usage of particular categories or individuals; raw data were inaccessible. However, my interest was in the broad patterns of consistent differences in the time use of males and females, which makes these limitations less important than they might at first seem.

Scheuch's (1972, p. 74) conclusions based on his review of research methodology that preceded the 1965 inquiry are important in this regard:

> A variety of observations during the pretests provided us with preliminary evidence concerning the trustworthiness of reports of specific types of behavior. <u>We learned that activities that are routinized, provided they take up longer periods of time, can be ascertained even with rather superficial procedures, and are little affected by faulty performance of the interviewer</u>; examples are sleep, major meals, and work outside the home. However, routinized behavior of short duration (e.g. brushing teeth, shopping for incidentals) is very sensitive to differences in data collection and interviewer performance. The same applies to all activities that accompany other behavior (i.e., secondary activities). . . . Thus, any time-budget report contains data of widely varying reliability and validity [emphasis added].

It is evident that there are great difficulties in evaluating detailed data from time-budget studies. However, since routine activities of relatively long duration are a major focus here, the problems are fewer.

As is indicated in the above quotation, secondary activities are difficult to record accurately. Scheuch (1972, p. 77) found evidence that "the more a person is part of an industrial society with a very high density of communication, and the more educated a person, the more likely he is to do a number of activities simultaneously." The greater simplicity of time usage of workers in the 1920s and 1930s may thus compensate somewhat for the less adequate methodology employed in the studies of that period (this is discussed below). In general, Soviet cities do not compare to those of Western Europe and the United States with respect to the complexity of activities, the availability of services, and the "density of communication." This is evident to anyone who has visited Soviet cities. Time usage in rural areas is undoubtedly even less complex. It is significant that much of the time-budget data comes from cities in the eastern regions of the RSFSR where the severe climate and recent development and population growth have made for a far simpler existence than in cities such as Moscow, Leningrad, or Kiev. These factors also contribute somewhat to the confidence one may place in the validity of the general findings based on the time-budget studies.

There are considerable seasonal variations in the use of time. This, of course, further complicates the comparison of time-budgets. During the summer, for example, the time spent on housework by men generally increases, for they are able to devote more time to gardening. The severity of the Russian winter in most areas obviously has a profound influence on the time spent on a wide range of activities. Time-budget studies usually are conducted in the warmer months of the year, and only rarely are data available from the same region for more than one season.

A more serious problem arises with the variation in time usage during the week. The better studies indicate time usage separately for workdays, days off, and the day prior to the day off. Considerable research by Soviet social scientists has been devoted to the study of differences in the use of time on these days that come about as a result of either changes in the schedule of work shifts or changes in the number of days worked per week or hours worked per day. I have not analyzed variations in time usage for different days of the week, but rather attempted wherever sufficient data are available to calculate the weekly expenditure of time, or used the expenditures for some longer period. This often entailed the appropriate weighting of time usage reported for two or three different types of days during a week. To further facilitate comparison and to focus upon only the large differences in time usage, time spent on each category is shown as a percentage of the total unit of time. The Soviet sources may report the time spent on activities per average 24-hour period during the week, per weekday, day off, and day prior to the day off, or even per month or year. For the most part, only in the case of the rather small but highly significant amount of time spent on study and raising one's qualifications have I shown the actual time spent per day.

The discussion of sampling techniques utilized by the Soviet investigators is generally either absent or obscure. It is often quite clear, however, that the methods leave much to be desired. The study of Pskov was unique in that a representative sample of the population of the entire city and suburbs was drawn. This was because the city was included in the aforementioned 1965 multinational endeavor, and procedures had to conform with the specifications agreed upon by other countries (Szalai 1973). Sometimes, as in the case of the study of Erevan, we are told that the sample includes a certain proportion of the industrial work force and that it is representative of workers in a particular region (Petrosyan 1966, p. 87). At other times—and far more frequently—a number of industrial enterprises in a region are selected. Occasionally there is mention of some form of sampling technique such as a random selection of individuals from reportedly representative workshops. In the large-scale study of several regions conducted by the Central Statistical Bureau of the Russian Republic in September 1959, the families studied were the same as those that had been "systematically" selected for a study of personal income and monetary expenditures (Artemov 1967, p. 74). It is often stated that factories have been selected because they are especially productive and successful. In research conducted in Kiev in 1962, for example, we are told that the factories under study are "leading enterprises in their branches in the Kiev economic district" (Goncharenko et al. 1963, p. 52). If anything, therefore, it can be assumed that the workers in the studies are materially better off than the average worker, and any conclusions with regard to the achievements of women as a result of the fruits of industrialization are exaggerated.

I am concerned here with differences between the time-budgets of male and female workers with, at a minimum, controls for age and family and employment status—variables having a major.impact on daily activities. However, the cross-classification of data is extremely limited in Soviet sources. Comparisons of sex differences by social class, income and education, for example, are often available (see Bolgov 1964; Baikova 1970; Gordon and Klopov 1972; Patrushev 1963). The absence of controls for age and family status make most of the material useless. Even in the cases where there is considerable effort to take these variables into consideration, there is an utter failure to indicate anything about the spouses of the married individuals under investigation. I have yet to find a single study that includes such data.

The fact that such a large proportion of Soviet women are engaged in full-time employment makes the situation a bit less difficult to assess. However, among older age groups the deficit of males makes it likely that many women who are working do not have husbands. Soviet studies do not show the difference between the time usage of older women who do have husbands present and those who do not.

The methods of data collection have varied somewhat over time and appear to be improving as time use becomes more complex. Most research undertaken during the 1920s and 1930s involved having each individual relate from memory the amount of time spent on particular activities over a given period in the past (Kryazhev 1966, p. 42). In the studies by Strumilin (1957, p. 271) in 1922-24, workers answered questionnaires concerning their time usage both on weekdays and days off. In addition, the workers were asked to list the amount of time spent per month on activities that they engaged in infrequently, such as laundering, taking a bath, and attending performances or shows. These monthly expenditures were then included in the daily budgets as one-thirtieth of the time reported.

The method was not considered very accurate, for the respondents usually did not remember activities taking less than between 5 and 15 minutes. In the studies done since 1958, rather than reporting the amount of time spent on particular categories of time, those involved were asked to list their time expenditures in chronological order. At first, all activities from the time of awakening on one day until the time of awakening on the next day were included. This was found to be somewhat inaccurate and was replaced with instructions to list activities from 6:00 a. m. until the same hour on the following day (Kryazhev 1966, pp. 42-45; Artemov 1967, pp. 52-53).

Prior to the study the participants would be briefed about the objectives (Bibik 1961, p. 13). In more recent studies the preparations prior to the day when the time expenditures were to be recorded apparently became more extensive. The respondents were asked to list all their activities on the previous day in chronological order. It was felt that this would facilitate remembering the order and timing of activities that would transpire on the following day. The researchers checked the accuracy with which the respondents recorded their time usage and probed for omissions (Kryazhev 1966, pp. 45-46).

Time-Budget Research of the 1920s and 1930s

My discussion here is restricted primarily to the work of Strumilin (1957; 1964), for the detail and sophistication of the findings reported from his studies of the early 1920s make it possible to compare this research with that conducted since 1958. What complicates the use of the early research is the fact that it was expressly undertaken to provide information for those directing the economy:

> The main objective was to stimulate the productive forces of the emerging socialist planning system. Economics, as a science of needs, resources and constraints, imposed its objective and qualitative method; time was treated as money. Social differences were given less consideration than common progress. Indicators were expressed as average time devoted within a global population, to activities which were not finely analyzed. . . .
>
> After 1960, methods changed. Sociology was no longer reduced to social economics. It gained a place of its own alongside philosophy. Objective methods became more exacting (Dumazedier 1974, p. 46).

The available results from the several large studies from the 1930s are particularly hard to compare. Investigators who conducted an extensive study in Leningrad in the winter of 1931-32 claimed that their research showed a substantial reduction since 1923 in the time spent on housework and an increase in the time spent sleeping and studying by both male and female workers (Lebedev-Patreiko et al. 1933, pp. 38-40). This appears to be largely the result of the authors' desire to show that progress has been made. Their gross comparison lacks any control for differences in sample composition. The 1931-32 sample included workers as young as eight years old, but there is no presentation of results that simultaneously cross-classifies time use by sex, age, and marital status. In my own analysis of the data in the book's appendix on time-budgets of working males and females by family size, I found no support for the authors' contentions. Other studies from this era also suffer from peculiarities in the classification of time, the reporting of time use for only one day of the week, and a lack of adequate attention to differences between social categories. However, the results appear to deviate little from those of Strumilin (see Baikova 1965, p. 51; Kingsbury and Fairchild 1935, pp. 251, 290; Bolgov 1973, p. 51).

The earliest Soviet time-budget study of industrial workers was conducted in December 1922. As was often the practice, this research supplemented one of the periodic studies of monetary budgets. All the 267 adult members of 76 families were included. There were approximately 47 female and 98 male industrial workers (Strumilin 1957, pp. 271-75). Because of the small size of the sample and the fact that the data were available for weekday time usage only, the findings do not warrant further attention. They are, however, quite comparable to those from the considerably larger study conducted during the following winter.

The 1923-24 study included 1,253 adults, but only 313 male and 147 female workers. Strumilin (1957, pp. 288-89) indicates that the workers included in the study came from all the chief branches of industry. Single workers are grossly underrepresented. Though they constituted 56 percent of the industrial labor force in 1897, only 7 percent of the female workers and 6 percent of the male workers in this study were unmarried. The express purpose of the research was to study families and not workers in general.

While the sampling technique is not described, Strumilin (1957, p. 288) does note that half the workers were drawn from 10 small industrial regions of Russia, the "provinces," and the remainder came from the "capitals"—Moscow and Petrograd (present-day Leningrad). However, the 1923 census of the urban population indicates that only 15 percent of the urban proletariat were residing in the capitals. The sample of office workers was drawn solely from Moscow and Petrograd. The data used to construct Table 5.1 came from estimates of the monthly expenditure of time which Strumilin based on time-budgets from weekdays and the day off.

These characteristics of the sample actually made it more comparable to the samples of the 1960s, for the latter were drawn almost

TABLE 5.1

General Time-Budget of Workers, December 1923 to January 1924
(figures in percent of a month)

Category	Number	Work and Time Connected	Housework	Free Time	Physiological Needs	Total
Males						
Moscow[a]	(56)	31	7	20	42	100
Petrograd[a]	(67)	30	7	22	42	101
Provinces[a]	(149)	32	8	18	42	99
Capitals[b]	(41)	32	6	21	42	101
Females						
Moscow[a]	(38)	30	24	6	40	100
Petrograd[a]	(26)	30	22	8	40	100
Provinces[a]	(59)	30	22	11	37	100
Capitals[b]	(24)	29	17	14	40	100

[a]These figures are based on time-budgets of factory workers. "Provinces" refers to Ivano-Vosnesensk, Nizhnyi-Novgorod, Kostroma, Vladimir, Bryansk, Ekaterinoslav, Tula, Tambov, Simbirsk, and Arkhangel'sk (Strumilin 1957, p. 288).

[b]These figures are based on time-budgets of office workers in Petrograd and Moscow.

Source: Based on figures in Strumilin (1957, pp. 708-20).

exclusively from very large cities and did not include persons under age 16—undoubtedly, a very substantial proportion of the unmarried working population in the 1920s.

Table 5.1 shows that in the early 1920s the differences between the pattern of male and female time use were very distinct and consistent. Though both spent about an equal amount of time on formal work, females had in excess of three times as much housework as men. For employed females these domestic responsibilities averaged between one-fifth and one-fourth of every 24 hours. The extra time of men was largely devoted to free-time activities.

The variations from this pattern can largely be explained by differences in the age and marital status of the women. Older and/or married women are more likely to have larger families to care for. Thus, we find that in the provinces, for example, only 29 percent of the women were 35 or older, whereas in Moscow and Petrograd this was true of 50 percent and 62 percent respectively. It is not surprising, therefore, that the provincial women have more free time.

The smaller amount of free time among females in Moscow can be explained by the fact that all of them were married. Though there are discrepancies in the figures presented by Strumilin (1957, pp. 289, 708-20), it appears that about 19 percent of the females from Leningrad and 10 percent of those from the provinces were single.

An important aspect of free time related to occupational advancement is the time spent on what was then called "self-education." This included activities such as reading newspapers, books, and magazines, attending clubs, schools, and lectures, and going to exhibits and museums (Strumilin 1959, p. 315). Female workers in Moscow, Petrograd and the provinces spent, respectively, 0.2, 0.3, and 0.6 hours per day on self-education. The figures for males varied between 1.7 and 2.2 hours per day—a sharp and unmistakable contrast (Strumilin 1957, pp. 708-20).

The female office workers in Petrograd and Moscow deviate somewhat from the other groups. The pattern of time use of these workers suggests that they are young, though there are no data on this. (See my comments above on the effect of age and marital status on time use.) They are probably well educated. Both these characterisitics are reflected in the considerable amount of time they spent on "self-education" (1.4 hours per day). Despite this, however, the amount of free time they had was far less than that of any group of the males, and they did nearly three times as much housework as male office workers. Neither urban living nor age, occupation or education seriously alter the pattern of sex differences.

Before considering the contemporary studies and comparing the findings with those from the 1920s, it is important to consider briefly the implications of the detail Strumilin presents regarding domestic chores. This detail makes it clear that the sexual division of labor is entirely understated by the gross housework categories employed in contemporary studies. Two examples serve to illustrate this quite clearly.

About half or more of the time that women spent on housework was devoted to preparing food. This was about twice the comparable proportion for men. What is concealed by this main category of housework, however, is the fact that 77 percent of the time working men spent preparing food was devoted to carrying water and cutting wood, while the comparable figure for women was only 10 percent.

The proportion of the time devoted to housework that is spent caring for children is about the same for men and women, but this too conceals a great difference in task allocation.[1] Seventy-eight percent of the time spent caring for children by male industrial workers was devoted to teaching grammar and only 16 percent was devoted to the care of infants; the figures for females are, respectively, 4 and 55 percent! There are many other such examples which provide convincing evidence of the inadequacy of gross categories of housework (Strumilin 1957, pp. 307, 311-12). But what is certain is that the broad differences in the time allocation of males and females revealed by looking at the four main categories (work, housework, free time, and time spent on physiological needs) merely hint at the myriad of more subtle differences in the chores of daily living. This is much the same problem faced in Chapter 4 with regard to occupational categories.

Contemporary Studies

To make general comparisons with earlier studies, I collected all the research that provided sufficient information to determine the weekly distribution of time in the four categories of what is called the "general time-budget." It was necessary to exclude studies that were deficient in this respect. However, parts of these are discussed in later sections. Still other studies were eliminated because of the small sample size. Thus, for example, certain studies of Leningrad (Belyaev et al. 1962), Kazan (Zhuravlev 1969), Moscow (Petrosyan 1965, p. 131; Kryazhev and Markovich 1962) and Novosibirsk (Artemov 1967, pp. 154-56) were found to be unacceptable.

There were several cases in which multiple presentations of the same data in different sources showed discrepancies. The most recent reports were chosen in these cases, for, as previously mentioned, there are definite signs of greater sophistication in the more recent research and discussion.

With only three exceptions, all the studies included factory workers, office workers, and engineering-technical personnel from selected industrial enterprises. The study of Mirnyi was based on a sample of 10 percent of all those working in industry and institutions of the city (Kokarev et al. 1970, p. 189); the sample from Pskov included all types of employed persons (Kolpakov and Patrushev 1971, p. 82) and the 1966

TABLE 5.2

Cities Included in the Time-Budget Studies in 1959, by Republic and Population

Republic	City	Population, 1959
RSFSR	Gorkii[a]	941,962
	Irkutsk	365,893
	Ivanovo[a]	335,161
	Kostroma	171,720
	Krasnoyarsk[a]	412,375
	Mirnyi	5,695
	Moscow	5,045,905
	Novokuznetsk	277,671
	Pskov	81,073
	Sverdlovsk[a]	778,602
Ukraine	Dnepropetrovsk	660,832
	Kiev	1,109,840
	Zaporozh'e	449,200
Armenia	Erevan	493,494

[a]Data also available from the region having the same name.
Source: Ts.S.U. 1963, pp. 30-38; 1972a, pp. 43, 45, 47, 49.

study of the four cities of Dnepropetrovsk, Zaporozh'e, Odessa, and Kostroma included factory workers and no engineering-technical personnel or office workers (Gordon and Klopov 1972a, p. 28).

Table 5.2 shows that the cities included in the selected time-budget studies are located mainly though not exclusively in the Russian Republic. (The one city located in Armenia is the capital of the republic, it has a very large population and probably a large proportion of the workers are of Russian nationality. Cities in the Ukraine should be even more akin to those located in European Russia. The greatest variation probably exists among the cities located in different regions within the RSFSR.) With the exception of Mirnyi, Pavlovskii Posad, and Pskov, all the cities had populations of well over 100,000 in 1959. In 1965, when the Pskov study was conducted, the population of the city had reached 115,000, and by the time of the 1963 study of Ivanovo and Krasnoyarsk these cities had populations exceeding one-half million (Kolpakov and Patrushev 1971, p. 82). However, only 51 percent of the urban population of the Russian Republic lived in cities of over 100,000 in 1959. The figure rose only six percentage points by 1970 (Ts.S.U. 1972a, p. 62). There is thus a blatant underrepresentation of small and, perhaps, medium-sized cities.

Although data are available from workers in the oblasts of Rostov, Sverdlovsk, Ivanovo, and Gorkii, as well as Krasnoyarsk Krai, they too, for the most part, probably either resided in very large cities or not very far from them. Pavlovskii Posad, one of the only two small cities, is located about 50 miles outside Moscow. The effects of any egalitarian ideology and of industrialization are likely to be more potent in large cities and, if anything, this sampling should have exaggerated those influences.

All the data from studies in 1963 were collected during May and June (Tumanov 1964, p. 74; Kolpakov and Patrushev 1971, p. 82; Patrushev 1966, p. 97). The study of Mirnyi was probably done in the spring; that in Pskov and the 1959 study of Krasnoyarsk were conducted in autumn; the study of Erevan was done in June; and there are strong indications that the 1966 study of Dnepropetrovsk and other cities was done during the summer months (Kokarev et al. 1970, p. 188; Kolpakov and Patrushev 1971, p. 82; Baikova 1970, p. 93; Gordon and Klopov 1972a, pp. 28-30). There is only one study that sources indicate to have been definitely conducted during the winter months (February-March of 1962), and that was done in Moscow. The sample included only workers and employees in a locomotive and diesel enterprise (Mialkin 1962, p. 24). Information is unavailable on the season in which the remaining studies (Kiev, Kostroma, Moscow, and other cities in about 1959, and Novokuznetsk) were conducted, but given the understandable penchant to avoid the brutal Russian winter, it is probable that most, if not all, were undertaken during relatively warm months. This is a very significant difference between these and the studies of the 1920s and 1930s—a point I shall return to below.

The study sites in Siberia are especially distinguished by their severe climate and youthful population. These factors have a profound influence on time usage and warrant a separate consideration of the regions. In Table 5. 3 I have arrayed the findings from the Siberian studies. The columns are in chronological order and, coincidentally, also in order of their geographic location. Mirnyi is deep in Eastern Siberia (Yakutsk Autonomous Soviet Socialist Republic), while all the others stretch across Western Siberia, with Novokuznetsk the most westerly. In Novokuznetsk during half the year the mean temperature does not go above freezing, although there may be as many as 30 days when the temperature exceeds 68 degrees Fahrenheit (Economist Intelligence Unit 1963, p. 28); Mirnyi, on the other extreme, has eight months of winter and a short, relatively warm summer (Kokarev et al. 1970, p. 190).

The important characteristic of the Siberian cities is that they are and have been growing rapidly and thus contain a large proportion of young migrants. This is particularly true of Mirnyi, where the authors specifically note that the abundance of young and single workers has inflated the amount of free time. The amount of housework done by men is, they say, high in comparison to that in cities of European Russia due to the high proportion of women working and the relatively

TABLE 5.3

General Time-Budget of Male and Female Workers in Siberian Cities
(figures in percent of a week)

	Novokuznetsk	Krasnoyarsk Krai		Krasnoyarsk City		Irkutsk[b]	Mirnyi
	1959(?)	1959	1963	1959	1963	1963	1966
Males							
N	n. a.	n. a.[a]	n. a.[a]	n. a.	(595)	n. a.	n. a.[c]
Work and time connected	35	36	33	36	32	36	31
Housework	10	11	9	9	8	10	9
Physiological needs	35	38	37	38	37	36	38
Free time	21	15	20	17	23	18	23
Total	101	100	99	100	100	100	101
Females							
N	n. a.	n. a.[a]	n. a.[a]	n. a.	(364)	n. a.	n. a.[c]
Work and time connected	36	34	31	35	31	34	30
Housework	21	19	20	20	19	16	20
Physiological needs	34	36	35	34	34	33	35
Free time	9	12	14	12	16	16	15
Total	100	101	100	101	100	99	100

n. a.: data not available.

[a]It has been reported that the 1959 study of Krasnoyarsk Krai included about 1,000 workers and the 1963 study of the region included about three times that number (Baikova 1970, p. 93).

[b]The respondents from this study were workers in machine-construction enterprises (Tumanov 1964, p. 74).

[c]A total of 371 employees of the diamond-extracting enterprises were included. The sample reportedly was largely made up of males and constituted 10 percent of the city's working population (Kokarev 1970, p. 189).

Sources: Patrushev 1966, p. 88; Kokarev et al. 1970, pp. 188-90; Petrosyan 1965, pp. 94-96; Tumanov 1964, pp. 74, 77-78, 84; Prudenskii 1972, p. 296; Kolpakov and Patrushev 1971, p. 83.

large number of men without wives. Time spent on housework is also increased by the poor quality of the houses (many lack running water and central heating) and the lack of communal everyday services (Kokarev et al. 1970).

I found no data on the growth of the population prior to 1959, but the 1970 census (Ts. S. U. 1972a, p. 42) shows that the population of Mirnyi has more than quadrupled since 1959. This is not an isolated industrial city unexposed to the ideology of population centers. As is probably true of workers in larger cities of Western Siberia, the young migrants have come largely from regions located in the European part of the Soviet Union and to a lesser extent from the Irkutsk, Chitinsk, and other oblasts of Eastern Siberia (Kokarev et al. 1970, p. 190). The population of Irkutsk has increased 146 percent between 1939 and 1959, while that of Krasnoyarsk and Novokuznetsk has increased 217 percent and 209 percent respectively (Ts. S. U. 1963, pp. 30-38).[2] Of course, these latter three cities already exceeded one-quarter million population in 1959 (see Table 5. 2).

Another factor which may explain the relatively large amount of free time particularly in Krasnoyarsk is the type of workers included in the study. The free time of both males and females in Krasnoyarsk is greater than that in most of the cities of Siberia as well as those in the western regions of the USSR from which data are available. Soviet investigators explain that this is due to the fact that the workers in this area, unlike those of many other regions, are employed primarily in heavy industry. The workers in such factories have both a higher education and income. They can better afford household appliances, improved housing, etc. and also will be less inclined to seek extra income by spending their spare time on private agricultural endeavors (Kolpakov and Patrushev 1971, p. 84).

The decline in the time spent working in Krasnoyarsk between 1959 and 1963 is due to the shortening of the workday by one hour (Prudenskii 1972, p. 296). Both men and women appear to have benefited by having decreased housework and increased free time, though men did gain more free time than women. However, differences in methodology and sampling make precise longitudinal comparison very difficult.[3] (The effect of altered work schedules is discussed at greater length in a later section.)

The above factors appear to have resulted in some significant differences between the average figures of the Siberian cities and those of the cities west of the Urals (see Table 5. 4). Table C. 1 shows the sample sizes and time-budgets for cities west of the Urals. Some of the difference between the time use in these sites and those in Siberia is an artifact of the time classification. The category "other" in several of the studies conducted in the regions west of the Urals includes time elsewhere classified under housework. This aspect is usually travel associated with completing domestic chores (see footnote d, Table C. 1). Siberian women spent more time working but may have had

TABLE 5.4

Average Time-Budget Figures from Studies Conducted during the 1920s and the 1960s
(figures in percent of a week)

	Males			Females		
		1960s			1960s	
	1920s	Siberia	West[a]	1920s	Siberia	West[a]
Work and time connected with work	31.0	34.1	30.5	30.0	33.0	29.5
Housework	7.0	9.4	8.1	21.3	19.3	18.4
Total work	38.0	43.5	38.6	51.3	52.3	47.9
Physiological needs	42.0	37.0	39.7	39.3	34.4	38.1
Free time	20.3	19.6	20.5	9.8	13.4	12.7
Total	100.3	100.1	98.8[b]	100.4	100.1	98.7[b]

[a]Regions west of the Urals.

[b]These totals are below 100 percent because of the category "other" included in time-budgets of these regions (see Table C.1, Appendix C).

Source: Table 5.3 and Table C.1.

slightly more "free time" as a result of time devoted to physiological needs. Again, the larger amount of housework done by men probably is not attributable to their greater willingness to help their wives, but rather to the large number of bachelors in an environment where they cannot purchase all the services that a wife usually assumes (cf. Skolnick 1973, pp. 32-33).

What is most significant here is the difference between the 1920s and the 1960s. These are certainly attributable in part to differences in time classification and the methods of conducting the research. However, the very slight increase in the housework of men and the decline for women, as well as the greater free time of women in the 1960s, can largely be explained by a rather obvious factor: the season during which the studies were conducted. As already noted, the studies in the 1960s the proportion of time spent on housework that men devoted Strumilin chose the depths of winter. This significantly influences domestic chores.

From those studies reporting relevant data, I found that during the 1960s the proportion of time spent on housework which men devoted to gardening and care of livestock varied between 13 and 44 percent; it averaged 30 percent. It is not surprising that this figure was far lower in January and February of 1923-24. Such activities occupied 4 percent of the housework time of male workers in Moscow, 13 percent in Petrograd, and 5 percent among the office workers. The only deviation from this pattern was among the workers in the provinces (the figure was 28 percent) where the workers apparently owned cows and goats that required attention throughout the year (Strumilin 1957, pp. 300, 708-20). The average figure for the 1920s was only 8 percent. Since the housework of men increased by only 17 percent between the 1920s and the 1960s, this can probably be explained solely by the seasonal differences in activities rather than any change in the quantity of housework done by men.

There is the possibility that workers in Moscow and Leningrad in the 1920s did not own plots of land as workers often do today. (This is discussed at greater length later in this chapter.) Since we lack data on the use of time by workers in the summer, this issue is difficult to resolve. It is more probable, however, that a great many returned to the rural areas in summer to aid other family members with planting and harvesting or, perhaps, returned to the countryside during their days off in the warmer months. Kushner (1970, Chapter vi), in his well-known study of the village of Viriatino, discusses the importance of prerevolutionary migrant miners who spread revolutionary literature upon their periodic returns to the countryside. Wolf (1969) noted the close and crucial link between Russian peasants and industrial workers in the first years of the twentieth century. Kogan (1970) found that even today industrial workers may frequently return to relatives in villages mainly for rest and the exchange of goods, but also in some cases to help out with the agricultural chores.

Seasonal differences also influence female time-budgets. In the 1960s during the summer months many children attended summer camp, reducing the time that mothers had to devote to their care (Trufanov 1970, p. 143). Also, there is greater impetus during warm months to devote more time to outdoor activities in lieu of sedentary winter pursuits such as knitting and crocheting. The latter expenditures may sometimes be classified as "free time," while the former are considered housework.

In the early time-budget studies "care of children" was not distinguished from "upbringing of children". In the 1960s the former is usually subsumed under housework, but the latter is a free-time pursuit (cf. Gordon and Klopov 1972a, p. 130). The effect of both these artifacts of the classification of activities is to inflate the time recorded as housework in the 1920s and that recorded as free time in the 1960s.

This points to some of the serious problems involved with classifying time. There is much current discussion of the issues involved here. See, for example, Javeau 1974.

Unlike their male counterparts, working women devote only a small amount of time to gardening relative to that spent on other household chores. It is significant that Soviet researchers have suggested that it may be inappropriate to classify gardening as housework, for "today it is not so much a source of extra income as a form of rest, a means of relating to nature, etc." (Gordon and Klopov 1972a, p. 37). This, of course, would mean that the housework of men is overestimated.

In sum, three points are worth emphasizing here: (1) The reduction of housework is relatively small; (2) this reduction is not the result of men assuming a greater portion of domestic responsibilities; and (3) the greatest change is probably more apparent than real—largely a product of extraneous factors such as the season, the composition of the samples, and differences in time classification.

The temporal continuity in the differences between male and female time usage parallels findings regarding the degree of geographic continuity. Robinson et al. (1973) examined the combined time spent on work, including associated travel, and housework by employed males and females in cities of the 1965 12-nation study. Despite the extreme differences in technological development between such sites as Lima, Peru, Kragujevac, Yugoslavia and Jackson, Michigan, it was found that these activities occupied 43 percent of the workday and 16 percent of the day off of employed men and 49 percent of the workday and 26 percent of the day off of employed women, while "the variation by site occupies a range of much less than plus or minus 10 percent around these averages" (1973, pp. 127-28).

The temporal trend is supported by Vanek's (1973) comparison of time usage in the United States between the 1930s and the 1960s. She concluded that there has been little change in the total time employed and nonemployed women spend on housework. Rather, with the spread of modern household technology there has been a shift from the expenditure of time on "maintenance aspects of housework" to "managerial and interactional tasks" (1973, Chapters 3 and 4)—a finding consistent with assertions by Tilly and Scott (1975). Woman's greater place in the factory or office has not vastly altered her place in the home.

VARIATIONS BY AGE

The attitudes of young Soviet working women appear to be different from those of their older counterparts (see Chapter 3). That age is a significant variable is, of course, widely acknowledged. In his classic article on the subject, Kingsley Davis (1974) asserts that youth is more receptive to change and is more idealistic than older generations and that this is particularly evident in societies experiencing rapid social change. The close relationship between age and education in the Soviet Union (see Table A. 6 and Gordon and Klopov 1972b, p. 10) should, as evidence from the United States suggests, enhance the differences between groups of older and younger women:

> The Daniel Yankelovich polling agency told us several years ago . . . that the really important "gap" was not

> so much the widely publicized "generation gap" as the less publicized "education gap." There were, by and large, as many differences between young college and noncollege youth as between youth and their parents. For, in general, less-educated persons tend to be somewhat older as well as more conservative than the better educated and conversely, older persons tend to be less well educated than younger. Thus, any comparison of older with younger women involves comparing quite different populations. Any cross-section comparison of women of different ages tells us as much about their schooling as it does about their age, if not more (Bernard 1975, p. 167).

However, just as the data do not make it possible to tease out the confounding influences of age and education, so too it is not possible to separate the impact of age from that of life-cycle stage. What the evidence does suggest is that the latter is the most profound factor influencing female time use and that there is little indication that young men are more willing than generations before them to assume household chores.

There are four studies from which data by sex and age were available (see Table C. 2). Again, particular characteristics of individual studies give rise to considerable variation in the findings. These include, among other things, the season and the year the study was conducted, the geographic location, and the age groupings. Also, the data from two studies show weekly time usage while those from the other two are for workdays only.

Perhaps the most significant study is that of Pskov. The large sample represented the entire working population of the city. Of course, Pskov may be a poor representative of characteristic Russian cities. The very small size of the samples of groups over age 50 lead us to seriously question findings based on this group. Since there were only two women aged 50 and older in Krasnoyarsk Krai, this group is excluded from the analysis below.

The greatest change in time usage occurs at about age 25, when both males and females are starting to form their own families. (Data from the 1963 study of Krasnoyarsk City show that among those under 25 years old, 81 percent were unmarried and an additional 23 percent were married but without any children. In age group 26 to 35 only 19 percent were unmarried, while 47 percent were married with children [Artemov et al. 1967, p. 92]. See also Table 3. 6.) Figure 1 shows that there is a very sharp increase in the housework of females in all the studies, with a leveling off when they are somewhere in their 30s. For males the increase is far less dramatic. The age breakdown is very broad and certainly leaves much to be desired, but the patterns revealed are fairly consistent.

FIGURE 1

Percentage of Time Spent on Housework by Workers in Krasnoyarsk Krai, Erevan, Pskov, and Rostov, Sverdlovsk, Gorkii, and Ivanovsk Oblasts, by Age and Sex
(the upper lines are for females and the lower lines are for males)

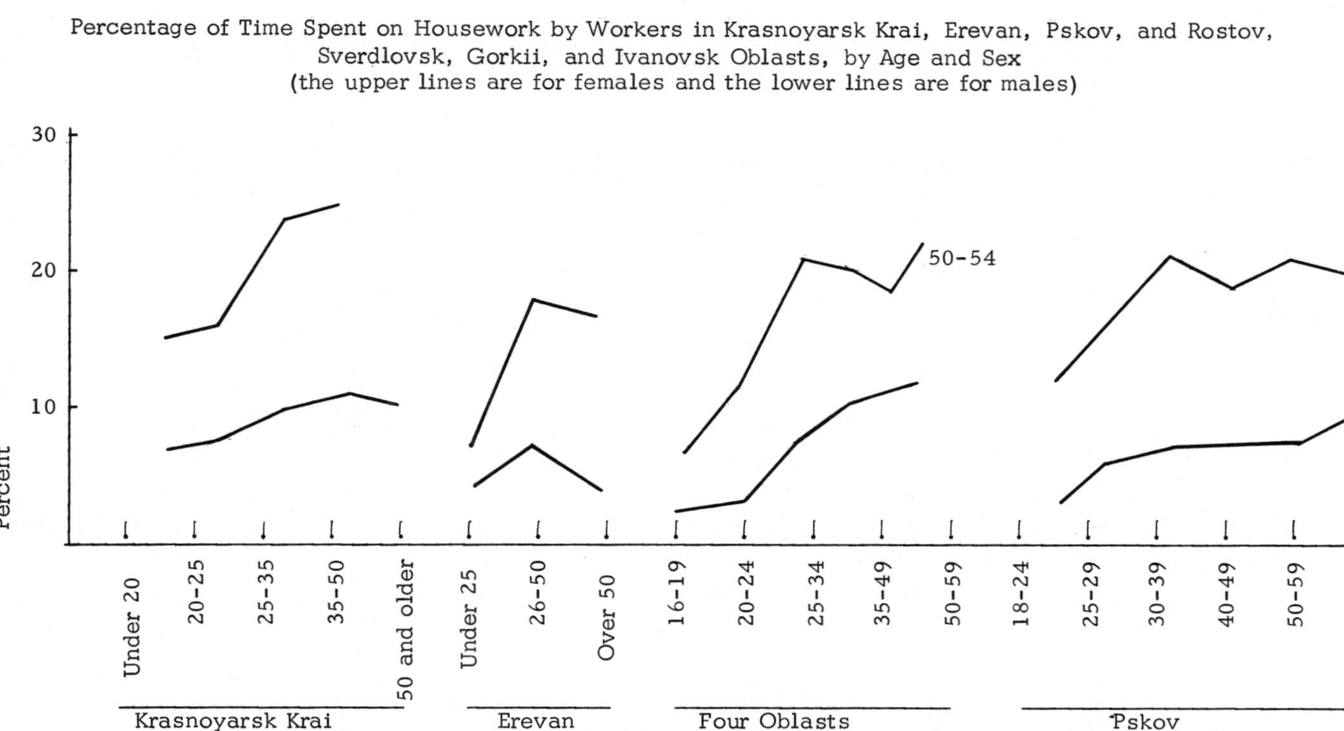

Source: Data from Table C.2.

FIGURE 2

Percentage of Free Time of Workers in Krasnoyarsk Krai, Erevan, Pskov, and Rostov, Sverdlovsk, Gorkii, and Ivanovsk Oblasts, by Age and Sex
(the upper lines are for males and the lower ones are for females)

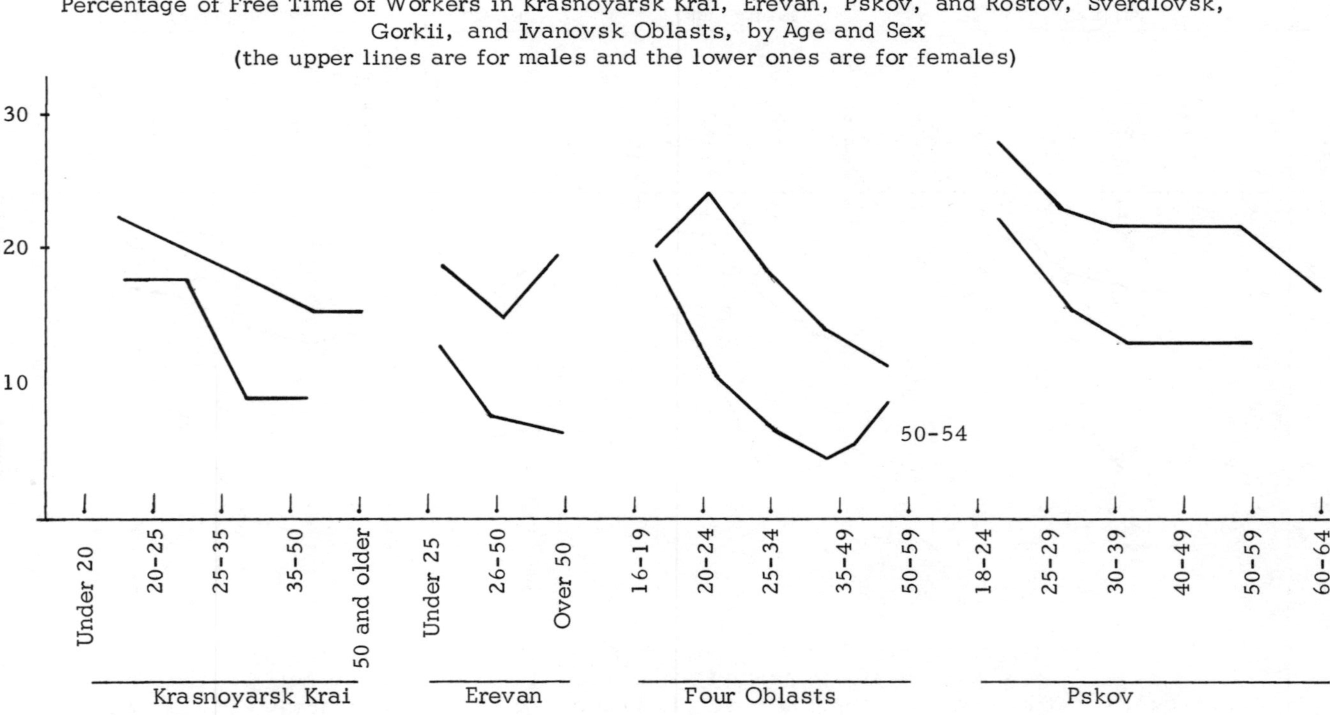

Source: Data from Table C. 2.

There is somewhat less consistency in the data shown in Figure 2, although it is apparent that over most of their life span the gap in free time between males and females remains quite stable.[4] Prior to marriage it appears to be relatively small, while on the other end of the continuum there is some evidence that it may again decline among older men and women. (The gap increases, according to the evidence from the Erevan study; data from Krasnoyarsk Krai are inadequate. It is possible that the sample of older persons in Erevan is quite small. This increased gap may also be explained by the fact that in this Armenian city the older generation may have been more conservative and had larger families. Older women were also more likely to have husbands than were those in the Russian cities. The sex ratios of the urban population in the RSFSR aged 50 to 54 and 55 to 59 were, respectively, 62 and 50, while in Armenia the comparable figures were 80 and 69 [Ts. S. U. 1972b, pp. 18-19, 66-67]. Evidence below indicates that the husband's presence may increase the amount of housework done by married women.) Data from a large study conducted in Leningrad in 1931 indicate a very similar pattern (Kingsbury and Fairchild 1935, pp. 251, 290).

Not surprisingly, there is a sharp distinction between the amount of time women under about age 25 spent on studies and the amount spent by the age groups older than this. There is also a very sharp decline for men, however, at a much slower rate than that of women. Whereas women in their early 20s spent about as much time studying as did men, in the next age group males spent about twice the time on this activity, and the ratio increases considerably in the still older groups. In Krasnoyarsk, Pskov, and the four oblasts, by age 50 there were at least some men still studying whereas no women were doing so (see Table C. 2). I assume that the average figures indicate that some men were studying for a considerable amount of time, rather than that large numbers engaged in this activity for only a short time.

VARIATIONS BY FAMILY STATUS

Few data are available on time usage by family status. There is usually a lack of controls for age, social class, and other important variables. However, the findings are consistent and support those based on variations by age: housework increases and free time decreases when a woman marries. The sharpest increase in housework and decrease in free time occurs with the birth of the first child; the trend continues, though at a slower rate with the birth of more children. In some cases there is evidence that older children may help out somewhat with household chores. The presence of relatives, presumably grandparents, who are not employed in the labor force reduces the housework of the working mothers. And, lastly, it is evident that younger children generally demand more time than do older children. The even sparser material on males shows similar patterns; however, men always have far more free time and far less housework. These data come from a diversity of regions including Krasnoyarsk (Artemov et al. 1967, pp. 84-87), Moscow (Kryazhev 1966, pp. 105-7), Erevan, and Kostroma (Petrosyan 1965, pp. 103, 106-9) and Pskov (Kolpakov and Patrushev 1971, p. 73; Szalai (ed.) 1972, pp. 640-57).

The data from a study of Moscow in the early 1960s (Kryazhev 1966, pp. 105-7) are of special interest, for they are restricted to a single age and income group. The respondents were working women between the ages 20 and 40 from families with an income per family member of between 35 and 50 rubles. In none of the families was there an adult who was neither working in industry nor engaged in full-time studies. The size of the sample is not stated.

Women with only one child under age one spent 42 hours per week doing housework; those with a child aged one to three spent 21 hours and those with a child three to seven years old and seven to sixteen years old spent, respectively, 33 and 25 hours per week on housework. No explanation is provided for the low figure among those with a child aged one to three (Kryazhev 1966, p. 106).

Single women in the study spent 1.3 hours per day (it is not clear whether this is an average day of the week or a weekday) on housework. Those married without children spent 2.1 hours; those married with one child spent 3.7 hours, while those with two or more children spent 4.5 hours. The indexed figures are, respectively, 100, 156, 262, and 337 (Kryazhev 1966, p. 105).

Recent research in several enterprises of Minsk, Belorussia confirms that women are often compelled to decide between a career or children. One respondent stated the following: "I am categorically against sitting at home. But to work like a man and to be weighed down by the home is also impossible. This rules out having more than one child" (Yurkevich 1970, p. 47). Litvinenko (1971, p. 42), an outspoken Soviet feminist, concurs with these sentiments: ". . . the woman must make a choice: either a child or raising her qualifications and advancing in her career. More frequently she chooses the latter." Finally, a female Soviet professor of law concludes that the reason why women are so underrepresented in top positions is that they are "overburdened with the care of children and housework; [they] are physically incapable of devoting to managerial work the great deal of time which it requires" (Berezovskaya 1975, p. 12). These points will be elaborated upon below.

A comparison of males and females can, perhaps, best be assessed from the data of the 1966 study of the large cities of Dnepropetrovsk, Zaporozh'e, Kostroma, and Odessa and the smaller city of Pavlovskii Posad. The study included only factory workers, and thus there is some limited degree of control for social class. Again, the pattern is a familiar one already largely revealed by the material on variations by age. The housework of females always exceeds that of males; for both sexes it increases with marriage and after the birth of children. However, the

FIGURE 3

Hours Per Week Spent on Housework and Care of Children in Pavlovskii Posad and the Large Cities of Dnepropetrovsk, Zaporozh'e, Kostroma, and Odessa, by Family Status and Sex, 1966
(the broken line indicates missing data)

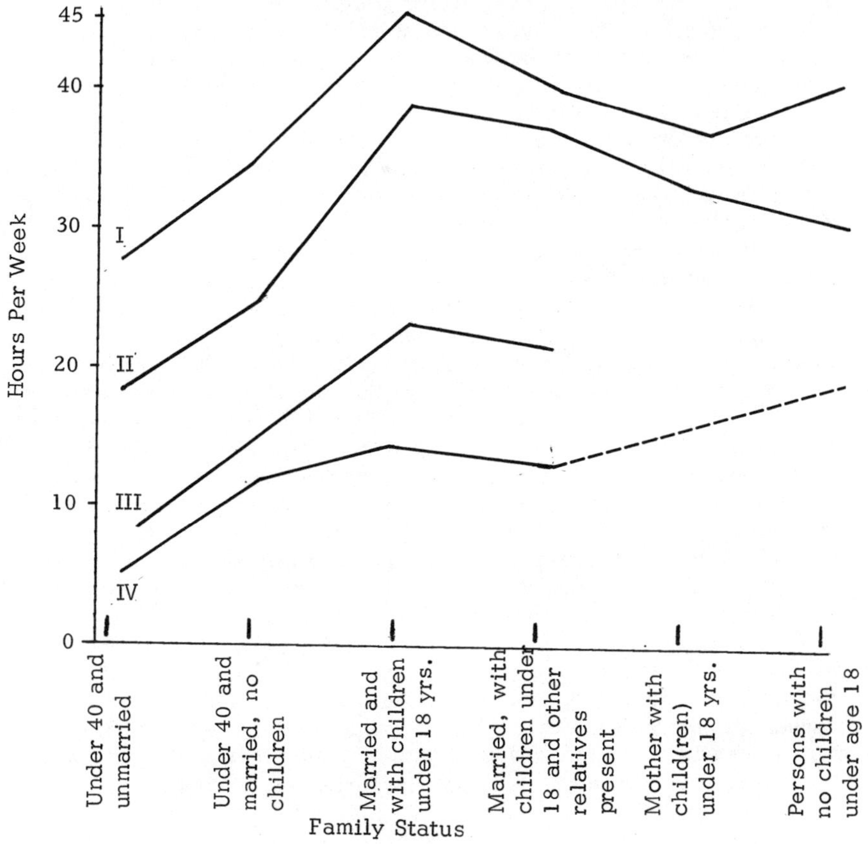

Notation:

I = females in Pavlovskii Posad.
II = females in the four large cities.
III = males in Pavlovskii Posad.
IV = males in the four large cities.

Source: Gordon and Klopov 1972b, pp. 14-15, 19.

increase is far greater for females than for males and the contrast is especially great when men and women in large cities are compared (see Figure 3).

The amount of housework in Pavlovskii Posad is greater for a number of reasons. The workers in this city have a lower age at marriage and a higher birth rate. They tend more frequently to have gardens as compared to workers in large cities. Housing conditions were far worse in the small city, where in few cases were there any running water, sewerage systems, or the provision of gas. In addition, in Pavlovskii Posad only 28 percent of the workers questioned had an education exceeding seventh grade, while in the large cities 49 percent had such an education (Gordon and Klopov 1972a, pp. 140-42). Evidence to be discussed below will more clearly show the influence of living conditions on sex differences in time use. Note, however, that married men with children appear to have benefited especially from the conveniences of urban life.

Figure 3 also shows that the presence of other relatives has only a small influence in reducing housework. This is a further indication of the need for children's institutions (see Chapter 3). Of course, in this case both relatives who are working as well as those who spend all their time doing housework are included. The influence of having a *retired* grandparent in the home may, therefore, be underestimated.

A pattern which seems to have particularly surprised Soviet analysts (cf. Levikov 1973, p. 65) is that the absence of a husband *reduces* the amount of housework of the working mother. Not only do men not help their wives, but the care of a husband is an added chore. Data from Krasnoyarsk in 1963 (Artemov et al. 1967, p. 87) and Erevan (Petrosyan 1965, p. 106), containing the only other material relevant to this, support the finding. The latter study shows that among mothers having one child and a husband present the time spent on housework ("care of self" is included in the category) is 5.4 hours per weekday, while among mothers with one child and no husband housework takes 4.9 hours. Until better data that control for the age of the mother and the number of children are available, obviously no definitive conclusion can be drawn. It is interesting to note, though, that a Western observer of the Soviet scene has argued that the women are finding husbands to be "a bad investment":

> The concept of man as a breadwinner for the family is falling by the wayside. A tendency is growing for women to have children outside of wedlock, so that they can fulfill their maternal instincts without taking on wifely chores (Marcelle Bernstein as quoted in Rowbotham 1972, p. 167).

The likelihood that few older persons were included in the study, as well as some problems with the data,[5] lead one to be particularly skeptical about the reported time use of those over age 40 with no children under age 18. There is also an absence of data on the other members of the family living with those in this group. Thus, we do not know what proportion of the women have a husband present or are living with their children and/or grandchildren. Other data show that only 12 percent of the female workers and 26 percent of the male workers over age 40 and with no children under 18 spent any time caring for children. The males in this group spent 6.7 hours and the females 17.3 hours per week caring for and bringing up children (Gordon and Klopov 1972a, p. 133; 1972b, p. 20). The average figures for the whole group are thus based on two very different groups.

CONSEQUENCES OF WOMEN'S DOUBLE BURDEN

The amount of time spent on housework has a profound influence on the worker's free time. The ramifications of sex differences in this respect are vividly illustrated by the figures in Table 5.5. The findings clearly parallel those based on age (see Figure 2). The advantages of not having a husband are again apparent: working mothers in this situation average 1.2 hours more free time per week than do those with husbands.

That career advancement is more impeded by motherhood than by fatherhood is quite evident from the figures on study time. The time working women can allocate to this, though initially at a comparable level, very quickly drops far below that of their male counterparts as they enter marriage and bear children. The presence of other relatives in the home frees more time for study—about as much as does the absence of a husband!

The pattern repeats itself in the large-scale study of Pskov. The time spent on study and organizational participation by single men is 80 minutes per average day of the week. This category is approximately equivalent to what in other studies is included under "study and self-education" plus "public work." It includes such activities as attending classes and lectures, doing homework, religious participation, and work in job-related, civic, political, and other organizations (Szalai [ed.] 1972, pp. 565-66). Marriage brings a decline to 52 minutes, while married men with children average 46 minutes on the activity. The comparable figures for females are 49, 18, and 21 (Szalai [ed.] 1972, p. 653). The reason why the time for single women is so low relative to that for single men—unlike the findings of other studies—is that "single" in this case refers to persons who never married as well as to those who are divorced or widowed (Szalai [ed.] 1972, p. 500). Single males are far more likely to be young and never married, while single females would be more likely to be divorced or widowed and older.

The data strongly support findings in the previous chapter, which indicated that males were able to advance farther than females in their

TABLE 5.5

Free Time and Time Spent Studying by Male and Female Workers in Dneptropetrovsk, Zoporozh'e, Kostroma, and Odessa, by Family Status, 1966 (hours per week)

	Free Time			Study and Self-Education*		
	Males	Females	Males as Percent of Females	Males	Females	Males as Percent of Females
Unmarried/Under 40	40.0	31.8	(1.26)	10.1	9.1	(1.11)
Married/Under 40, with no children	32.5	21.2	(1.53)	7.5	3.5	(2.14)
Married couple with children under age 18	28.9	12.4	(2.33)	3.3	1.0	(3.30)
Married couple with children under age 18, with other relatives present in the family	28.5	13.9	(2.05)	3.6	1.5	(2.40)
Mother with child(ren) under age 18	—	13.6	—	—	1.4	—
Over age 40 with no children under age 18	27.3	16.0	(1.71)	0.0	0.0	—

*It is not precisely clear what activities are considered to be included under "self-education." However, it does not include ordinary reading of newspapers, books and magazines at home. The category probably corresponds to what is elsewhere called "study and raising qualifications."

Source: Based on data from Gordon and Klopov 1972b, pp. 34-35.

spheres of employment and had greater opportunity to raise their educational achievement in later stages of life. Family responsibilities clearly have a far greater effect on females than on males in limiting their free time, and particularly the time they have to advance their education for job-related purposes. Heavy household responsibilities also deter women from seeking demanding occupations or from pursuing a career. Soviet sociological investigations of the problems of working mothers consistently confirm these conclusions.

A study of female workers in five industrial enterprises in Leningrad revealed a close connection between women's family status and their performance on the job:

> The majority of the female workers are conscientious and fulfill and overfulfill the production plans. . . . However, only 8 percent of the women take part in the innovator and inventor movement. . . . It is here that we see the influence of the "two responsibilities" of women. In order to be in this movement a person must raise his professional level, become acquainted with the experience of others, read special literature, remain at work after the shift, and, lastly, think about production problems when at work and, not infrequently, when at home. Women, especially if they are mothers, strive continuously to spend more nonwork time fulfilling their many domestic responsibilities. Moreover, many female workers stated that when at work they cannot put the house and children out of their mind. The women value jobs requiring simple automatic responses that can be performed adequately despite these mental distractions (Kharchev and Golod 1969, p. 442).

A female Soviet investigator has noted the same phenomenon and argues that this inflates the importance of the husband's occupation:

> Women do indeed choose easier jobs, with convenient hours, close to home and with pleasant co-workers and managers, but not because they lack initiative. They choose these jobs because their combination of social roles is difficult. In a study at Moscow and Penza factories women were asked whether they found it hard to combine family obligations with jobs; 25 percent replied "very hard," 31 percent "hard" and 44 percent "bearable." When asked which tired them most, work, home, children or shopping, they said all of them were tiring.
>
> Why be surprised if women show less initiative on the job? Women accept mechanical tasks because they are tired from their double load, and the mechanical work in turn does not stimulate creative thought. It is poorly

> paid, so the husband takes the role of the chief breadwinner. The implicit assumption is that most housework is the woman's task (Pavlova 1971, p. 16).

Once the husband's job is defined as primary, it is the wife who must then make the adjustments needed to foster his career. The geographic mobility of the family is determined by the husband's job and the resources of the family must undoubtedly be devoted far more to advancing his work qualifications. A Soviet commentator notes that when there is a choice between spending more time on the job or doing domestic chores, "a women's deferring to the needs of her family is considered valid, but a man's doing so would lead to ridicule not only by his friends but also by his superiors" (Tsimbalyuk 1974).

A study of sewing factories in Lithuania conducted between 1966 and 1967 showed that only 8.6 percent of the women were able to engage in studies to raise their work qualifications. Sixty percent of those not studying stated that family responsibilities prevented them from doing so (Panova 1970). Research conducted among female workers in several enterprises in Moscow, Penza, and Leningrad revealed that only about 20 to 25 percent of the women felt that the potential existed for them to raise their qualifications. Single women were twice as likely as married women to express this. Comparable data for men were unavailable (Slesarev and Yankova 1969, p. 422).

A woman from Omsk complains, "I have the feeling that in a female's life there remains to be abolished only the 'stops' (*ostanovki*) for sleep. Everything happens at a heightened and convulsive pace" (quoted in Kuznetsova 1973, p. 12). Many women do not fail to see the direct connection between their "double burden" and the lack of cooperation they get from their husbands:

> Although women are now legally equal to men, male psychology has not changed. For many women, marriage means a working day equal to a man's, plus another working day at home. Men seldom view marriage as a joint venture. A man I know is a good example. When he married, he couldn't boil water and he felt imposed upon if his wife asked him to go to the bakery. After his divorce, he lived alone and became a wonderful cook and housekeeper. But when he remarried he reverted completely to type (Yunina 1971, p. 28).

The male point of view expressed in letters to the Soviet press well illustrates the kind of deeply ingrained chauvinism that many women must contend with:

> "Everybody agrees that it is necessary to liberate women from hard physical labor," Comrad Nebitov from Gatchina wrote, "but why separate a woman from the kitchen? Why

> deprive her of additional opportunities to manifest love and consideration for her husband? If only you could see with what tender attention my wife follows the trajectory of my first probing spoon from a plate of soup!"
>
> . . . Here is the view of Comrad Vanyushin from Kaluga province: ". . . Free a woman from the kitchen and you give her freedom to be a silly hen. Who needs such a woman? Woman is supposed to adorn the family hearth, just as flowers adorn the meadows" (quoted in Kuznetsova 1967, p. 7).

Besides seriously impeding their occupational mobility, this situation has detrimental effects on women's physical and psychological well-being. In the study of women working in enterprises in Moscow, Leningrad, and Penza, 70 percent reported that they frequently felt fatigued at work. Analysis of material from polyclinics and health centers showed that women workers were ill almost twice as frequently as men. However, the average duration of women's illnesses is far shorter than that of men. The Soviet investigators note that "this is evidently explained by the fact that women with families cannot allow themselves to stay in bed for a long time because all the household responsibilities rest on their shoulders" (Slesarev and Yankova 1969, p. 423).

The extreme regimen of housework and employment saps both a woman's "physical and emotional strength. As a result many women grow old early, don't have time to take care of themselves, lose their femininity and attractiveness, and become quarrelsome and irritable" (Kharchev 1970, p. 65). Elsewhere, a female Soviet commentator observes that because of housework, "many a pretty young girl turns into a dowdy, unkempt drudge after marriage" (quoted in Baskina 1968, p. 14). The limitations on women's "cultural growth" stemming from family responsibilities may further reduce the woman's desirability: "The inequality in cultural levels of husbands and wives not infrequently leads to family conflicts and sometimes even to the breakup of the family" (Labzin 1965, p. 101).

A 1969 study of three factories in Minsk, Belorussia disclosed that among those couples sharing household burdens equally about 60 percent had happy marriages and only 6 percent had unhappy ones (Yurkevich 1970, p. 190). In cases where the wife did all or almost all the housework, only 22 percent had happy and over 40 percent had unhappy marriages. Where the husband "helped" the wife the proportion of happy marriages was midway between that in the two above situations. The findings were based solely on interviews with the wives.

A Soviet investigator of divorce in Novosibirsk concluded that the "lack of willingness of a number of men to take part in the division of labor" has been a serious reason for divorce. This reason was most often stated by skilled factory workers and highly skilled office workers and least likely to be the cause of divorce among collective farm workers and housewives (Musatov 1967, p. 30). This, perhaps, indicates that women in the latter groups have less tolerance for their husbands' failure to take an active role in doing housework.

CLASS DIFFERENCES IN TIME USAGE

If industrialization promotes egalitarian relationships it may be expected that working men and women in the middle and upper class would be more likely to manifest this than those in the lower class. The former should be more exposed to modern beliefs and have the material well-being to take advantage of modern household technology and service enterprises. Unfortunately, for political and other reasons, this is a particularly difficult variable to investigate and measure with the data usually available from Soviet sources.

Determining the class structure of the Soviet Union is a major problem in itself. No worthwhile data (with, perhaps, the exception of the Pskov study discussed below) directly relate time usage and class. In general, looking at the time usage of males and females by educational achievement or income is not fruitful, because there are no controls for such crucial variables as age and family status. That there is a definite relationship between, for example, income and family status is well illustrated by Gordon and Klopov (1972b, p. 8) and Artemov et al. (1967, p. 91). The latter report that in the study of Krasnoyarsk City in 1963, on the one hand, 95 percent of those having an income per family member of less than 50 rubles per month—the lowest income category—were married with children; none were unmarried. On the other hand, among those in the highest income category—more than 75 rubles per month per family member—55 percent were unmarried and only 28 percent were married with children.

There are, however, some data relating to social class that are quite revealing. The Pskov study shows time use of high and low white-collar workers as well as of skilled and unskilled blue-collar workers (see Table C. 3). The data reveal that males with high white-collar jobs spend significantly more time at work and connected with work than other male groups or females in the same social category. It would not be surprising if women in this top group had less demanding and less prestigious occupations than their male counterparts. The time spent by men on housework is <u>uniform</u> in all the groups, although it may be slightly higher among the unskilled (a difference of one percentage point). Among the women the time spent on housework declines from 18 percent of the day to only 14 percent as one moves from the unskilled blue-collar to the high white-collar group. The larger burden of housework may be due to a lack of appliances, poor housing, etc. However, one cannot dismiss the possibility that variations in, for example, family status are also involved.

Both the time that women spend satisfying physiological needs and their free time are always less than that of men. The difference between the free time of males and females varies little, though it is highest among the high white-collar group and lowest (a two-percentage-point difference) among the two middle groups. Yet the time spent studying and participating in organizations by low-collar female employees is still only 61 percent of that of male low white-collar workers. With respect to this specific aspect of free time, females, again, are relatively less well off in the high white-collar group. Their time expenditure is 45 percent of that of men. The comparable figure in the skilled blue-collar group was 55 percent.

Thus, there is no sign that male-female differences decline in the upper social classes. Women benefit largely from the reduction in the total housework burden and apparently not from the help of more "liberated" husbands.[6] Relative to women in blue-collar occupations, white-collar female workers have greater time for study and organizational participation. However, this pattern is even more extreme among the men.

Another study (Trufanov 1970) that provides significant data bearing on social class differences was undertaken in Leningrad during the summer of 1966. The study was conducted in eight large industrial enterprises and three scientific research institutes. Workers were apparently classified according to the character of their work and then selected randomly from within each group. In all, there were eight occupational categories. The workers registered their time use for two weekdays, the day prior to the day off and the day off. There was a total of 2,564 24-hour time-budgets (Trufanov 1970, p. 129). The actual number of respondents is not stated, but if there were four time-budgets per person, then the sample size was obviously 641.

The presentation of the data in the article by Trufanov (1970) showed only the time expenditure on days off and on weekdays. From this I caluculated the weekly expenditures of time. The results indicate that those in the study were probably representative of the most advanced strata in Soviet society in terms of occupational prestige and its usual correlates. The average of the expenditures of time on housework by females in the eight occupational categories was 16.8 percent of their weekly time-budget. The average of the weekly time in the previously discussed studies was about two percentage points higher. The free time of women averages 16.5 percent of the week in this Leningrad study, while in the other studies the average figure is about 13.0 percent (see Table 5.4). Similarly, the men have more free time and less housework than in the studies we have considered so far; the differences are less extreme for the women.

To compare males and females with similar types of work, Table 5.6 shows the ratio of male to female time use by occupational category. In only one category, skilled physical work that is unmechanized, does the amount of time spent on housework by men reach substantially

TABLE 5.6

Ratio of the Weekly Time Spent by Males to That by Females on Four Time Categories, by Type of Work, Leningrad, 1966

	Work and Time Connected	Housework	Physiological Needs	Free Time
Physical Unskilled	1.00	0.52	1.06	1.52
Skilled Physical				
Mechanized	1.05	0.54	1.01	1.27
Unmechanized	0.99	0.66	1.00	1.33
Medium Skilled Mental Work	1.02	0.52	0.97	1.57
Highly Skilled Combining Mental and Physical Work	1.08	0.50	1.00	1.36
Mental Work				
Skilled	1.03	0.47	0.98	1.59
Highly skilled	1.07	0.52	1.03	1.26
Heads of work collectives	1.08	0.43	1.03	1.25

Source: Based on data in Trufanov 1966, pp. 130-31, 134.

above half that done by women. Though it is difficult to order these occupations precisely in terms of prestige, income, educational requirements, etc., it is apparent that the relative amount of housework done by men is not significantly influenced by this dimension. In fact, in the obviously most prestigious work category, heads of work collectives, the ratio of male to female time spent on housework reaches its nadir. The amount of housework done by females as well as that done by males is lowest among heads of work collectives, but whatever has reduced this burden has not made it more equally divided.

In many job categories the males spend more time working than do the females. Again, this is probably a sign that they have more demanding occupations that are likely to command both a higher salary and greater prestige.[7] In those areas where the men's work burden is particularly high (in addition to the one area where men's housework is high relative to the women) the free time of men and women is far more comparable. In the remaining three cases the free time of men is over one and one-half times that of women. Among those doing highly skilled mental work and heads of work collectives, it should be noted that the men not only work longer but also spend more time satisfying physiological needs.

The data used to calculate the figures shown in Table 5.6 indicate that there is a substantial difference in the time spent on housework by female unskilled "physical" workers and female heads of work collectives. However, differences between the other groups of women are quite small (never more than three percentage points), and their direction is difficult to interpret. The same is true for the men. The variation in free time is even less among both the males and females. Differences in family status, age, and other variables undoubtedly play an important role here. It is not possible to assess their influence. However, the findings appear to constitute important evidence that this occupational dimension does not significantly alter the relative position of women.

Other sources confirm that female professionals are still heavily burdened with household chores. In an extensive review of the time-budget studies particularly of 1959 and 1963, the Soviet investigators note (Baikova et al. 1965, p. 65):

> The large expenditures of nonwork time on housework prevents many female workers, engineers and specialists from working at their full intellectual capacity and from raising their cultural level. This significantly affects their work. Imagine an engineer or doctor not reading the latest special literature. Can he be the best specialist? I think not. And yet at between 35 to 40 years of age, when a female specialist has reached greatest maturity, housework occupies up to 42 percent of her nonwork time (time not spent on physiological needs or at work and connected with work).

It is not surprising that "male managers (and sometimes even women!) consider it more advantageous to use the funds of the enterprise to train men because there is more profit from them" (Litvinenko 1971, p. 42; cf. Dodge 1966, pp. 48-50). Slesarev and Yankova (1969, p. 423) found that women lose about one year out of four as a result of their giving birth, caring for sick children and other members of the family, and taking leave when ill. This does not solely apply to factory workers. In a study of industrial enterprises of Leningrad, it was found that with regard to care of children "the husband helps least of all among the office workers, and most of all among the unskilled workers" (Kharchev and Golod 1969, p. 499). The following is an apparently typical situation that well illustrates the findings from the time-budget studies:

> I have some friends—a man and wife who are both doctors of science, both professors. Both head large laboratories, read papers at international congresses and publish their scientific works; their salaries are identical. But in addition the wife must think of their daughter's upbringing, and see that there are always starched shirts in the dresser for her husband and that the table is set when guests arrive (Libedinskaya 1967, p. 14).

The relationship between education and time usage supports the above findings. Educational attainment is related to occupational status but, as already indicated, perhaps even more closely associated with age.

Incidentally, Inkeles and Bauer (1968, pp. 6, 198) concluded on the basis of the Harvard Project interviews (the sample was comprised of persons who had left the Soviet Union mainly between 1943-46 but also as late as 1950-51) that "as in the United States, Sweden and elsewhere, the better educated a woman is in the Soviet Union the greater is the likelihood that she will fail to find a husband. This holds for all women ages 25 to 55 taken together and for particular age classes." Whether this is true today or accurately reflected the population at the time those interviewed had emigrated is debatable. However, it is an interesting point to consider, since the absence of the husband appears to mean less housework for the woman.

It is, therefore, likely that a large number of factors contribute to education being inversely related to the time spent on housework and directly related to the amount of free time (see Table C.4). What is most significant, however, is the fact that the ratio of time spent by men on housework to that spent by women is exceedingly stable in the three studies from which data are available. There is no indication that the share of domestic chores men assume is related to their level of educational achievement.

ADAPTATIONS TO THE FIVE-DAY WORKWEEK

With the advance of industrialization, it has become possible to reduce the workweek. Soviet researchers have been particularly concerned with the effect of various changes in the length and structure of the time spent working. Unfortunately, most of the Soviet studies of the effect of innovative work schedules provide insufficient information for analyzing sex differences.[8] However, a 1966 study of four large cities and the small city of Pavlovskii Posad does provide considerable evidence that is relevant. The study shows the effect of moving from a six-day workweek to a five-day workweek while still maintaining the same number of hours worked.

It should be noted that there are no data on the same workers prior to and following the changeover to the five-day work schedule. The assumption that those presently on the six-day workweek have the same family status, living conditions, educational attainment, etc. as those on the five-day workweek is not adequately demonstrated in the literature.

There may also be a problem with the sample size. Apparently, far more worked the original six-day schedule. Since only about 550 male and 350 female workers were included in the entire sample from the large cities, the number of workers on the five-day schedule included in the study may have been quite small (Gordon and Klopov 1972a, pp. 29-30).

The data show that since the factory workers have to go to their place of work only five times a week instead of six, there is a reduction in the time spent travelling to work as well as waiting for and changing work shifts (Levin 1971, p. 112). In some cases time working appears to have been reduced as well. In large cities this has led to an increase in the free time and a decrease in the housework of both men and women, although, as is usual, the increase in the free time of men may be slightly greater. For women in Pavlovskii Posad, on the other hand, the five-day work schedule is associated with an increase in the time spent on housework and a slight decline (less than two percentage points, however) in the free time. For males there appears to be no significant change in time usage, although there is a one percentage point increase in housework (see Table C. 5).

There were more precise figures available on the change in the time spent on housework alone on Saturday, Sunday, and a weekday. This shows that the weekly decline for men is somewhat greater than that of women in the large cities. Thus, males working a 6-day work-week do 49 percent as much housework as women, while those on a 5-day workweek do only 42 percent as much. From this data it is evident that in Pavlovskii Posad the housework of both men and women shows about the same proportional increase paralleling the decline in the number of workdays (Kolpakov and Patrashev 1971, p. 121). In Pavlovskii Posad the weekly time spent on housework by males increased from 17.3 to 19.0 hours, while that of females grew from 36.4 to 40.5 hours (Kolpakov and Patrushev 1971, p. 121).

Soviet investigators attribute the increase in housework in small cities largely to the added time spent in private subsidiary agriculture. As was found to be the case in a study of another small city, Nerekhta, the low salary of the workers provides a sufficient incentive for them to acquire income from their private plots of land and to use extra time to enhance that income (Levin 1971, p. 114; Kolpakov and Patrushev 1971, p. 121).

The changeover to the five-day workweek has led to a growth in gardening even among workers in large cities. In 1967 almost 1.6 million workers had collective gardens (Kolpakov and Patrushev 1971, p. 140). In Dnepropetrovsk, Zaporozh'e, Odessa, and Kostroma 29 percent of those questioned had either private plots or collective gardens. There apparently has also been a recent rapid growth in collective gardening among workers in the Urals and Siberia. In Novosibirsk some 40 percent of the population engages in collective gardening. This is probably a sign of the desire for more income as well as the lack of compelling alternative uses for extra time. For many men work in the garden may be a form of recreation, more appropriately classified as a free-time activity than as housework (Gordon and Klopov 1972a, p. 37).

A study of Taganrog has shown that there is considerable dissatisfaction among women who have recently changed to the five-day work schedule. The city is located in the Rostov Oblast, RSFSR. This industrial center of 250,000 persons is reportedly typical of cities in the Russian Republic with populations between 100,000 and 500,000 (Gordon and Pimashevskaya 1972, p. 89). Unlike the study of large cities in

1966, that of Taganrog included office workers and engineering-technical personnel in addition to factory workers. It should also be pointed out that the changeover to the five-day workweek for the workers in the Taganrog study had only recently taken place, while those on this new schedule in the 1966 study had considerably more time to adjust to the altered routine before they were questioned.

Unfortunately, the actual time-budgets are not presented; but, in general, the data that are given indicate that women have not benefited as much as men from the changeover to the five-day workweek (Gordon and Pimashevskaya 1972, pp. 40-44). The data show that almost 90 percent of the women working a six-day workweek intended, following the changeover to a five-day schedule, to spend one of the two days off on household affairs and to spend the second day on rest and leisure. However, only about 60 percent of those actually on a five-day workweek were able to accomplish this (p. 88).

The Soviet investigators largely attribute the changeover's failure to achieve the expected results to problems of urban living and a lack of institutional accomodations to the new work schedule. When the increased or altered demand for service institutions cannot be satisfied, it is difficult to economize housework. The longer workday means that workers are seeking services at a later hour—a time when they are less available. Demand has also markedly increased on days off. Adjustments need to be made in the transportation system to serve workers travelling at different hours (1972, pp. 95-98). The difficulties for women appear to be particularly acute as a result of their responsibility for caring for children. The stores close at seven o'clock, while the kindergartens are open only between eight and six during the day. The limited time for shopping forces women to bring their children with them. There are complaints from workers who begin work before the kindergartens open. Women also find that many household shores such as preparing food cannot wait until Saturday, and therefore must be done with greater difficulty during the lengthened workday (1972, pp. 98-105).

ADVANTAGES OF CITY LIVING

The increasing concentration of the population in urban centers with growing services has been the outcome of the progress of economic development and decisions regarding the allocation of resources. The impact of the change in the locus of daily living is well illustrated by the 1965 study of Pskov, which examines the difference in the housework and child care tasks of those living in the city center, Administrativnyi region, and those in Lopatino, located on the outskirts of the city. Administrativnyi is the area of the city with the greatest concentration of food stores and other service institutions. It also has some of the best housing conditions. Lopatino, on the other hand, shows little sign of industrial growth, is dominated by housing of a rural type, and has between 29 and 86 percent fewer food stores and other types of stores than does the city center (Kolpakov and Patrushev 1971, pp. 139-45).

The investigators found that, in general, the improvement of everyday life and the better organization of public services has benefited men more than women. The household tasks traditionally reserved for men are likely to be the first reduced or eliminated. These included carrying fuel and water, cleaning the area around the house, and caring for the garden. They found that whereas 4.5 percent of those in Administrativnyi had gardens, 50.8 percent had them in Lopatino. Males in Lopatino spent 5.3 and females 3.9 hours per week on the three activities listed above. This time was almost 80 percent less for males and 90 percent less for females living in the city center; however, these activities constituted a far greater part of the housework activities of males than of females. (In this context housework does not refer to all domestic tasks. In their discussion of regional differences Kolpakov and Patrushev (1971, pp. 143-46) divide domestic tasks into three categories: (1) care of children; (2) purchases and visits to everyday institutions, including time spent travelling and waiting for transportation connected with these activities; and (3) the remaining household tasks in and around the home. In this and the following paragraph there is a discussion of each of these aspects considered separately as well as together.) Thus, whereas in Lopatino men did 37 percent as much housework as women, in Administrativnyi men did only 33 percent as much (Kolpakov and Patrushev 1971, pp. 139-43, 145).

The ratio of the time spent by men on child care, purchases, and everyday services of the time spent by women was higher in the center than in the outskirts of the city. While males in Lopatino spent only about 33 percent as much time as females on these activities, in Administrativnyi they spent 43 percent as much time on child care and about 49 percent as much time as women on purchases and services. However, in both regions the total time spent on domestic tasks by males was between 36 and 38 percent of the expenditure by female workers. In Administrativnyi as compared to Lopatino women spent about seven hours less per week on domestic activities; the corresponding figure for men was two hours (Kolpakov and Patrushev 1971, pp. 143-45). There is a decline in the burden but it is not, again, more equally divided.

This points to the conclusion that with improved housing conditions and better service enterprises men benefit more than women, particularly with respect to the reduction in the proportion of time they spend on the dull and tedious aspects of household chores. Even in Administrativnyi, women spent 18 percent of their weekly time-budget engaged in housework and related tasks—about the average found in time-budgets of the 1960s. The figure for Lopatino, on the other hand, was about the average found in the 1920s. For males the picture is approximately the reverse. Men spent just under 7 percent of their weekly time-budget on housework in Administrativnyi—about the same as the time spent in the 1920s—while in Lopatino they spent 8 percent of their weekly time-budget on this activity or about the average for the 1960s! Plus ca change, plus c'est la meme chose.

After noting that female workers do all the housework in 81.5 percent of the families studied in Leningrad, in between 47 and 90 percent of those in Moscow, and in 97 percent of those studied in Kostroma, a female Soviet commentator wrote: "It is true that the more technology in the home the more willing men are to undertake household chores. But how often do couples make use of machines in everyday life?" (Baskina 1972, p. 12).[9] Moreover, as is witnessed by the following statement of one Soviet woman, the use of machines does not by itself imply that less time will be needed for tasks previously done completely by hand:

> Yes, a washing machine frees me from heavy physical work . . . but now if there is the slightest spot on the linen I toss it into the washing machine. But after all the washing machine doesn't iron. Now the time that I formerly spent washing clothing, I now spend ironing. If there had not been a washing machine in the house I would not so quickly toss the linen into the wash-basin. Everyday appliances free the housewife from heavy physical strains—shaking out rugs, washing clothing, heating and carrying water, but the time that it takes to carry out all household tasks has remained the same as it used to be (quoted in Marok 1973, p. 13).

CONCLUSION

Lenin clearly recognized how housework stifled women's development. In the light of the evidence in this chapter, his 1919 statement on the subject is profoundly ironic:

> Notwithstanding all the liberating laws that have been passed, woman continues to be a domestic slave, because petty housework crushes, strangles, stultifies and degrades her, chains her to the kitchen and to the nursery, wastes her labor on barbarously unproductive, petty, nerve-racking, stultifying and crushing drudgery. The real emancipation of women, real communism, will begin only when a mass struggle (led by the proletariat) is started against this petty domestic economy, or rather when it is transformed on a mass scale into large-scale socialist economy (The Woman Question 1951, p. 56). [Emphasis in original.]

The Soviet studies have made it possible to compare male and female time use between the 1920s and the 1960s and to varying degrees to measure the impact of education, occupation, social class, the nature of the work schedule, and the availability of urban conveniences on the sex differences.

In sum, the change in the domestic burdens of working women which resulted from industrialization and the ideology associated with it has been exceedingly limited. Change in the sphere of employment has been unmistakable, yet it has not altered domestic living as reflected in time use. But it is clear that the double burden that marriage and children bring for the working woman has a profound influence on her labor-force participation and aspirations. Males avoid onerous housework, are less influenced by change in family status, and appear to benefit far more from improved living conditions. Should the demands of a man's job conflict with doing his share of housework, he can depend upon his wife to complete the latter and facilitate his occupational advancement. It appears that only single women can compete equally with men and that marriage and especially the bearing of children severely curtail not only their career prospects but their satisfaction with daily living in general.[10]

NOTES

1. This included what in the 1960s was generally classified separately as "care of children" and "upbringing of children."

2. The average increase in population between 1939 and 1959 in the seven cities listed in Table 5.2 that are located in the northwestern part of the Russian Republic was 130 percent (this excludes Sverdlovsk, which grew 184 percent, as it is located farther east in the Urals). The figure for the RSFSR as a whole was only about 109 percent over the two decades (Ts. S. U. 1963, pp. 11, 30-38).

3. In 1966 Patrushev (1966, p. 88) reported data from the study of Krasnoyarsk Krai that showed, contrary to Prudenskii's findings presented in Table 5.3, that with the changeover to the seven-hour workday the housework of women increased slightly. Several things are possible. Prudenskii (1972, p. 296), six years after Patrushev's efforts, may have recalculated or changed the categories. Alternatively, Patrushev and Prudenskii may be referring to different parts of the same study; or, lastly, the data reported by Prudenskii may actually refer to the city of Krasnoyarsk and not to the Krai.

4. Kolpakov and Prudenskii (1966, p. 220) present data on the weekly free time of workers in Sverdlovsk, Rostov, Ivanovsk, and Gorkii oblasts. The data show the same pattern as that in Table C.2 based on workdays only. The amount of time for both males and females is predictably higher (there is more free time on days off) in each age group, but the gap between the sexes remains approximately the same.

5. It is necessary to note that the amount of housework is somewhat understated for the group under age 40 with no children and the group over age 40 with no children under 18 years old. The expenditure of time caring for children in these two cases could not be included with housework, for it was unavailable. However, the combined time spent on "upbringing of children" and "caring for children" in large cities we know amounted to only between 10 and 20 minutes per week in the former group and to just under 3 hours for women and 1.3 hours for men in the latter group (Gordon and Klopov 1972a, p. 131).

6. A real deficiency with the data is that it is not possible to directly determine the family division of labor from material on individuals (cf. Goode 1968, pp. 324-26). The proportion of couples in which both are from the same social class is difficult to assess. The consistency in male time use, however, makes this less of a problem.

7. Trufanov (1970, pp. 132-33) indicates that highly qualified scientific-technical workers, especially men, spend more time than other groups travelling to and from work. This, he explains, is due to the difficulty in finding such specialized work close to one's residence.

8. See, for example, Patrushev 1966, pp. 192-94; Chufarova 1961; Levin 1971, pp. 116-17; Artemov et al. 1967, pp. 107-10, 144-48; and Kolpakov and Patrushev 1971, p. 218.

9. Slesarev and Yankova (1969, p. 428) note that women are more likely to have washing machines than refrigerators not only because the former are cheaper but also because washing machines increase the housework done by men. This is due to the fact that "operating a machine is 'traditionally masculine' work and for that reason it does not contradict the traditional conceptions of prestige."

10. Havens (1973, pp. 978-79) found that in the United States in 1960 there was an almost perfect inverse correlation (-.89) between income grouping and the proportion of the females who were married with spouse present.

CHAPTER

6

WORK AND FAMILY IN RURAL RUSSIA

THE RURAL HOUSEHOLD

In their review of Soviet ethnographic research, Dunn and Dunn (1967, p. 47) found that the family unit retains vital functions despite the transformation of agriculture during the Soviet period:

> The family is still the social unit which most powerfully influences the individual. . . .
>
> The household is collectively the owner of the buildings, tools and livestock used in the private economy and of the products of the economy. . . . The concept of common household property in theory extends even to income received in cash and in kind by members of the household for labor days and to articles bought with money so received.

The Dunns (1967, p. 76) argue that the family unit has been bolstered by the extreme lack of alternative institutions for handling domestic chores:

> In places where for reasons of overall policy the state is unable to assume certain necessary functions (providing adequate day-care facilities for preschool children, supplying labor-saving devices in large quantities, or making public catering available either directly or through the kolkhoz), these tasks must devolve on the family.

In 1964 only 4 percent of the total electricity consumed in the USSR went to rural areas; half of this was used for productive purposes. During the preceding decade the rates charged for electricity were prohibitive for most collective farms. This obviously prevented the acquisition of modern appliances and also made it impossible to furnish the population with "permanent and smooth-running child-care facilities or large-scale public catering." The Dunns report that "in most kolkhoz (collective farms) of central Russia day-care and preschool facilities either do not function at all or operate only during the peak agricultural season" (1967, pp. 60, 68). A rather extensive study of families in the RSFSR in June 1962 showed that per 10,000 collective farm families there were 3 refrigerators, 50 washing machines, 4 vacuum cleaners, and 0.1 floor polishers. The figures for industrial workers were 290, 1,001, 10, and 230 respectively (Baikova et al. 1965, p. 210).

A study of several collective farms in Soviet Russia in 1965-66 revealed that 61.5 percent of the women not working in social production attributed this to the lack of facilities for the care of preschool-age children (Bolgov and Smolentsev 1970, p. 183). That the problem persists is evident from complaints in the Soviet press:

> Tatyana Okolelova, wife of a driver and mother of two boys who are still young enough to need a nursery school, writes from . . . Stavropol Territory. . . . "The harvest is about to begin, and every man counts. Yet young mothers in the village have to stay home because they have no place to send their children" (Novplyansky 1972, p. 37).

It is clear, also, that it is not simply a question of a lack of resources:

> True, V. Baranov, Director of Distant Collective Farm, takes a dim view of the day-care center; he is not taking the necessary steps to renovate an old building or to finish building a new one. . . . Can a major matter—a matter of state importance—be made ultimately dependent on the attitude of a farm director? If he wants to, he will concern himself with youngsters; if he does not want to, he will delay or postpone the matter. . . .
>
> How long, one wonders, will a matter of such importance to the harvest as day-care centers be left uncontrolled and dependent upon "goodwill"? Or is it still necessary to go on explaining the importance of day-care centers to certain managers, to appeal to their consciences? (Ibid.)

There is also a lack of basic facilities such as indoor plumbing. This apparently is most distressing to young people who resent having to use bathhouses. The Dunns (1967, p. 61) found this to be "one of the most persistent topics for complaint in the press."

The conservative influence of older generations appears to be quite strong. It is difficult to assess the extent to which three generations live together, for the distribution of private plots of land is based on the number of economically independent households. Peasants may falsify their reports to Soviet ethnographers, leading to an undercount of large households. Yet research done in the 1960s in three diverse collective farms in Orlov Oblast, RSFSR, showed that one-quarter to one-third of the families consisted of three generations. Two studies of central Russian peasantry done in the early and late 1950s indicate that about 20 percent of the families had this structure (Dunn and Dunn 1967, pp. 70, 71-72; Kolbanovskii 1970, p. 212). The Dunns (1967, p. 73) note that:

> At least in the Kalinin Oblast study, . . . the nuclear family is not considered ideal by the people themselves. . . . Anokhina and Shmeleva state specifically that it is not considered proper to leave old parents alone, and that, furthermore, when one or both parents are still living and are domiciled with the children, the grandfather (or in his absence the grandmother) is usually considered the head of the family.

Ties beyond the nuclear family are sustained through mutual aid in a large number of recurring activities (1967, p. 75).

The conservatism of the older generation is enhanced by neglect. The population in rural areas in general, and women in particular, are less exposed to the ideology of industrial centers. This is apparent, for example, from the data on media usage (discussed later in this chapter). Cultural facilities are limited, and whatever resources are available are oriented towards young people. Serious efforts to change the religious beliefs of the older generation, for example, do not have high priority:

> The middle-aged and elderly tend to be left to their own devices. But where an appreciable portion of childrearing is done by grandparents in order to permit the mothers to work the older generation is not without social influence. Thus, the common Soviet attitude which tends to dismiss the older section of the population from consideration in matters of policy is at least open to question (Dunn and Dunn 1967, p. 65; see Whyte 1970).

CHANGING EDUCATIONAL ACHIEVEMENT

The growing educational attainment of the young has reduced the influence of the older generations. This may be particularly salutary for women:

> The difference between the educational achievement of young rural residents and their parents is very large.

TABLE 6.1

Education of the Rural Population of the RSFSR, by Age and Sex, 1959
(persons per 1,000 population)

	Higher		Incomplete Higher, Secondary and Incomplete Secondary		Primary and Incomplete 7-Year		Less Than Primary[a]	
	Males	Females	Males	Females	Males	Females	Males	Females
10-19	0.0	0.0	279	347	442	387	279	266
20-24	4	10	483	568	461	325	52	97
25-29	14	22	252	297	622	485	122	196
30-34	15	14	366	377	529	454	90	155
35-39	29	12	424	316	428	385	119	287
40-44	22	5	275	110	461	246	242	639
45-49	14	3	128	32	380	118	478	847
50-54	12	2	85	25	342	114	561	859
55-59	11	2	71	20	322	82	596	896
60-64	7	1	49	15	287	60	657	924
65-69	4	1	35	10	250	47	711	942
70 and older	2	0.4	20	6	156	25	822	968.6
Total	10	6	269	218	442	265	279	511

[a]These are residual figures.

Source: Based on figures in Ts. S. U. 1963, p. 107.

> The better education of the youth is the foundation of their moral authority and independence. This is reflected especially in the position of women, and this changes the whole structure of relations in the family. The young generation of rural women also differ from their mothers and mothers-in-law in their income, the character of their work, in their mode of life, in prestige and in family roles. There is a significant and increasing proportion of young women in skilled work. To a very large extent young women are now oriented not to housework, but to activities outside the home (Arutyunyan 1971, 211-12).

Table 6.1 shows the very rapid change that has been taking place. Note particularly the difference in the educational achievement of females below age 40 as compared to the older women. Whereas 29 percent of those women 35-39 had less than a primary education, the figure for those 40-44 was 64 percent. In the age groups below 35 the proportion of women with secondary and higher education actually exceeds that of the men. It may be, however, that as in urban areas men are completing their education later in life. This is suggested by the particularly high level of education of males aged 35-39.

As would be expected on the basis of the age-specific data for 1959, by 1970 the educational attainment of the total female rural population was far more comparable to that of males. In 1959 the ratios of the proportion of males to the proportion of females by the educational groupings listed in Table 6.1 were, respectively, 1.7, 1.2, 1.7, and 0.5. In 1970 the figures were 1.3, 1.2, 1.4, and 0.7 (based on the figures in Table 6.1 and Ts.S.U. 1972c, pp. 56-57).

THE CONTRAST BETWEEN STATE AND COLLECTIVE FARMS

The impact which technological advancement may have on the status of women in rural areas can be assessed to some degree by comparing their position on collective and state farms. The latter, where far fewer workers reside, have benefited from considerably better material conditions, a greater mechanization of work, and a younger and better educated labor force.

Table 6.2 shows that the higher educational attainment of state as compared to collective farms paralleled a decrease in the difference between male and female achievement in this respect. To a large extent this is probably a reflection of the younger age structure of the state farms (Monich 1973, p. 16).

The 1962 study of families in Soviet Russia showed that 29 out of every 1,000 state farm families had a washing machine. This figure is almost six times that for collective farm workers (Baikova et al. 1965, p. 210). The ages of state farm employees have generally been far more

TABLE 6.2

Educational Achievement, by Sex, on State and Collective Farms in the RSFSR, 1959

	Higher	Incomplete Higher and Secondary Specialized	Secondary General and Incomplete Secondary	Primary and Incomplete 7-Year	Less Than Primary
Females					
Collective	1	7	173	316	503
State	5	18	215	350	412
Males					
Collective	2	12	220	484	282
State	9	26	225	505	235
Ratio M/F					
Collective	2.00	1.71	1.27	1.53	0.56
State	1.80	1.44	1.05	1.44	0.57

Source: Based on figures in Ts.S.U. 1963, pp. 222, 225.

stable and considerably higher than those of collective farm workers.[1] The wages of even state farm workers, however, have in the past been far below those of industrial workers (Volin 1970, p. 528):

> An average wage of more than 600 [old] rubles for state farm workers compares favorably with less than 400 rubles of average earnings by kolkhozniks in collective farms; but it still lags considerably behind the average nonagricultural wage of more than 900 rubles which, with high prices, connotes a very low standard of living.

The state farm has higher labor productivity and far less private ownership of plots of land. Government involvement may be somewhat greater on the state farms, though the difference between the two types of farms in this regard "is so greatly diluted by the pervasive control of the state that it hardly exists." State farms are often created when new areas are being put to productive use. However, very frequently many have been formed from the conversion of collective farms (Volin 1970, pp. 526-31).

Data from a study on expenditures by families of farm and industrial workers in 1961 showed that state farm workers spent 3.8 times as much money as collective farm workers on "cultural everyday expenditures." This included things such as communal services and transportation. It is also significant to note that they spent between 2.1 and 2.8 times as much on articles for culture and recreation and activities such as going to movies and theaters. Industrial workers spent only slightly more money on these latter activities than did state farm workers, but they spent 8.3 times as much as collective farm workers and twice as much as state farm workers on "cultural everyday needs" (Arutyunyan 1971, p. 145).

Thus, state farm workers may be somewhat more exposed to urban ideologies as a result of their higher education, and, in some cases, greater involvement of the state, the younger age structure of the population, and the greater expenditure on cultural activities. If such an exposure promotes egalitarianism, this should be evident from the contrast between state and collective farms.

THE SEXUAL COMPOSITION OF THE LABOR FORCE

The literature dealing with occupations in agriculture usually distinguishes among several groupings. The description of these by Kolbanovskii (1970) is particularly useful for understanding the significance of the difference between the way males and females are distributed in the occupations.

The group at the bottom of the hierarchy consists of unskilled workers engaged in fieldwork. The tasks they perform are simple, repetitive, physically demanding, largely unmechanized, and seasonal. In winter these workers tend animals that are primarily kept on their private plots of land. Kolbanovskii (1970, pp. 210, 81) contends that the irregular employment plus the heavy involvement in housework and private agriculture "animates the private ownership psychology" and leads to the persistence of traditional sex roles.

Only slightly more prestigious is the work of those who tend animals in the socialized sector: milkmaids, stablemen, shepherds, poultry workers, etc. Though these workers are paid somewhat more than the first group, their work is also physically demanding and requires little skill. They work long hours and have short breaks. As in the case of the first group, Kolbanovskii (1970, pp. 209, 87) explains that this group also shows little change in family relationships:

> The limitation in the realization of the spiritual needs of the family adversely affects the orientation to higher moral values and reanimates and strengthens the influence of tradition—the habits of the past in the consciousness and actions of the individual.

This is the type of work that drives the rural young to the cities. In the following passage the Soviet investigator refers to one overwhelmingly female occupation to illustrate the point:

> Their working day on the dairy sections lasts 14 to 16 hours, breaks included. Owing to the shortage of

> manpower, the dairymaids are not always able to take vacations, days off and holidays. A dairymaid is on the job twice as long as any other workers. Such conditions lead to a shortage of cadres, and this complicates working conditions still more (Ilyin 1972, p. 9).

The machine operators, agricultural specialists, and construction workers differ considerably from the groups above. They have a much higher income and their everyday life is more comfortable and better organized. They "strive to judiciously utilize their free time." They engage in tasks that involve considerable skill and training (Kobanovskii 1970, pp. 86-87, 209).

Finally, the last two groups consist of the leading personnel on the farms and those engaged in the service sector; salesmen, postmen, kindergarten workers, etc. Those in leading roles are highly trained and have much work experience (Kolbanovskii 1970, p. 88).

Apparently, those workers engaged in field work and animal tending do not have the income to obtain goods and services that would lighten household tasks. They are more likely to do work in the private economy and to be less exposed and attuned to an ideology opposed to the traditional division of labor in the family. It might be expected, therefore, that in the higher occupational groups the household burdens would be somewhat less; that men would share more in the remaining tasks; and that women would have more free time which they could use to advance in their jobs. Data given below show that this is not the case.

A detailed comparison of the occupations of state and collective farms is possible with data from the 1959 census. (The 1970 census omits this breakdown of data.) The categories approximately correspond to those distinguished by Kolbanovskii (see Table 6. 3). Women are extremely underrepresented in the top two main categories of workers. The fact that 43. 9 percent of the workers on state farms (as opposed to 61. 0 percent of collective farmers) are females means that the exclusion of females from these categories is far greater on the collective farm. On the other extreme, women clearly predominate among those in the bottom two main categories consisting of the least desirable occupations.

What is more significant is the fact that on state farms 46 percent of the males and only 3 percent of the females were tractor and combine drivers. There was a far smaller percentage difference on the less mechanized collective farms: only about 1 percent of the females and 16 percent of the males were engaged in this type of work. On collective farms 62 percent of the males and 78 percent of the females were in nonspecialized farm work, but on state farms only 23 percent of the males as compared to 54 percent of the females were in this most arduous and least prestigious work. (The larger proportion of the labor force outside of nonspecialized agriculture on state farms has meant that more workers are in occupations that segregate a great deal.

TABLE 6.3

State and Collective Farm Workers in the RSFSR, by Occupation and Sex, 1959

	State			Collective		
	Males	Females	Percent Female	Males	Females	Percent Female
Administrative and supervisory personnel	66,998	12,931	16.2	271,760	37,465	12.1
Heads of livestock poultry farms	3,085	1,354	30.5	54,406	13,695	20.1
Brigadiers of field brigades	9,547	2,327	19.6	104,990	15,281	12.7
Brigadiers of livestock brigades	17,075	5,454	24.2	10,925	2,435	18.2
Other brigades	37,291	3,796	9.2	101,439	6,054	5.6
Skilled workers and junior personnel	732,118	9,238	1.2	731,816	31,915	0.4
Bookkeepers	3,392	1,439	29.8	13,425	3,731	21.8
Tractor and combine drivers	714,296	4,698	0.7	664,598	6,629	1.0
Implement handlers and workers on agricultural machines	14,174	731	4.9	51,080	1,153	2.2
Field-team leaders	256	2,370	90.0	2,713	20,402	88.3
Specialized agricultural workers	398,194	531,673	57.2	766,092	1,499,973	66.2
Workers in plant breeding and food production	14,168	36,065	72.0	68,342	197,660	83.8
Cattle farm workers	86,340	82,773	49.0	131,989	273,780	67.5
Milking personnel	1,206	186,234	99.4	4,454	608,398	99.3
Stablemen and grooms	175,034	28,205	13.9	286,900	41,939	12.8
Swineherds	6,046	88,428	93.6	16,912	216,628	92.8
Herdsmen, drovers, shepherds	75,192	20,177	21.2	176,397	48,432	21.5
Other livestock workers	19,515	26,994	58.0	35,143	16,107	31.4
Poultry workers	1,348	29,480	95.6	2,458	62,035	96.2
Beekeepers	8,540	2,679	23.9	29,570	6,358	17.7
Orchard and vineyard workers	6,880	16,743	70.9	9,946	10,665	51.7
Vegetable and melon growers	2,980	13.179	81.6	3,716	17,742	82.7
Irrigators	945	716	43.1	265	229	46.4
Nonspecialized agricultural workers	354,240	655,737	65.0	2,904,810	5,741,586	66.4
Total	1,551,550	1,209,579	43.9	4,674,478	7,310,939	61.0

Source: Based on figures in Ts.S.U. 1963, pp. 276-77.

Of course, there is probably considerable segregation in the tasks of nonspecialized workers that is concealed by the lack of subcategories. Using the categories available, the unstandardized measure of segregation was 62 for state farms as opposed to only 30 for collective farms. That this is the result of the distribution of the labor force and not a difference in the extent to which females are under- or overrepresented in the occupations is evidenced by the standardized figures: 57 for the state farms and 63 for the collective farms. These figures are based on the data in Table 6. 3.)

Though these are only cross-sectional data, they strongly suggest that technological progress has provided far greater opportunities for males than for females. Note, however, that in collective farms the probability of a male being an administrator or supervisor is about eleven times as great as that of a female, whereas the comparable figure on state farms is "only" about four times as great as that of a female.

These findings are confirmed by other data in the 1959 census.[2] Table 6. 4 shows that between 1939 and 1959 the proportion of males and females in the category "other occupations and nonspecialized workers" declined about equally for both males and females. (The decline would probably have been far greater for males had this category not included "other occupations.") The proportion of the males in cattle farm work, etc. also declined. However, the proportion of females among these animal tenders increased, while males showed a very substantial shift into work with tractors and combines. In 1939, 8 percent of the males were in the latter occupation; by 1959 the figure reached 22 percent as compared to less than 0. 1 percent of the females.

The contrast is most striking in the youngest age group. An exceedingly small proportion of the males are engaged in animal tending (. 03), and an inordinate concentration in tractor and combine work (. 36). Almost the exact opposite is true of the comparably aged females. The figures, respectively, are . 25 and . 02. In fact, in all three age groups and in the total working population for 1939 and 1959 the proportion of the women in "other occupations" and "cattle farm workers" varies between . 97 and . 99.

Women constitute a substantially larger percentage of the heads of farms and brigadiers aged 20-29 as compared to the older groups. Yet between 1939 and 1959, in the labor force as a whole, women came to be less well represented among the heads of farms. The percentage of women among these workers declined from 26 to 21.

The measures of segregation indicate that overall the segregation of males and females has remained very constant, although the labor force has shifted into occupations in which women were already either highly over- or underrepresented. This is precisely what was revealed by the contrast between state and collective farms. The standardized measure of sex-role differentiation among those aged 20 to 29 was 59. This increased to 66 in the age group 40 to 49, though it declines again to 59 in the oldest group. However, the unstandardized measure, representing the differences between the actual distributions of males and

TABLE 6.4

Frequency Distribution of Agrarian Workers in the RSFSR, by Sex, 1939 and 1959, and by Selected Age Groups, 1959

	20-29	40-49	55-59	1959	1939
Females					
Heads of livestock and poultry farms	.000	.002	.001	.002	.003
Brigadiers of field brigades	.002	.002	.001	.002	.002
Brigadiers of livestock brigades	.001	.001	.000	.001	.001
Other brigadiers	.001	.001	.001	.001	.001
Field-team leaders	.003	.003	.001	.003	.007
Tractor and combine workers	.002	.001	.000	.001	.000
Cattle farm workers, milkmaids, stablemen and grooms, swineherds and poultry workers	.248	.158	.062	.188	.083
Shepherds, herdsmen	.009	.008	.006	.008	.003
Orchard and vineyard workers, vegetable and melon growers	.007	.007	.005	.007	.005
Other occupations and nonspecialized workers	.726	.817	.924	.787	.894
Total	.999	1.000	1.001	1.000	.999
Males					
Heads of livestock and poultry farms	.003	.022	.015	.009	.013
Brigadiers of field brigades	.012	.035	.018	.018	.040
Brigadiers of livestock brigades	.002	.010	.006	.004	.008
Other brigadiers	.010	.048	.015	.020	.014
Field-team leaders	.000	.001	.001	.000	.001
Tractor and combine workers	.362	.149	.018	.219	.081
Cattle farm workers, milkmaids, stablemen and grooms, swineherds and poultry workers	.029	.175	.202	.113	.146
Shepherds, herdsmen	.026	.056	.061	.040	.036
Orchard and vineyard workers, vegetable and melon growers	.002	.005	.009	.004	.004
Other occupations and nonspecialized workers	.552	.500	.655	.571	.657
Total	.998	1.001	1.000	.998	1.000

Source: Based on figures in Ts.S.U. 1963, pp. 276-77.

females, declines from 40 in the youngest group to 32 among those 40 to 49 and to 27 among those 50 to 59. The measure was considerably lower in 1939 (24) than it was in 1959 (30), although the standardized equivalent was about 60 at both dates. (See my comment above based on data in Table 6.3.)

There has been a considerable growth in the number of rural residents working in industry. A study of collective and state farms in Belorussia between 1964 and 1969 showed that these workers were "predominantly male." On the other hand, there was also a considerable growth in the "personnel engaged in physical labor at various institutions and enterprises in the sphere of the service industries, public health, education, and culture." Women comprise 80.2 percent of these workers (Monich 1973, pp. 18-19). Thus these developments parallel the increased differentiation found in the urban areas.

Monich sees the concentration of relatively well educated women in the service sphere as a sign of their lack of opportunities in other areas of the rural economy:

> How are we to explain the fact that a portion of the working class comprised chiefly of unskilled labor has proved to be similar in educational level to industrial and agricultural workers of the skilled occupations? In our opinion, this is to be explained in significant measure by the limited availability of skilled work in rural localities for women with comparatively advanced general education. Another cause, in our view, is the fact that physical, manual labor in the service sphere is less heavy, and working conditions here are easier and better than for analogous work in farming (1973, p. 18).

Another Soviet investigator found a similar situation among urban women, though he sees familial responsibilities as being the primary problem:

> Under present conditions a part of the women do not have a sufficient level of education, specialization or have lost their professional qualifications as a result of a long absence from work connected with the upbringing of children. Not infrequently these women consent to any type of work either in material production or in the service sphere (Mikhailyuk 1970, pp. 54-55).

As will be made clear by data presented below, rural women also face these constraints.

The rapidly growing service industries may have been an answer to some of the problems of women, but there is little indication that this area will become increasingly mechanized or that there will be a grwoing demand for skilled labor (Monich 1973, p. 19).

Overall, the opportunities for women in the rural areas appear bleak. This makes the tremendous expansion of the number of women in professional and semiprofessional occupations in primarily urban areas all the more significant. Women are not making any substantial gains in obtaining access to the leading or better paying positions in agriculture, especially those involved with operating machines. More recent evidence confirms that this situation has persisted despite the fact that "the educational level of women is entirely adequate for them to qualify as equipment operators and mechanics":

> Thus, according to . . . [a] survey by the Central Statistical Administration, among 2,530 tractor and truck drivers, there were 5 women altogether. A peculiar division of labor has arisen between men and women: The sphere of mechanized work is a male privilege and that of manual labor is reserved to women. The time is ripe to change this situation, as a matter of need (Monich 1973, pp. 12-13).

Kharchev, probably the foremost sociologist of the family in the USSR, has openly condemned the blatantly unjust but unchanging sexual division of labor:

> It is necessary to note that in our society it is detrimental to have men monopolizing administrative responsibilities in many collective farms. . . . This does not pertain to men who need to occupy leading posts in the collective farm, but rather to the very frequent cases of evasion by the "strong sex" of work directly in the sphere of agricultural production in the name of their especial personal interests simply because desk work proves to be more advantageous. "Not infrequently in the villages," stated one of the correspondents of Sovetskaya rossiya (October 9, 1959), "one can find healthy men, who, preferring to be where things are easier, evade work and do nothing. Much of the basic work is left to women." As a result production suffers (a man can do the physical work of many women but this cannot be said about desk work) and there is a moral deterioration, for working according to the principal "wherever it is easier" is simply shameful parasitism (1964, p. 260).

Finally, it is necessary to consider the several rural occupations that are listed as professional or semiprofessional. In 1959 these included: (1) agronomists and zootechnicians; (2) veterinary doctors; (3) veterinary technicians and feldshers (surgeon's assistant); and (4) foresters and forest assessors. In 1959 women constituted 55 percent of the workers aged 20-29 in all four categories. The figures for the age groups 40-49 and 55-59 were, respectively, only 25 and 5 percent.

Women constituted 59 percent of the workers of all ages in these categories—four times the figure in 1939. The number of males in the occupations declined from 155,000 to 147,000 over the 20-year period, while the number of females grew from 27,000 to 101,000. Although the classification of occupations differed in the 1970 census, the material available suggests that the percentage of women remained stable in the period after 1959 (Ts. S. U. 1963, pp. 256, 246-47, 287, 283; 1973b, p. 172).

But these changes in the professional occupations may be of questionable significance for two reasons, both because professional workers constitute only a very small proportion of the agrarian labor force (less than 2 percent) and because these occupations apparently have rather low prestige. In a study of a state farm in the Melitopol'skii region of the Ukraine, whereas 90 percent of the parents questioned wished their children to become professionals, none wished them to become agronomists or veterinarians. Parents were quoted as saying, "Let them study, only not in agricultural institutions." Education is recognized to be the main channel of mobility; real mobility, however, is out of rural areas and into cities that have far more cultural facilities and "all the amenities of everyday life and the possibility to improve one's material well-being" (Arutyunyan 1968, p. 77). The agrarian professions may have provided opportunities for women probably because men were seeking urban employment. Dunn and Dunn (1967, p. 191) conclude that "social mobility, especially for women, means mobility out of the rural environment" (1967, p. 191).

Female intellectuals have considerable difficulty finding husbands in rural areas. This is indicated by Perevedentsev (1972, p. 13) in an article on schoolteachers in rural areas. Females find it difficult to find husbands among their peers because there are so few male teachers, but also, Perevedentsev argues, because these women were not brought up to be "housewives." They are actively involved in their professions and "this does not make them highly desirable wives for rural men." In the villages spinsters are pitied, whereas in the cities "it is easier to get married and it is easier to get along without a husband." This results in a high turnover of female teachers in rural areas.

RURAL TIME-BUDGET STUDIES

Contemporary time-budget studies of rural regions have been conducted since 1969 (see Artemov et al. 1967, p. 59), though data has been published primarily from studies undertaken between 1963 and 1966. The regions studied were located in the western part of the Russian Republic with the one exception of Vinnitsk, Ukraine. Table 6.5 provides data on most studies which I will discuss in this chapter.[3] I will first consider the data from the 1963 and 1964 studies from which it was possible to reconstruct the weekly time use by workers in both summer and

TABLE 6.5

Information on Time-Budget Studies of Collective and State Farms Conducted in the USSR between 1923 and 1966

Region	Year	Season	Type and Number of Farms	Sample	Persons in the Sample	Number of 24-Hour Time Budgets
Sverdlovsk, Rostov, and Gorkii Oblasts	1963	Summer	5 state and 64 collective farms	1600 families	216[a] 1893[a]	284 2580
Stavropolskii Krai, Moscow, and Vinnitsk Oblasts	1964	Summer and winter	4 collective farms	247 families	634 (16 and older)	1902
Mari Autonomous Republic	1965-66	Summer and winter	4 collective farms	387 families	1767 (16 and older)	n. a.
Voronezh Guberniya	1923	Summer	Individual peasant households	29 households	71 (age unknown)	n. a.
Leningrad, Moscow, Kiev, Odessa, and Sverdlovsk Oblasts, Kuibyshev Krai, Azov-Chernomorsk Krai, Belorussia	1934	All 4 seasons	Collective farms	---	Approximately 4000 (12 years and older)	n. a.

n. a.: data not available.

[a]Workers included in the study.

Sources: Artemov et al. 1967, pp. 61, 65; Baikova et al., 1965, p. 221; Bolgov and Smolentsev 1970, pp. 163-67; Strumilin 1964, pp. 167-70; Gosplan 1935, p. 388.

winter separately in collective and state farms. The data available from the 1965-66 study are used for comparisons by sex and occupation later in the chapter.

The largest contemporary study was done in 1963. It was undertaken in conjunction with the study of factory workers in those same oblasts. The study in 1964 reportedly included 10 to 12 percent of the households in the regions where the collective farms were located (Baikova et al. 1965, p. 212), while that in 1965-1966 included .07 percent of the households in the Mari ASSR (Bolgov and Smolentsev 1970, p. 194). The sampling techniques are inadequately described or not mentioned.

I have used the same basic categories as those employed in the analysis of time-budgets from urban areas, although housework is shown as a category apart from the time spent on private subsidiary agriculture—an activity certainly not very different from much of the work in the socialized sector. Thus, Table 6. 6 shows work and time connected with work (in the contemporary studies this refers only to work in the socialized sector), work in private subsidiary agriculture, and housework all as subcategories of "total work."

I should note at this point that a considerable part of the produce of the country has always come from the private plots of the farmers:

> In 1970 the private sector accounted for 65 percent of the produce in the entire country, 38 percent of the vegetables, 35 percent of the meat, 36 percent of the milk, and 53 percent of the eggs and 19 percent of the wool. Altogether, 12 percent of the country's agricultural commodity output was raised privately—8 percent of the produce and 14 percent of the animal husbandry products. . . .
>
> In 1970 for the entire U. S. S. R., 6, 500, 000 hectares, or 2. 94 percent of all plowland, were worked privately. (Of this total 4, 000, 000 hectares was land belonging to collective farms and representing 3. 6 percent of their land (Makarova 1972, p. 13).

Women's work in private subsidiary agriculture consists of the care of cattle and poultry kept on the private plot as well as work in the small gardens. Men erect and repair buildings, prepare wood products, and do the heavy work involved in preparing plots for sowing (Bolgov and Smolentsev 1970, pp. 171-72; Dunn and Dunn 1967, p. 59).

It is clear from the analysis of time-budgets of urban areas that it is of utmost importance to control for family status and/or age. The data required for such controls, however, are unavailable. Age differences between males and females in rural areas are quite extreme. Thus, in 1959, while there were 108 men per 100 women in the age group 20 to 24 and 99 men per 100 women in the age group 25 to 29, the sex ratios in the three age groups 30 to 35, 45 to 49, and 55 to 59 were, respectively, 63, 52, and 41 (Ts. S. U. 1963, p. 61). This is reflected

TABLE 6.6

General Time-Budgets of State and Collective Farm Workers, by Sex, According to Available Studies, 1923, 1934, 1963, and 1964
(percent of average day of week)

	1963 Kolkhoz[a]	1963 Sovkhoz[b]	1964 Summer	1964 Winter	1934 Summer	1923 Summer	1934 Winter	1923 Winter
Males								
Total work	50	43	51	34	49	58	40	21
Work and time connected	39	32	42	27	48	52	38	12
Private sub. agric.	11	11	5	1				
Housework			4	6	1	6	2	9
Physiological needs	37	40	37	42	40	31	44	44
Free time	11	15	12	23	11	11	15	35
Other	1	1	0	0	0	0		
Total	99	99	100	99	100	100	99	100
Females								
Total work	56	52	58	48	55	63	45	55
Work and time connected	29	28	28	16	33	34	19	17
Private sub. agric.	27	24	15	2				
Housework			15	30	22	29	26	38
Physiological needs	35	37	36	39	41	33	44	40
Free time	7	9	5	13	6	4	10	6
Other	2	2	0	0	0	0	0	0
Total	100	100	100	99	101	100	99	101

[a]Collective farm.
[b]State farm.
Sources: Based on figures in Artemov et al. 1967, pp. 62, 64; Baikova et al. 1965, pp. 223-24; Gosplan 1935, pp. 380-83; Strumilin 1964, pp. 169-70. Further information on the studies is available in Table 6.7.

in the time-budget data of the 1960s (see Table 6. 8): the obviously older women averaged considerably less time at work in the socialized sector than did the men. It is difficult to judge whether the total work time of males and females would have been more comparable had their ages been more comparable. This is a serious shortcoming.

It is evident that there is considerable seasonal variation in the time use of the farm workers. Column 4 of Table 6. 6 shows the only contemporary data collected during the winter. During the cold weather both males and females have considerably more free time and spend more time satisfying physiological needs than in summer. However, note that the decline in agricultural work for women was paralleled by a substantial increase in housework during the winter. Males, on the other hand, benefit from the decline in work in the socialized sector and in private subsidiary agriculture by having increased free time. Thus, the difference between the work time of males and females reaches its peak during the winter. When males have more time, there is no sign that they take a greater share of the housework.

The household tasks of men are about the same in summer and winter. For women, however, there are substantial changes. In summer 64 percent of the time women spend doing housework is devoted to preparing food. In winter this takes slightly more time but constitutes only 37 percent of the time spent on housework. There is a major increase in time women spend on the category "other." This increases from 4 percent in summer to 27 percent in winter. This category probably includes sewing and knitting (Baikova et al. 1965, p. 223). Men, of course, do not engage in these activities.

There is a considerably reduced work burden of men on state as opposed to collective farms. The decline for women is far less. If there are improved conditions on the state farms, these conditions appear to be benefiting men more than women. Again, the crucial variable may be age and not material conditions.

Overall, the data on weekly time usage estimated from the 1964 and 1963 studies show the familiar pattern of extreme differences between males and females. During the summer men have on the average about 1. 8 hours more free time and time to spend satisfying their physiological needs. During the winter the figure reaches about 3. 1 hours!

Soviet scholars often make comparisons between the studies of the 1960s and that of 1923 to show the extent of progress in rural areas. The latter research was apparently done in June in connection with an agricultural exhibition that year. But time usage in both summer and winter is recorded, suggesting that the peasants were expected to recall how they spent their time during the winter! The original plan entailed the study of twelve provinces but had to be reduced to the study of only one—Voronezh, RSFSR. Only 71 time-budgets were gathered from 29 households. Strumilin (1964, pp. 166-67) conceded that the data did not warrant "detailed scientific analysis," but did contend that, in general, they were sufficiently representative. There appear to be substantial grounds to question his judgment.

The 1934 study is more extensive than any research done since that time and is by far more credible than the 1923 study. The study includes regions in European Russia as well as Belorussia, the Ukraine, and one in Central Asia (see Table 6. 5). Only the approximately 2, 500 "housewives" and "heads of family" (they are exclusively males) are of interest here, for they are representative of adult males and females. Contemporary studies include only those 16 and older.

Columns 5 through 8 of Table 6. 6 show why comparisons with 1923 rather than 1934 are more frequently found in the literature. Women worked less and had more free time and time for physiological needs in the summer and winter of 1934 than they did in 1964. A comparison with 1923, however, shows that there has indeed been improvement, but not since 1934. For men, work in the summer of 1923 was considerably greater than in later years; however, unlike the situation for women, this was well compensated for by the very much reduced workload in winter. Comparing 1934 and 1964 we see that men have benefited by at least having a reduced workload in winter. The onerous position of women shows remarkable stability over the 30 years.

It should also be noted that the work of men is primarily in "social production," while that of women is in the less prestigious areas of housework and, in recent times, the private economy. However, younger women probably do spend more of their working hours in the socialized sector.

Women use their more scarce free time somewhat differently from men. Though there is some ambiguity in the data, women seem to spend far less of their free time on the mass media: listening to the radio, watching television, going to the movies, reading newspapers, journals, and books. They also spend a larger proportion of their free time on inactive rest and visiting. Both men and women spend more time on inactive rest in the collective farm as opposed to the state farm (Churakov 1967, p. 92; Baikova et al. 1965, pp. 223-24). A Soviet investigator explains that this more passive use of time is due to the lack of facilities for alternative uses of free time. Such deficiencies as these are reportedly convincing young people to leave the farms (Churakov 1967, p. 93).

Other research bearing on the use of free time was conducted in three collective farms in the Orlov Oblast of the Russian Republic between 1963 and 1969. In this study the farms were selected because of their varying degrees of economic success. The results showed considerable differences in the use of media by males and females. The percentage of men who regularly read political literature varied between 8 and 9. 3, whereas the comparable figures for women were only 1. 0 to 1. 5 percent. Between 58. 4 and 68 percent of the men regularly read a newspaper and between 69. 5 and 82 percent listened to the radio for information on domestic and international affairs. The corresponding figures for women were 14 to 18 percent for the former and 40 to 45 percent for the latter (1970, p. 163). The dominance of men in the domestic and work spheres is paralleled by their position

TABLE 6.7

Percentage of Family Members Doing Most of the Housework in Three Villages in Moscow Oblast, by Occupational Group, n.d.

	Husband and Wife	Husband	Wife	Grand-mother	Children under 16	Total
Leaders and specialists	18	5	72	5	0	100.0
Office workers	23	9	61	6	0	99.0
Machine operators	23	7	67	3	0	100.0
Unskilled physical workers	29	5	59	6	0.9	99.9

Source: Arutyunyan 1971, 216.

with regard to the mediation of the outside world. (Again, without controls for age the comparison is seriously deficient.)

CLASS DIFFERENCES IN FAMILY LIFE

A study of Moscow and Riazan Oblasts showed that two-thirds of those questioned responded negatively when asked whether they thought it better for a wife to engage solely in housework and the upbringing of children if it were financially feasible. The higher the skill of the woman, the more likely she valued work outside the home and the less likely was she to express a preference to engage solely in housework and raising of children. Thirty-one percent of the male office workers and machine operators, as opposed to only 20 percent of the males doing manual work, felt that if it were possible women should engage solely in housework and child care (Arutyunyan 1971, pp. 187, 214). Other data suggest that the adherence by men to the belief that women should assume domestic chores only was related to the men's willingness to share such work. Thus, on the basis of the figures in Table 6.7 the Soviet investigator concluded:

> In families of workers in skilled and unskilled physical occupations where the income of the wife comprises a substantial portion of the family budget, the proportion of men taking an active part in housework is more than in other groups. The work burden of leaders and

TABLE 6.8

Summer General Time-Budget of Workers in Mari ASSR, by Sex and Type of Work, 1965-66[a]

	Males		Males and females[b]			Females	
	Fieldwork	Livestock	Construction	Machine Operators	Personnel in Administration & Services	Fieldwork	Livestock
N	(73)	(41)	n. a.	n. a.	n. a.	(176)	(118)
Total work	39	46	45	43	43	65	54
Work and time connected	33	38	37	37	35	32	34
Private sub. agric.	3	5	5	1	3	12	10
Housework	3	3	3	5	5	11	10
Physiological needs	37	35	35	37	36	33	32
Free time	17	11	15	18	15	6	9
Total	93	92	95	98	94	94	95

n. a.: data not available.

[a]Figures represent percentage of a week calculated from time use on weekdays, days off and holidays, and the day before the day off.

[b]There were a total of 164 men and 9 women in these three categories.

Source: Based on data in Bolgov and Smolentsev 1970, pp. 168-69.

TABLE 6.9

Total Free Time and Time Spent Studying and Raising Qualifications among Workers on the Collective Farm Rossii, by Sex and Type of Work

	Fieldworkers	Livestock Workers	Machine Operators	Administrators & Specialists	Service Personnel
Males					
Free time as a percentage of the week	16	9	15	17	16
Study and raising qualifications (hours per week)	3.6	2.3	4.3	2.7	6.9
Females					
Free time as a percentage of the week	10	8	---[a]	8	6
Study and raising qualifications (hours per week)	0.9	2.1	---[a]	2.0	0.2

[a]There were no females in this category.

Source: Based on data in Baikova et al. 1965, pp. 248, 249. This study was conducted during the spring. No date is stated.

> specialists leads them to have less time to help in carrying out household tasks (Arutyunyan 1971, pp. 215-16).

These findings clearly parallel those based on data from urban areas.

Table 6. 8 shows that the housework done by men does not vary "significantly" by occupation.[4] The slightly greater average amount of housework done by machine operators and administrative and service personnel is probably due to the fact that there are several women included in the sample (the females are least likely to be construction workers). The working burden of male field workers is particularly low, contrasting markedly with their female counterparts. This is apparently due to the fact that males in this occupation are only temporarily in this line of work. Much of their free time is likely to be spent studying and advancing their skills through training. A Soviet source indicates that whereas 95 percent of the women in the least skilled jobs on collective farms are likely to remain in such work, the figure for men is only 54 percent. As is confirmed by the census data, males have far greater occupational mobility than do females (Arutyunyan 1968, p. 78).

The data in Table 6. 9 from a different study show more clearly the differences by sex in free time. As in Table 6. 8 it is apparent that males and females in livestock work have the most comparable free time, although the 1965-66 study shows that men compensate for this low figure by having considerably more time than the females for satisfying their physiological needs. In all other cases males have far more free time than their female counterparts. The male-female difference is perhaps most glaring in the time spent on study and raising qualifications. This clearly illustrates that, as in urban areas, men are able to continue to get the training for career advancement while they are working, while females find that combining housework and their jobs prevents them from engaging in such activities.

CONCLUSION

It would certainly appear that in rural areas strong resistance to change has been fostered by the preservation of the functions and structure of the peasant family unit. One Soviet investigator has noted that tradition has thus upheld the dominant position of the male as head of the household, the _khozyain_:

> Most of all the position of head of the household is strengthened by the designation "head of the kolkhoz homestead." It is in the name of this individual that the house and personal plot with buildings is recorded.

> The head of the kolkhoz is also responsible for the financial obligations to the government (paying of taxes, loans, and the arranging for insurance) (Pimenova 1971, pp. 38-39, 42).

When the interests of the family as a unit take precedence over those of the individual members, this appears, at least in this rural setting, to have imposed far greater constraints upon females than upon males.

Females in rural Russia have much more limited opportunities than their urban counterparts. Again, there is evidence that males benefit far more easily and rapidly from technological advancement.

Higher educational attainment and greater exposure to urban ideas does not appear to produce a sexual division of labor in the family that demands equal free time from working men and women.[5] Instead, the evidence suggests that a wife's service to the family frees her husband to devote additional time to study and advance the skills that make his occupational mobility possible. But the occupational segregation among young workers suggests that even single women cannot compete equally with men for the higher status occupations that are available. It is only through their migrating to cities that substantial career advancement has become possible for women.

NOTES

1. In 1966 guaranteed annual income and state pensions were introduced for all collective farm workers (Monich 1970, p. 15). During at least the last decade wages of collective farm workers appear to be increasing relative to those of state farm workers (see Matthews 1972, pp. 64-65).

2. Data from the 1970 census are so limited as to make comparisons by sex worthless. There is, for example, no indication of the number of female tractor and combine operators. The few categories that are presented show little change (Ts. S. U. 1973b, p. 171).

3. The time-budget studies from rural areas suffer from the same types of problems as do those from urban areas. However, the far sparser data from rural studies make them more difficult to analyze. It is, again, likely that the samples overrepresent the more prosperous workers. Thus, if there has been any improvement in the position of women one would expect it to be revealed here more so than in truly representative samples.

4. Note that the totals in Table 6. 8 often add up to far less than 100 percent. Among livestock workers only 92 percent of the male and 95 percent of the female time usage is accounted for. These inaccuracies certainly warrant caution. However, what proves significant here is the consistency of the pattern of male-female differences in the entire table; these differences are confirmed by Table 6. 9.

5. It is quite significant that a study conducted in the rural areas of Moscow Oblast showed that 25 percent of the intelligentsia contended that it was legitimate to punish a wife; the figure for other social groups in the population was either equal to this or lower (Barker 1972, p. 184).

CHAPTER 7
CONCLUSION

CHANGE AND CONTINUITY

The educational and occupational achievement of Soviet Russian women is unmistakable. Nevertheless, occupational segregation by sex has persisted probably since the early post-World War II period. As is shown in Chapter 4, this has mixed implications. On the one hand, there is considerable underrepresentation of women in top positions in government, industry, and the professions. This has certainly had an adverse effect on their ability to influence policy decisions—a fact Soviet women do not fail to appreciate. Thus, as a solution to the deficiencies in the provision of services, a female investigator suggests:

> Why not create another ministry in our country—a united ministry of everyday services? And a woman should be appointed minister of it, one who once had to shoulder all the burdens of housework herself. Give her funds and broad powers. Allow her to display initiative without having each of her measures approved at several levels, and believe me, the new Minister will find hundreds of ways to take care of the everyday needs of her countrywomen (Libedinskaya 1967, p. 14).

Also, women's wages tend to be below those of men because of the far larger concentration of women in fields in which remuneration has been low and increasing at a slower pace. Finally, in many nonprofessional occupations women predominated among those doing the least mechanized and least desirable tasks.

On the other hand, different does not necessarily mean unequal, and measures of dissimilarity may conceal very significant changes in the structure of the labor force that have had positive consequences for women. As should be quite evident from the previous chapter, the shift of women out of agriculture has been extremely propitious. Despite the unchanging segregation in the professional and semiprofessional occupations, the number of women in this sector has increased far more rapidly than that of men. Women's employment pattern has become increasingly different from that of men, for a far larger proportion of the latter have been drawn into nonprofessional occupations. This is evidence that women are getting a substantial return from their high educational attainment. Finally, especially the occupational segregation of increasing numbers of professional women may promote both their organization and critical awareness (cf. Lipset and Dobson 1972). In this respect the relationship between men and women may be analogous to that of youth and adults. In both cases the change in the locus of activities away from the family has ultimately increased segregation. In their report on youth in America, Coleman et al. argue that this contributes to social change:

> Youth that are in close and continual contact with adults are often in close and continual supervision by them. This, and the close contact itself, leads youth to be near-replicas of these adults and less free to bring about social change. A degree of segregation from adults increases the change that a new generation can bring about. Adults often regard youth-initiated change with some fear, but it is one of the major means by which societies change to meet new conditions (1974, p. 132).

In a comparable way Soviet women may have gained greater ability to challenge decisions and institutional arrangements that are contrary to their interests.

There is a lack of evidence on the change over time in the relative influence of husbands and wives on family decision making. Several contemporary studies indicate that women have considerable authority. In a Minsk study of married couples the investigator asked who made the decisions with regard to monetary expenditures, the correct way to raise the children, and the activities to be undertaken during leisure time. He discovered that though there were substantial differences in the views of husbands and wives, they concurred that with regard to all three areas the wife alone made the decisions more often than the husband alone. Decisions were made jointly in 49 to 69 percent of the cases according to the males, and in 41 to 51 percent of the cases according to the females (Yurkevich 1970, pp. 187-90). Another study of urban families also showed that most decisions were made jointly, although women had considerably more authority than men with regard to domestic affairs. Even on collective farms, though the head of the family most frequently represented the family at meetings, it was found that women played an active role in discussion and voting (Pimenova 1971).

However, the inadequacy of decision making as a measure of the "spread of egalitarianism" or of the "companionship marriage" is profoundly evident when one considers the division of labor in the home (cf. Blood and Wolfe 1960; Blood 1963). As is shown in Chapter 5, the persisting sex differences in the time spent on housework and the amount of free time contrast very markedly with women's changing extrafamilial status. It is significant that though the authority of wives appears to be greatest with regard to family finances, this influence does not result in a high priority on appliances that would ease the burden of housework. The following passage illustrates that there is an underlying power structure that is easily concealed when one concentrates solely on who makes a decision:

> Kharchev and Golod found that the possession of appliances was related to professional and cultural attainment. As a whole there is still a lack of everyday technology. The problem is not attributable to material deficiencies but to the psychological orientation of the couple's decisions as to what to purchase. Sixty-four percent of the families of female workers in Kostroma have radios, 75 percent have televisions, but only 13.5 percent have vacuums, and 0.4 percent have floor polishers. This is because the couples put greater importance on their cultural interests and needs. The authors have a more pessimistic conclusion: Machines that could lighten household chores are still of little value to the women themselves and to their husbands. The influence of the husband is obviously stronger. This is shown clearly by other research. . . . If women were completely free from the influence of their husbands and their full dependence on them for purchases, they, obviously, would buy those appliances to lighten housework (Baskina 1972, p. 12).

This may partly explain why mothers without a husband present have less housework. Men influence the criteria women use to make a decision.

THE INTERCONNECTION BETWEEN WORK AND FAMILY LIFE

To some extent the continuities in the position of women in the family and their restricted occupational mobility can be understood in terms of the institutional arrangements which over time have reinforced one another.

That a woman's domestic role profoundly influences her ability to succeed in her occupation was appreciated by Lenin:

> As long as women are engaged in housework their position is still a restricted one. In order to achieve the complete emancipation of women and to make them really equal with men, we must have social economy, and the participation of women in general productive labor. Then women will occupy the same position as men. This, of course, does not mean that women must be exactly equal with men in productivity of labor, amount of labor, its duration, conditions of labor, etc. But it does mean that women shall not be in an oppressed position compared with men. You all know that even with fullest equality, women are still in an actual position of inferioirity because of the housework thrust upon them (The Woman Question 1951, p. 52).

The greater concern was not with occupational segregation—something which Lenin saw as fully warranted—but rather with the constraints of family life which were to persist throughout the Soviet period.

The heavy domestic repsonsibilities of women reinforces and is reinforced by a differential emphasis on the occupational role of men and women. The husband's career has greater priority because he often earns a higher salary or has the greater potential for occupational advancement. This priority further impedes the advancement of the wife and increases the importance of her role as wife and mother. This suggests that the balancing of the sex ratio in recent decades may have increased the stress on woman's domestic role and her facilitating the occupational advancement of her husband.

A woman's commitment is often divided between work and family. When female workers in a number of industrial enterprises in Moscow were asked about the relative importance of their occupational, "social-political" and "family-everyday" roles, 92 percent responded that they were equally important (Yankova 1972, p. 12). The time-budget data show that a woman is not as likely as man to be able to find the time for studies necessary to further her skills and attain higher level positions. Many managers are convinced that women are not as valuable employees as men and that the investment of resources in their training is not as worthwhile.

The inadequate child-care facilities mean that women must take considerable time to care for infants and older children when they are sick. They also must often travel considerable distances to drop off and pick up their children. Managers are less than sympathetic, and often appear to be more inspired to rectify the situation by hiring the increasingly available males than to invest in or press for the necessary service facilities. This is well exemplified by the problems of a female employee at a state bank:

> Her boss . . . took the utilitarian attitude that an employee at home on maternity leave has become only so much

> deadweight to the organization and is no longer of any concern to him. Such executives would probably prefer that there be no vacations at all and that all women employees be transformed into men (Novoplyansky 1973, p. 27).

By not making special provisions for women, the employers make it all the more difficult for females to satisfy the demands put upon them. Furthermore, the managers' low expectations influence the women's self-concepts:

> Managers do not believe in the ability of women to successfully learn the new technology. In practice this makes more difficult the proportional division of the complex and simple labor between men and women.
>
> The lack of faith of the managers motivates the women to have doubts about their own ability (Danilova 1968, p. 36).

Danilova notes that this also has the obvious consequence of limiting women's aspirations, and so the cycle goes on.

The managers also have considerable influence over the type of training received by boys and girls in school. After reviewing recent developments that have further impeded women from obtaining technical training, the Soviet investigator concluded the following:

> One doubts the advisability of the practice of planning admissions to state professional-technical schools according to sex on the basis of the demands of directors of enterprises, who announce only the need for boys even in those professions in which female labor may be used. As a result it turns out that girls are taught primarily those professions in which there was traditionally an extensive use of female labor (Mikhailyuk 1970, pp. 79-80).

Indications are that women constitute about 20 to 25 percent of those in vocational-technical schools (Sharapov 1969, p. 11; Panova 1970, p. 88). However, the training girls receive apparently differs considerably from that of boys. A study of professional-technical schools in Odessa revealed that females constituted 85 to 90 percent of those studying dressmaking, sewing, plastering, and house painting. There were _no_ women in schools that gave the training needed to become various types of specialized machinists, brigadiers for railroad repair, construction engineers, electric welders, brick installers, ship motor mechanics, and other auxiliary workers. Females constituted only about 10 to 15 percent in schools for adjusters of machines with programmed mechanisms, electricians, adjusters of thermoplastic machines, metal craftsmen who repair machinery, and other specialists (Mikhailyuk 1970, p. 80).

Studies of school-age children show very substantial differences in the occupational aspirations of boys and girls (Vodzinskaya 1970; Yanowitz and Dodge 1969). The orientations and abilities of males and females are clearly formed prior to their entrance into the school system. Working mothers have already experienced sex-specific socialization in their families of origin and throughout their education; they have already learned of the prejudices of managers and the discrimination they face should they seek certain high-level positions or fields reserved for men. They have felt the incredible constraints entailed in combining housework and child care with full-time employment, the resultant fatigue and, perhaps, marital discord, the failure of husbands to take a substantial share of domestic responsibilities, the impediments to advancing their work qualifications, etc. They may have little reason to believe that their daughters' lot will be radically different, and the preparation they will give them for adult life will contrast markedly from that which they impart to their sons. In a letter to the Soviet press a woman recently wrote:

> The moral preparation of women for the tremendous social changes which have taken place in our country must be inculcated from early childhood. At present we find an incredibly staunch inertia in the upbringing of girls. Their own parents give them the specific orientation, which in the future leads to the particular differences between the life aspirations of men and women. . . .
>
> [The characteristics of female psychology] are most of all the result of the way in which girls are raised, which to a significant degree is predicated upon the social conceptions of the role of women (quoted in Belkin 1973, p. 14).

Equally distinct is the socialization of males:

> Men consider the family to be of secondary importance. Since childhood they are taught to believe that they must be good breadwinners, but little is said to them about the need to be a good family man. Even in school girls are taught the skills of doing housework, boys are exclusively oriented to production. The whole system of upbringing and the actual relationships of men teach them to be shy about discussing family affairs, to be embarrassed by their love for their wife and children. Even in the first days after marriage the young husband does not rush home directly after work. He demonstrates to his friends that he is not hurrying to be home, that there is

> nothing he is missing and that his having a family is not something so serious that it requires that he change his habits (Tsimbalyuk 1974).

This naturally has a profound effect on relations within the family. Not surprisingly, the son emulates his father: "The circle repeats itself."

"IDEALIZED FEMININITY"

It is the marked change in women's occupational and educational attainment during Soviet Russia's industrial development in the midst of the continuities discussed above that seriously challenges much conventional thinking on the subject.

In Chapter 1 I reviewed theories that suggested that the change should have resulted in growing egalitarianism in the family and reduced occupational segregation by sex. The evidence is clear that these are not imperatives directly associated with industrialization. Rather, the situation in Soviet Russia confirms the theory advanced by Scott and Tilly (1975).

Female employment in industry initially was not a sign of a change in values—a change that would also manifest itself in family relations. To the contrary, it represented the response to changing costs and opportunities on the part of a population adhering to preindustrial values. As in the past, women made their contribution to the survival of the family household, but now the locus of activity was the factory rather than the home. A gradual change in values did take place in the course of industrialization, but the change was to result in a greater emphasis on women's domestic functions and not in a reduction of the difference between the roles of men and women. This was not consistent with traditional beliefs, but rather developed with the emergence of the middle class:

> Goode assumes that the idea of "women's proper place," with its connotations of complete dependency and idealized femininity is a traditional value. In fact, it is a rather recently accepted middle class value not at all inconsistent with notions of "rights and responsibilities of the individual." The division of labor within the family which assigned the husband the role of breadwinner and the wife the role of domestic manager and moral guardian emerged clearly only in the nineteenth century and was associated with the growth of the middle class and the diffusion of its values (Scott and Tilly 1975, p, 41).

In Soviet Russia conditions required to support a middle-class style of living and value system were to emerge far later than in Western Europe. Only in recent decades have the severe economic conditions and the shortage of males finally abated. One need only remember, for example, the extreme shortage of housing that has existed throughout the Soviet period. This is important, for it would seem that the nature of family relations and privacy are closely linked (Aries 1962; Laslett 1973).

It is not yet clear what the most crucial factors are that produce middle-class values, nor whether they are the same in Western Europe as in Soviet Russia. This is an important subject for further research. The spread of middle-class values may be a product of increased prosperity that has reduced the need for women to work or at least to work full time (Scott and Tilly 1975). Factors that have promoted the diffusion of ideas (urbanization, education, the development of mass media, etc.) are probably significant. Also, decline in the labor-force participation of adolescents (see Table 4.1) with the extension of schooling has increased the length of childhood and certainly contributed to the increased emphasis on tasks involving children. This too requires the achievement of a certain level of prosperity.

In Chapter 4 I presented evidence of the apparently growing emphasis on women taking care of their own children. The reader may recall, for example, the statement by a Soviet demographer that "nurseries were a necessity in their own time, but now we are wealthy enough not to have to deprive a child of its mother's affection" (Urlanis 1971, p. 11).

The importance of what Scott and Tilly call "idealized femininity" is very evident from statements in the Soviet press. The following comment, for example, seems utterly incongruous in a nation where women constitute more than half of the full-time labor force and predominate among those in the professional and semiprofessional occupations (Shim 1967, p. 13):

> Is it possible to emancipate an additional segment of women from the handbarrow? Is it possible to reduce the working day for women? Is it possible to evaluate justly her labor in raising a family, in rearing children, recognizing this as one of the principal areas of labor? Finally, is it possible to change our habitual attitude, that ill-starred stereotype, and create an atmosphere of decent respect and chivalry? An unvarying, general atmosphere that would make stereotyped lessons of gallantry superfluous, that would make it unnecessary to learn from the newspapers to take one's hat off before a woman and let her go first.

Or note the pleas of a male graduate student responding to a female's letter decrying the vacuousness of gallantry:

> Girls for all your equality with us men, stay feminine, gentle and weak (in the best, Marxist sense of this concept), stay beautiful not only internally but also in your manners (Kurgansky 1967, p. 11).

That these views are also held by educated women is evidenced by the complaints of an ardent Soviet feminist (Litvinenko 1971, p. 40):

> In the press one finds the opinion of female readers supporting the notion that children and family are the very first and sanctified functions of a woman. These women, though, are in the intelligentsia. They feel that they are bright and capable and can make their way in the world and work at their professions. The others, they feel, are not capable of anything besides housework and deserve what they get.

Also manifesting this complex of beliefs to some degree is the persistence of occupational segregation and the growing concentration of women in the tertiary sector of the economy. There clearly exists a distinct conception of women's work and this covers aspects of both their domestic and their occupational roles.

THE ABSENCE OF DISRUPTIVE CAPITALISM

The premise of the above explanation of continuity is that recently emerging values have supported differences in sex roles. But it is not possible with the data available to trace these values over time nor to reject the notion that they are entirely inconsistent with traditional values. Surely, for example, some of the conceptions of women's leadership capabilities and other aptitudes relative to men are not of recent origin. That a woman's place is in or near the home may have been a value that had to be dispensed with only as a result of the exigencies of the past. It is plausible that middle-class values reinforced and grew from values already extant in the traditional culture. What I am suggesting here is that the continuing influence of traditional values might also explain the absence of change in family relations and in certain aspects of female labor-force participation. This may have been a product of the traditional social structure having been relatively undisturbed by the full development of capitalism at the time of the 1917 Revolution (see Kushner 1970). Note even today the collective nature of the rural household as described in Chapter 5. Such an explanation is suggested by the writings of Marx and Engels.

In Chapter 1 I discussed evolutionary theory which pointed to the advantages that economically backward areas may derive from not being hindered by the institutions of the more advanced areas. Marx and

Engels suggest that the destruction of previous relations is performed by the evolution within a social system. The potential for change comes not from skipping stages but from experiencing them:

> The bourgeoisie, historically, has played a most revolutionary part. The bourgeoisie, wherever it has got the upper hand, has put an end to all feudal, partriarchal, idyllic relations. It has pitilessly torn asunder the motley feudal ties that bound man to his "natural superior".
> . . .
> The bourgeoisie has torn away from the family its sentimental veil, and has reduced the family relation to a mere money relation (1968, pp. 37-38).

This disruption is wrought by the rapid pace of economic development, which in Russia was to be fully achieved only during the Soviet period (Marx and Engels 1968, p. 38):

> Constant revolutionizing of production, uninterrupted disturbance of all social conditions, everlasting uncertainty and agitation distinguish the bourgeois epoch from all earlier ones. All fixed, fast-frozen relations, with their train of ancient and venerable prejudices and opinions are swept away, all new formed ones become antiquated before they ossify. . . . Man is at last compelled to face with sober senses, his real condition of life, and his relation with kind (Marx and Engels 1968, p. 38).

Because of the strength of the relationships among the peasantry, the early social experimentation after the 1917 Revolution was doomed to failure. Following the analysis of Eric R. Wolf (1971), however, it is the presence of just such a stratum that fosters revolution. The poorest peasants are the first to succumb to the effects of the market economy. It is the middle peasantry who are "the main bearers of peasant tradition" and who revolt in an attempt to remain conservative:

> . . . it is precisely this culturally conservative stratum that is most instrumental in dynamiting the peasant social order. This paradox dissolves, however, when we consider that it is also the middle peasant who is relatively the most vulnerable to economic changes wrought by commercialism, while his social relations remain encased within the traditional design. . . . it is precisely this stratum that depends most on traditional social relations of kin and mutual aid between neighbors; middle peasants suffer most when these relations are abrogated, just as

> they are least able to withstand the depredations of tax collectors or landlords (pp. 56-57).

Thus, the continuity in social relations between tsarist and Soviet Russia may be explained by the fact that the Revolution occurred before traditional social relations eroded sufficiently to provide the potential for change. As argued in the preceding section, however, should the progress of capitalism produce a large middle class rather than an impoverished proletariat, this too may impede the radical change in women's work.

THE MEANING OF WORK

One further consideration derives from Scott and Tilly's discussion of the values associated with work. It may be that the very emergence of middle-class values is what alters the meaning and the influence of female employment. One implication of this is that if Soviet women had withdrawn from the work force at some previous period, their participation in the labor force might have had a different meaning. The situation, again, may parallel that of youth. While the work of youth in modern industrial societies is a sign of the transition to adulthood, it has become such only because of their gradual separation from the labor force:

> We might remind ourselves that in a society where everyone worked, a society without protected childhood, institutionalized adolescence, or forced retirement, the performance of work was less a mark of maturity than it is in our own society, where the labor force forms so much smaller a proportion of the total population. . . . Thus, [in antebellum society] even though young people were fully incorporated into the labor force, they were not described as full adults. The usual definition of "youth" was actually very broad, from 15 to 25 (with slight variations), and youth was described not merely as the opposite of age but as a prolonged period of immaturity and lamentable irresponsibility (Coleman et al. 1974, p. 16).

This suggests that the meaning and significance of women's labor participation may be very different in the United States than in the Soviet Union. A woman judge or steelworker, for example, may constitute very much more of a discontinuity in a nation in which middle-class values and family living are already prevalent. Such a discontinuity may more seriously bring into question previous conceptions of women's role.

If a greater stress on "idealized femininity" is emerging in contemporary Soviet Russia, it may generate conflicts and tensions that create the potential for further change. Certainly in the United States the women's movement is very much a reaction to such values and may have been fostered and spread by recent changes in female employment. The sequence of change may be somewhat different among Soviet women, for the nature and extent of their occupational participation has for a long time been radically different from that of their American counterparts. The change of values (either from the strengthening of traditional conceptions or the spread of middle-class values) may generate considerable resistance in such a context. Letters from the Soviet press confirm that there is substantial divergence in the views of males and females.

The slowness of change in the family division of labor may initially have been a product of the persistence of preindustrial values. The fruits of industrial progress may have given rise to a set of values stressing women's roles as wives and mothers, but this may also have been the seed for further change. The very significnat changes in women's extrafamilial roles may begin to manifest themselves far more within the family. The conflicts with men may crystallize the organization and awareness of women that has already been fostered by higher education and occupational segregation.

APPENDIX A: EMPLOYMENT AND EDUCATIONAL ATTAINMENT

TABLE A.1

Percentage of Women among Executives and Professional Workers Occupying Various Posts in Industry in the USSR, December 1961 and 1963

	1961	1963
Total	32	34
Heads of enterprises	6	6
Chief engineers	16	16
Shop superintendents and deputy superintendents	12	12
Shift, sector, section, and shop-laboratory chiefs	24	22
Department, bureau, factory management group, and shop chiefs, and heads of factory central laboratories	20	20
Engineers (excluding economists and rate-setter engineers)	37	38
Technicians (excluding rate-setter technicians)	59	65
Foremen	20	20
Rate-setter engineers and technicians	59	62
Chief and senior bookkeepers	33	36
Engineer economists, economists, planners, statisticians	76	79

Source: Central Statistical Board 1963, p. 121.

TABLE A. 2

Percentage of Women among Executives and Professional Workers Occupying Various Posts in Building Organizations in the USSR in December 1961 and 1963

	1961	1963
Total	22	23
Heads of building organizations, subsidiary enterprises, leading specialists, work superintendents, heads of production departments and groups	5	n. a.
Engineers (excluding engineer economists, rate-setter technicians), architects	39	41
Technicians (excluding rate-setter technicians)	52	54
Foremen	13	12
Rate-setter engineers and technicians	62	67
Chief and senior bookkeepers	27	31
Engineer economists, economists, planners, statisticians	70	72

Source: Central Statistical Board 1963, p. 122; Ts. S. U. 1969b, p. 102.

TABLE A. 3

Percentage of Women among Scientific Workers in the USSR, 1960, 1968, and 1973

	1960	1968	1973
All scientific workers	36.0	38.9	39.6
Scientific workers holding academic degrees			
Doctor of Sciences	10.0	12.5	13.4
Candidate of Sciences	29.2	27.2	27.6
Scientific workers with academic titles			
Academician, corresponding member professor	7.0	9.4	10.2
Reader	17.0	20.7	22.1
Senior scientific worker	28.5	24.5	24.1
Junior scientific worker and assistant	50.9	50.0	49.5

Source: Based on figures in Ts. S. U. 1969a, p. 695; Ts. S. U. 1974, pp. 175-76.

TABLE A.4

Percentage of Female Teachers among Various School Personnel in the USSR

	1960-61	1969-70	1973-74
Directors of primary schools	69	54	80
Directors of 8-year schools	24	27	31
Directors of secondary schools	23	23	27
Assistant directors of 8-year schools	54	59	61
Assistant directors of secondary schools	53	59	64
Teachers of grades 1 to 4	87	87	64
Teachers of grades 5 to 7	76	} 75	} 80
Teachers of grades 8 to 11	67		
Teachers of music, singing, drawing, physical training, and vocational training	26	29	34

Source: Vestnik statistiki 1971 (1), p. 89; Central Statistical Board 1963, p. 125; Ts.S.U. 1974, p. 706.

TABLE A.5

Percentage of Females among Deputies in Various Government Bodies of the USSR, 1966, 1967, and 1970

	1966	1967	1970
Supreme Soviet of the USSR	28.0	n.a.	31
Soviet of the Union	28.9	n.a.	30
Soviet of Nationalities	27.1	n.a.	31
Supreme Soviets of Union Republics	n.a.	33.7	n.a.
Supreme Soviets of Autonomous Republics	n.a.	34.7	n.a.
Territorial, regional, area, district, city, rural, and settlement Soviets of Working People's Deputies	n.a.	42.8	45

n.a.: data not available.

Source: Ts.S.U. 1970, p. 33; Vestnik statistiki 1970 (1), p. 90.

TABLE A.6

Educational Achievement of the Urban Population of the RSFSR, by Age and Sex, 1959 and 1970
(number of persons per 1,000)

	Higher Education		Incomplete Higher and Specialized Secondary		General Secondary and Incomplete Secondary		Elementary		Less Than 4 Years	
	Male	Female	Male	Female	Male	Female	Male	Female	Male	Female
1959										
10 and older	45	35	84	86	342	329	383	258	146	292
10-19	0.0	0.0	9	119	376	472	402	325	187	84
20-29	33	47	111	165	420	483	405	261	31	44
30-39	63	64	114	127	400	430	382	297	41	82
40-49	73	35	115	73	264	185	375	272	173	435
50-54	90	28	90	42	176	130	353	231	291	569
55-59	96	27	79	36	161	113	329	185	335	639
60 and older	58	16	55	23	103	63	295	125	489	773
1970										
10 and older	68	55	106	114	438	395	293	228	95	208
10-19	---	---	8	15	420	467	433	388	139	130
20-29	48	71	161	246	688	632	96	43	7	8
30-39	122	119	150	186	439	462	258	191	31	42
40-49	100	75	129	129	384	437	340	278	47	80
50-54	97	50	141	102	343	269	323	296	96	283
55-59	82	31	114	58	228	145	354	242	222	524
60 and older	90	24	78	31	148	95	302	174	382	676

Source: Based on Ts.S.U. 1963, pp. 104-105; Ts.S.U. 1972, pp. 32-33.

TABLE A. 7

Educational Achievement of the Urban Population of the RSFSR in the Labor Force, 1959 and 1970
(persons per 1, 000 population)

	Higher Education	Incomplete Higher	Secondary Specialized	Secondary General	Incomplete Secondary	Elementary	Less Than Elementary
Males							
1959	36	9	63	52	268	424	148
1970	68	13	92	132	341	289	65
1970 as percent of 1959	(1.89)	(1.44)	(1.46)	(2.52)	(1.27	(0.68)	(0.44)
Females							
1959	35	10	82	68	257	277	271
1970	65	12	130	149	311	224	109
1970 as percent of 1959	(1.86)	(1.20)	(1.59)	(2.19)	(1.21)	(0.81)	(0.40)

Source: Based on figures in Ts. S. U. 1972c, p. 408.

APPENDIX B: THE CLASSIFICATION OF TIME

The following are the time-budget categories based on a questionnaire developed by the Institute of Economics and Organization of Production of the Siberian Division of the Academy of Science of the USSR and used for the study of Krasnoyarsk Krai in 1963 (Patrushev 1966, pp. 199-213).

A. Working time
   1. Time actually working
      a. Usual work
      b. Overtime work
   2. Time wasted and nonproductive expenditures of time
      a. Industrial gymnastics
      b. Time spent by mothers nursing their children
      c. Time spent changing work shifts

B. Time not working connected with work
   1. Travel to and from the place of work
      a. Walking to and from transportation stops
      b. Waiting for transportation
      c. Time travelling to work on communal transport and returning
      d. Walking to work and back (for those who do not use some means of transport)
      e. Travel to work by private means (motorcycle, bicycle) and return
   2. Time expenditures from the time of arrival at work until the beginning of work and from the end of work until the departure from the enterprise
      a. Traveling to the place of work and back within the enterprise
      b. Receiving orders and instructions
      c. Care of self before and after shifts (undressing, dressing, and washing)
   3. Lunch break
      a. Walking to and from the snack bar or cafeteria
      b. Waiting in line
      c. Eating
      d. Rest
      e. Exercises
      f. Meetings, conferences
      g. Fulfilling public tasks

C. Housework
   1. Time purchasing foods

a. Time travelling to and from the store
b. Time spent in the store purchasing edible products
c. Time going to the cafeteria for food to be eaten at home
d. Receiving a meal at the cafeteria to be eaten at home
e. Expenditure of time purchasing products at the market, including travel time

2. Time spent making other purchases
   a. Time spent going to the stores
   b. Time in the stores connected with purchases
   c. Time spent at the clothing and shoe shop (including time travelling)
3. Preparing food
   a. Lighting the stove, carrying out ashes, carrying fuel (for homes with stove heating)
   b. Carrying water
   c. Preparing and heating food
   d. Washing dishes after eating
4. Care of residence, furniture and appliances
   a. Cleaning of the premises
   b. Washing the floors
   c. Cleaning the yard (dirt, snow)
   d. Repair of the apartment, furniture, and everyday appliances, and other work in caring for the premises
   e. Going to workshops for the repair of furniture, everyday appliances
   f. Repair of motorcycle, bicycle, and care
5. Care of clothing, shoes, and linen
   a. Washing and ironing
   b. Household repairs of clothing and shoes
   c. Going to workshops for the repair of clothing and shoes, the coloring and cleaning of clothing
   d. Going to the laundry
   e. Household cleaning and of clothing and shoes
   f. Going to <u>prokatnykh punktov</u> (places to let out on hire)
6. Other aspects of housework
   a. Sewing and knitting
   b. Making household articles, utensils
   c. Stock up on fuel (transporting, loading, sawing)
   d. Work in the private subsidiary economy (care of livestock, poultry, the garden, etc.)
   e. Other aspects of housework
7. Care of children
   a. Care of infants during the day
   b. Care of infants at night
   c. Care of other children
   d. Bringing children to school, kindergartens, and yasles (day nurseries)

e. Going to children's hospitals and for doctor's consultations

D. Satisfying natural physiological needs

1. Care of self
   a. Dressing, brushing hair, washing (umyt'sya)
   b. Shaving at home
   c. Washing at home (nomyt'sya)
   d. Time travelling to and from baths and showers
   e. Time at baths and showers
   f. Time travelling to the hairdresser
   g. Waiting on line at the hairdresser
   h. Time at the hairdresser
   i. Time travelling to medical institutions
   j. Waiting to be received by the doctor
   k. Attendance at medical institutions (excluding time spent going there)
   l. Having medical procedures performed at home
2. Eating (not including lunch break at work)
   a. Time eating at home
   b. Time travelling to and from cafeterias, cafes, and tea houses
   c. Time spent eating in cafeterias, cafes, and tea houses
3. Sleep
   a. Sleep during the day
   b. Sleep at night

E. Free time

1. Study
   a. Preparing for lessons
   b. Time travelling to and from study institutions and production-technical courses
   c. Time spent in courses at study institutions (schools, college, technicums, institutes, etc.)
   d. Time spent in production-technical courses, in schools of pedagogical experience, etc.
   e. Reading literature in one's specialty (scientific books, journals)
   f. Time travelling to and from the library or reading rooms (to obtain literature in one's specialty or for courses, etc.)
   g. Time travelling to and from places where courses in the system of Party education are given
   h. Time at courses in the system of Party education (circles, seminars, night universities, etc.)
2. Self-education
   a. Reading the newspaper

b. Reading journal and artistic literature
c. Listening to lectures
d. Attendance at universities of culture (technical knowledge, etc.)
e. Reading scientific books and journals
f. Watching special television and radio programs
g. Studying foreign languages
h. Preparing scientific lectures and meetings
i. Participation in scientific-technical seminars, conferences and meetings
j. Time spent travelling to and from libraries and reading rooms (for the purpose of getting or reading newspapers, journals, and artistic literature)

3. Public Work
   a. Preparations for reports, for lectures for courses in the system of Party education, in production-technical courses, schools of pedagogical experience, universities of culture, technical knowledge
   b. Reading the reports and lectures
   c. Participation in meetings and conferences
   d. Fulfilling selective social responsibilities as a deputy, a member of the Party, union, or <u>komsomol</u> committee, etc.
   e. Participation in detachments for the preservation of social order
   f. Fulfilling tasks (participation in various committees) of Party, soviet, union, komsomol organizations, of NTO (Scientific Technical Department), etc.
   g. Participation in the work of public bureaus of economic analysis, design offices, economic and technical councils of enterprises, etc.
   h. Participation in collective voluntary work on Sunday (<u>voskresnik</u>)
   i. Fulfilling other public tasks
4. Activities with children
   a. Checking on preparations for school lessons
   b. Reading, games, conversations with children
   c. Walks with children
   d. Teaching children working habits (repairing and making furniture and household utensils, binding books, etc.)
   e. Meetings with teachers, attending parents' meetings
5. Physical culture and sports
   a. Physical exercise (besides those at work)
   b. Amateur sports activities, sports games (volleyball, football, skiing, ice skating, chess, checkers, tourism, etc.)
   c. Hunting and fishing

d. Activities in sports schools
e. Participation in competitions

6. Rest and amusement
   a. Listening to radio (excluding time spent simultaneously in other categories)
   b. Going to the movies
   c. Going to the theatre
   d. Going to concerts, clubs, houses of culture
   e. Going to exhibits and museums
   f. Parks, gardens, stadiums, social meetings (vecher otdykha), parades (massovykh gulyanii), etc.
   g. Singing, playing musical instruments at home
   h. Household table games (dominoes, checkers, chess, lotto, cards, etc.)
   i. Receiving guests and visiting relatives and acquaintances
   j. Inactive rest
   k. Other amusement (specify)
7. Creative activities and amateur endeavors (lyubitel' skii trud)
   a. Artistic embroidery and crocheting
   b. Photographic activities
   c. Radio construction
   d. Literary creations, drawing, sculpture
   e. Participation in amateur performances (dramatic, musical, literary, etc.)
   f. Inventive and streamlining activities (zanyatiya ratsional'uzatsiei i izobretatel'stvom)
   g. Care of flowers and aquariums
   h. Care of the garden
   i. Other amateur activities
8. Other expenditures of time
   a. Care of sick members of the family
   b. Going to church and the fulfillment of religious ceremonies
   c. Going to institutions concerning personal questions (police, savings bank, post office, district executive committee, receiving wages, information, etc.)
   d. Undivided time
9. Expenditures of time on the following while simultaneously spending time in an activity accounted for in another category
   a. Reading the paper
   b. Reading books and magazines
   c. Listening to the radio and television

APPENDIX C: TIME-BUDGETS OF WORKERS

TABLE C.1

General Time-Budget of Workers in Cities West of the Urals, 1960-66

City or Region	N	Work and Time Connected	Housework	Physiological Needs	Free Time	Other	Total
		Time-Budget Categories (percentages of week)					
Moscow, Novgorod, and Bolshev, 1958 or 1960							
Male	298	32	5	42	21	0	100
Female	648	30	11	45	14	0	100
Erevan, 1961							
Male	1345[b]	30	8	39	21	0	98
Female	4708[b]	31	19	37	10	0	97
Moscow Oblast, 1962							
Male	n. a.[c]	n. a.	8	n. a.	21	n. a.	n. a.
Female	n. a.[c]	n. a.	18	n. a.	15	0	n. a.
Kiev, 1962							
Male	101	31	5	39	25	0	100
Female	241	31	14	39	17	0	101
Ivanovo City, 1963							
Male	74	30	8	40	21	1[a]	99
Female	170	30	17	38	12	2[a]	99
Ivanovo Oblast, 1963							
Male	n. a.[d]	28	10	40	21	0	99
Female	n. a.[d]	29	19	39	12	1	100
Gorkii City, 1963							
Male	238	30	8	40	21	1[a]	100
Female	297	30	19	37	13	2[a]	101
Gorkii Oblast, 1963							
Male	n. a.[d]	31	8	40	19	0	98
Female	n. a.[d]	29	21	37	13	0	100
Rostov City, 1963							
Male	51	29	9	39	22	1[a]	100
Female	104	28	18	38	13	3[a]	100
Rostov Oblast, 1963							
Male	n. a.[d]	30	10	40	19	0	99
Female	n. a.[d]	28	22	37	13	1	101

Sverdlovsk City, 1963							
Male	99	30	8	39	21	2[a]	98
Female	182	29	20	37	13	2[a]	101
Sverdlovsk Oblast, 1963							
Male	n. a.[d]	31	10	39	19	0	99
Female	n. a.[d]	30	22	37	11	0	100
Pskov, 1965							
Male	1097	32	6	39	20	3[a]	100
Female	1574	29	17	38	13	3[a]	100
Kostroma, 1965-66							
Male	n. a.	n. a.	n. a.	n. a.	21	n. a.	n. a.
Female	n. a.	26-31	18-20	35-70	10-11	0	n. a.
Dnepropetrovsk, Zaporozh'e, Odessa, and Kostroma, 1966							
Male	350	32	11[e]	40[f]	16	3	102
Female	550	29	20[e]	36[f]	9	5	99

n. a.: data not available.

[a]Travel not connected with work. In other studies this is subsumed under several other categories. Kolpakov and Patrushev (1971, p. 82) explain that the particularly large amount of time spent on this activity in Pskov is due to the methodology employed in the study.

[b]Petrosyan (1966, p. 87) states that 3,363 factory and office workers and industrial-technical personnel aged 16 to 65 were included in the study. Petrosyan (1965, p. 24) also noted that 40 percent of the time-budgets returned came from men.

[c]Mialkin (1962, p. 24) indicates that 400 questionnaires on weekly time use were returned in this study. This is probably the total number of male and female respondents.

[d]From all four oblasts in the 1963 study there were drawn a total of 1,911 families of industrial workers, 369 families of industrial-technical personnel, and 141 families of office workers. Twenty percent of the families were from Rostov, 37 percent were from Sverdlovsk, 26 percent were from Gorkii, and 17 percent were Ivanovsk (Artemov et al. 1967, p. 54). The number of working members in these families is not available.

[e]This includes an aspect of care of children--"upbringing of children"--which is considered part of free time in other studies.

[f]This includes time spent on "inactive rest"--a category usually considered to be under free time.

Source: Based on Kokarev et al. 1963, p. 52; Kryazhev 1966, pp. 84, 86, 90-91; Mialkin 1962, p. 24; Kolpakov and Patrushev 1971, pp. 82-84; Levin 1971, pp. 104-7; Petrosyan 1966, pp. 95-96; Baikova et al. 1965, p. 53; Prudenskii 1972, p. 280; Gordon and Klopov 1972a, p. 20; 1972b, p. 11.

The categories in the Pskov study are a product of the specifications agreed upon for the 12-nation study of which this was a part (see Szalai 1972). Data for the cities of Ivanovo, Gorkii, Sverdlovsk, and Rostov on the Don as well as those for Krasnoyarsk in 1963 have been slightly adjusted by Kolpakov and Patrushev (1971, p. 82) to correspond to the Pskov classification of time. The data from the oblasts and krai with the same names were not reclassified.

TABLE C. 2

General Time-Budget of Workers in Krasnoyarsk Krai, Erevan, Four Oblasts, and Pskov, by Sex and Age Groups[a]

	Work and Time Connected with Work	Housework	Physiological Needs	Free Time	Study & Raising Qualifications	Other	N
Krasnoyarsk Krai							
September-October 1959							
Males							
Under 20	n. a.	7	n. a.	22	(8.6)[b]	0	[22]
20-25	n. a.	8	n. a.	20	(7.2)	0	[87]
25-35	n. a.	10	n. a.	18	(3.1)	0	[296]
35-50	n. a.	11	n. a.	16	(0.8)	0	[167]
50 and Older	n. a.	10	n. a.	16	(0.6)	0	[19]
Females							
Under 20	n. a.	13	n. a.	18	(4.0)[b]	0	[23]
20-25	n. a.	15	n. a.	18	(7.4)	0	[69]
25-35	n. a.	23	n. a.	10	(2.0)	0	[129]
35-50	n. a.	24	n. a.	10	(0.2)	0	[62]
50 and Older	n. a.	33	n. a.	4	(0.0)	0	[2]
Erevan, June 1961							
Males							
Under 25	36	5	38	19	(7.6)	2	n. a.
26-50	37	8	38	15	(1.5)	2	n. a.
Over 50	35	5	37	22	(0.0)	1	n. a.
Females							
Under 25	37	8	38	16	(8.2)	1	n. a.
26-50	37	18	35	9	(0.8)	1	n. a.
Over 50	36	17	38	8	(0.0)	1	n. a.
Rostov, Gorkii, Sverdlovsk, and Ivanovsk Oblasts							
June 1963							
Males							
16-19	35	2	40	23	(2.3)	1	n. a.
20-24	31	3	41	25	(10.2)	0	n. a.
25-34	35	7	38	19	(5.7)	1	n. a.
35-49	36	10	38	15	(1.0)	1	n. a.
50-54 55-59	37	11	38	13	(0.5)	0	n. a.

Females							
16-19	30	7	40	22	(7.8)	1	n. a.
20-24	36	12	38	13	(4.9)	1	n. a.
25-34	34	21	36	9	(1.6)	1	n. a.
35-49	35	20	36	7	(0.0)	1	n. a.
50-54	36	19	36	8	(0.0)	1	
55-59	26	22	40	11	(0.0)	1	
Pskov, October-November 1965							
Males							
18-24	30	3	39	24	(9.1)	4[c]	[88]
25-29	31	6	38	20	(6.3)	4[c]	[234]
30-39	32	7	39	19	(4.2)	3[c]	[400]
40-49	32	7	40	19	(3.5)	3[c]	[217]
50-59	32	7	40	19	(2.1)	2[c]	[141]
60-64	34	9	40	15	(0.0)	2[c]	[17]
Females							
18-24	27	11	39	19	(9.1)	4[c]	[176]
25-29	28	16	38	13	(2.8)	4[c]	[306]
30-39	28	20	38	11	(1.4)	3[c]	[494]
40-49	30	18	38	11	(1.4)	3[c]	[399]
50-59	29	20	38	11	(0.0)	3[c]	[184]
60-64	24	19	40	14	(0.0)	2[c]	[17]

n. a.: data not available.

[a]The figures from Pskov represent per cent of a week. All the others are in percent of a weekday. Figures in parentheses represent hours per week for Pskov and Krasnoyarsk; they represent hours per the six workdays of the week in the remaining two studies.

[b]It is significant to note that data presented by Kolpakov and Prudenskii (1966, p. 220) on the time per week spent studying by male and female workers in Krasnoyarsk Krai show approximately the same pattern as that shown here, based on data for workdays only. The only large difference is in the age group under 20 years old. The weekly data show that males this age spent 10.6 hours and the females 9.7 hours studying--figures far more comprable than those in the data based on workdays.

[c]This is the time spent on travel other than going to work. This is subsumed under several other categories in the other studies.

Sources: Based on data from Patrushev 1966, pp. 106-09; Baikova 1970, p. 90; Petrosyan 1965, pp. 100-01; Artemov et al. 1967, p. 85; Kolpakov and Patrushev 1971 pp. 214-15.

TABLE C. 3

General Time-Budget of Employed Men and Women in Pskov, by Social Class, 1965[a]

		White-collar		Blue-collar	
	Total	High	Low	Skilled	Unskilled
Males					
N	[813]	[154]	[138]	[428]	[93]
Work and time connected with it	35	37	34	35	35
Housework and child care	7	6	6	6	7
Physiological needs	40	41	40	40	40
Free time	16	19	17	16	15
Study and organizational participation	(51)	(67)	(70)	(44)	(34)
Total non-work travel	2	2	2	2	2
Total time[b]	(1462)	(1423)	(1452)	(1458)	(1452)
Females					
N	[1129]	[285]	[283]	[228]	[334]
Work and time connected with it	33	33	34	33	33
Housework and child care	16	14	14	16	18
Physiological needs	38	38	38	38	37
Free time	10	11	11	10	8
Study and organizational participation	(30)	(30)	(43)	(24)	(19)
Total non-work travel	3	3	3	3	4
Total time[b]	(1460)	(1459)	(1454)	(1459)	(1472)

[a]Figures represent percent of a workday; those in parentheses represent minutes per workday.

[b]To calculate the percentage distribution the actual time has been used rather than 1440 minutes.

Source: Based on data in Szalai (ed.) 1972, pp. 640-57, 670.

TABLE C.4

Free Time and Time Spent on Housework by Workers in Sverdlovsk, Krasnoyarsk Krai, and Dnepropetrovsk, Zaporozh'e, Kostroma, and Odessa, by Education and Sex[a]

	Sverdlovsk[b]			Krasnoyarsk Krai,[c] 1959			Cities,[d] 1966			
	Elementary	7-Year	Secondary and Higher	Under 4 Years	5-9 Years	Secondary & Incomplete Higher	Under 4 Years	5-7 Years	8-10 Years	Specialized
Housework										
Males	17.4	15.6	12.0	14.8	13.2	11.1	17.1	20.6	17.7	14.3
Females	31.2	26.4	22.2	32.4	26.7	23.6	45.2	39.3	40.8	35.4
Males/Females	0.56	0.59	0.54	0.46	0.49	0.47	0.38	0.52	0.43	0.40
Free Time										
Males	3.7	4.5	5.0	17.1	20.1	24.0	28.1	26.6	30.4	33.7
Females	2.3	2.9	3.4	8.7	14.5	18.7	10.9	13.6	16.2	14.1
Males/Females	1.61	1.55	1.47	1.97	1.39	1.28	2.58	1.96	1.88	2.39

[a]Precise data on sample size are available only for the Krasnoyarsk study which included 246 males and 97 females with less than a fourth-grade education, 265 males and 123 females with a fifth- to ninth-grade education, and 77 males and 65 females with a secondary or incomplete higher education (Baikova et al. 1965, p. 93).

[b]Date unknown. Figures represent hours per six weekdays.

[c]Figures represent hours per six weekdays.

[d]Dneptropetrovsk, Zaporozh'e, Kostroma, and Odessa. Figures represent hours per week.

Source: Based on figures from Petrosyan 1965, pp. 113-14; Patrushev 1966, p. 112; Gordon and Klopov 1972b, pp. 52-53.

TABLE C.5

General Time-Budget of Male and Female Workers on Five-Day and Six-Day Work Schedule in Pavlovskii Posad and Four Large Cities, 1966[a]
(figures in percent of a week)

	Males				Females			
	Six-Day Week		Five-Day Week		Six-Day Week		Five-Day Week	
	Pavlovskii Posad	Large Cities[a]	Pavlovskii Posad	Large Cities[a]	Pavlovskii Posad	Large Cities[a]	Pavlovskii Posad	Large Cities[a]
Work and time connected with work	30	33	27	32	30	32	29	29
Time connected with work	5	9	4	8	5	8	5	6
Housework	10	10	11	8	22	20	24	18
Physiological needs	43	38	43	38	39	38	40	38
Free time	18	19	18	22	9	12	8	14
Total	101	100	99	100	100	102	101	99

[a]The large cities are Dnepropetrovsk, Zaporozh'e, Odessa, and Kostroma.
Source: Based on data from Gordon and Levin (1968, p. 140) and Gordon and Pimashevskaya (1972, p. 24).

BIBLIOGRAPHY

Acker, Joan. 1973. "Women and Social Stratification: A Case of Intellectual Sexism." American Journal of Sociology 8 (January): 936-45.

Andrushkyavichenye, Ya. 1970. "Zhenskii trud i problemy svobodnovo vremeni." In Problemy byta, braka, i sem'i, ed. N. Solov'ev, pp. 78-86. Vil'nus, Lithuania: Mintis.

Arkhangel'skii, L. M., L. N. Kogan and V. K. Bakshutov (eds.). 1967. Dukhovnoe razvitie lichnosti. Sverdlovsk: Ural'skii gosudarstvennyi universtet imeni A. M. Gor'kovo.

Aries, Philippe. 1962. Centuries of Childhood: A Social History of Family Life. Translated by Robert Baldick. New York: Vintage.

Artemov, V. A. 1966. "O nekotorykh metodakh analiza byudzhetov vremeni trudyashchiksya." In Sotsiologicheskie issledovaniya: voprosy metodologii i metodiki, ed. R. V. Ryvkina, pp. 398-420. Novosibirsk: Novosibirskii gosudarstvennyi universitet.

Artemov, V. A., V. I. Bolgov, and O. V. Vol'skaya (eds.). 1967. Statistika byudzhetov vremeni trudyashchikhsya. Moscow: Statistika.

Arutyunyan, Yu. V. 1968. Opyt sotsiologicheskovo izucheniya sela. Moscow: Moskovskovo universiteta.

____. 1971. Sotsial'naya struktura sel'skovo naseleniya SSSR. Moscow: Mysl'.

Bahr, Stephen J. 1974. "Effects on Power and Division of Labor in the Family." In Working Mothers: An Evaluative Review of the Consequences for Wife, Husband and Child. ed. Lois Wladis Hoffman and F. Ivan Nye, pp. 167-85. San Francisco: Jossey Bass.

Baikova, V. G. 1970. "Svobodnoe vremya i problemy ideino-politicheskoi raboty sredi trudyashchikhsya." In Sotsial'nye issledovaniya, No. 6, ed. V. I. Bolgov, pp. 92-110. Moscow: Nauka.

Baikova, V. G., A. S. Duchal, and A. A. Zemtsov. 1965. Svobodnoe vremya i vsestronnee razvitie lichnosti. Moscow: Mysl'.

Baranov, A. N. 1971. "Gorodskaya sem'ya i lichnost'." In Sotsial'nye issledovaniya, No. 7: Metodologicheskie problemy issledovaniya byta, No. 7, ed. A. G. Kharchev and Z. A. Yankova, pp. 75-84. Moscow: Nauka.

Barker, G. R. 1972. "La femme en Union Sovietique." Sociologie et Societes 4 (November): 159-91.

Baskina, Ada. 1968. "Nedelya Round Table: Women and Work." Nedelya, (May 12), as translated in Current Abstracts of the Soviet Press 1 (3): 20-21.

_____. 1972. ". . . I doma s chasami v rukakh." Literaturnaya gazeta, March 8, p. 12.

Belkin, A. 1973. "Muzhchina i zhenshchina: stipanie psikhologicheskikh granei?" Literaturnaya gazeta, August 1, p. 13.

Belyaev, E. V., V. V. Vodzinskaia, A. G. Zdravomyslov, B. V. Ornatskii, A. S. Shaev, and V. A. Iadov. 1962. "Workers' Time-Budget Research: A Method of Concrete Sociological Investigation." Vestnik leningradskovo universiteta, seriia ekonomii, filosofii i prava 4 (1961), as translated in Soviet Sociology 1 (Summer): 44-57.

Berent, Jerzy. 1970a. "Causes of Fertility Decline in Eastern Europe and the Soviet Union, Part 1." Population Studies 24 (March): 35-58.

_____. 1970b "Causes of Fertility Decline in Eastern Europe and the Soviet Union, Part 2." Population Studies 24 (July): 247-92.

_____. 1970c Some Demographic Aspects of Female Employment in Eastern Europe and the U. S. S. R." International Labor Review 101 (February): 175-92.

Berezovskaya, S. 1975. "Prestizh—zabota nasha obshaya." Literaturnaya gazeta, June 25, p. 12.

Berman, Harold J. 1963. Justice in the U. S. S. R.: An Interpretation of the Soviet Law. New York: Vintage.

Bibik, L. 1962. "Investigating the Time-Budget of Collective Farmers." Biulleten' nauchnoi informatsii, trud i zarabotnaia plata 6 (1961), as translated in Problems of Economics 4 (12): 12-17.

Bibik, L., and M. Markovich. 1962. "Changes Occurring in the Structure of Free Time." Politicheskoe samoobrazovanie 7 (1962), as translated in Soviet Sociology 1 (Fall): 38-40.

Blood, Robert O., Jr. 1963. "The Measurement and Bases of Family Power: A Rejoinder." Marriage and Family Living 25 (November): 475-77.

Blood, Robert O., Jr. and Donald M. Wolfe. 1960. The Dynamics of Married Living. New York: Free Press.

Bogdanov, I. M. 1964. Gramotnost' obrazovanie v dorevolyutsionnoi rossii i v SSSR. Moscow: Statistika.

Bogue, Donald J. 1969. Principles of Demography. New York: John Wiley & Sons.

Bolgov, Vi. I. 1973. Byudzhet vremeni pri sotsializme: teoriya i metody issledovaniya. Moscow: Nauka.

Boserup, Ester. 1970. Women's Role in Economic Development. New York: St. Martin's.

Carr, Edward Hallett. 1970. Socialism in One Country: 1924-1926. Vol. 1. Baltimore: Penguin.

Central Statistical Board. See Central Statistical Board of the USSR Council of Ministers.

Central Statistical Board of the USSR Council of Ministers. 1963. Women and Children in the U. S. S. R.: Brief Statistical Returns. Moscow: Foreign Languages Publishing House.

Chufarova, G. 1962. "Work and Rest Schedules When Work Time Is Further Reduced (According to Data From the Ural State University)." Biulleten' nauchnoi informatii, trud i zarabotnaia plata No. 9 (1961), as translated in Problems of Economics 4 (April): 17-21.

Chuiko, L. 1972. "Molodozheni. Sotsial'nyi portret." Literaturnaya gazeta, March 1, p. 13.

Churakov, V. Ya. 1967. Ispol'zovanie trudovykh resursov v kolkhozakh i sovkhozakh. Moscow: Kolos.

Cohn, Stanley H. 1962. "The Gross National Product in the Soviet Union: Comparative Growth Rates." In Dimensions in Soviet Economic Power, pp. 68-89. Washington, D.C.: U. S. Government Printing Office.

____. 1970. "General Growth Performance of the Soviet Economy." In Economic Performance and Military Burden in the Soviet Union, pp. 9-17. Washington, D.C.: U. S. Government Printing Office.

Cole, John P. 1967. Geography of the U. S. S. R. Middlesex, England: Penguin.

____. 1965. "Long-Range Causes and Consequences of the Employment of Married Women." Journal of Marriage and the Family 27 (February): 43-47.

Cole, Robert E. 1973. "Functional Alternatives and Economic Development: An Empirical Example of Permanent Employment in Japan." American Sociological Review 38 (4): 424-38.

Coleman, James S. et al. 1974. Youth: Transition to Adulthood. Chicago: University of Chicago Press. The Coleman work is the Report of the Panel on Youth of the President's Science Advisory Committee. Coleman is the chairman and the report is generally associated with him. Others on the panel and listed on the book's cover are: Robert H. Bremner, Burton R. Clark, John B. Davis, Dorothy H. Eichorn, Zvi Griliches, Joseph F. Kett, Norman B. Ryder, Zahava Blum Doering, John M. Mays.

Collins, Randall. 1971. "A Conflict Theory of Sexual Stratification." Social Problems 19 (Summer): 3-12.

Connor, Walter D. 1972. Deviance in Soviet Society: Crime, Delinquency and Alcoholism. New York: Columbia University Press.

Cooney, Rosemary Santana. 1975. "Female Professional Work Opportunities: A Cross-National Study." Demography 12: 107-20.

Cuisenier, Jean, and Catherine Raguin. 1967. "De quelques transformations dans le systeme familial russe." Revue Francais de Sociologie 8 (October-December): 521-57.

Danilova, E. Z. 1968. Sotsial'nye problemy truda zhenshchiny-rabotnitsy. Moscow: Nauka.

Davis, Kingsley. 1974. "The Sociology of Parent-Youth Conflict." In The Family: Its Structures and Functions, ed. Rose Laub Coser, pp. 446-69. 2d edition. New York: St. Martin's.

"A Demographic Problem: Female Employment and the Birthrate." 1970. Voprosy ekonomiki 1969, No. 5, as translated in The Soviet Review 11 (Spring): 76-81.

Dodge, Norton T. 1966. Women in the Soviet Economy. Baltimore: John Hopkins Press.

Doletsky, S. 1970. "Two Points Higher Than a Dream." Komsomolskaya pravda, December 22, 1970, as translated in Current Digest of the Soviet Press 22 (52): 27.

Duchal, A. S. 1965. "Izmenenie struktury rabochevo i svobodnovo vremeni krest'yan za gody Sovetskoi vlasti." Voprosy filosofii 4: 74-80.

Dumazedier, Joffre. 1974. Sociology of Leisure. New York: Elsevier.

Dunn, Stephen P., and Ethel Dunn. 1967. The Peasants of Central Russia. New York: Holt, Rinehard and Winston.

The Economist Intelligence Unit and the Cartographic Department of Clarendon Press. 1963. Oxford Regional Economic Atlas: The U. S. S. R. and Eastern Europe. London: Oxford University Press.

The Emancipation of Women: From the Writings of V. I. Lenin. 1966. New York: International Publishers.

Farley, Reynolds, and Karl E. Taeuber. 968. "Population Trends and Residential Segregation since 1960." Science 159 (March): 953-56.

Feiffer, George. 1964. Justice in Moscow. New York: Dell.

Feshbach, Murray and Stephen Rapawy. 1973. "Labor Constraints in the Five-year Plan." In Soviet Economic Prospects for the Seventies, pp. 485-563. Washington, D.C.: U.S. Government Printing Office.

Field, Mark G., and Karin I. Flynn. 1970. "Worker, Mother, Housewife: Soviet Woman Today." In Sex Roles in Changing Society, ed. Georgene H. Seward and Robert C. Williamson, pp. 257-84. New York: Random House.

Fomin, V. G. 1967. Budzhet vremeni nauchnovo rabotnika. Novosibirsk: Nauka, sibirskoe otdelenie.

Geiger, H. Kent. 1968. The Family in Soviet Russia. Cambridge, Mass: Harvard University Press.

Gerschenkron, Alexander. 1965. Economic Backwardness in Historical Perspective: A Book of Essays. New York: Praeger.

Gillespie, Dair L. 1971. "Who Has the Power: The Marital Struggle." Journal of Marriage and the Family 33 (August): 445-58.

Gol'tsman, M. T. 1961. "Sostav stroitel'nykh rabochikh SSSR v gody pervoi pyatiletki (no materialam profsoyuznykh perepisi 1929 i 1932)." In Izmeneniya v chislennosti i sostave sovetskovo rabochevo klassa. ed. D. A. Baerskii, pp. 142-202. Moscow: Akademii nauk SSSR.

Goncharenko, M. P., V. B. Ananiichuk, M. V. Zkharenko, G. I. Kulaga, and L. P. Deribasova. 1963. "Methodology of a Study of Working

People's Time-Budgets, and Some Results." Nauchnye doklady vysshei shkoly: filosofskie nauki, 1963, No. 1, as translated in Soviet Sociology 2 (Summer): 52-61.

Goode, William J. 1964. The Family. New Jersey: Prentice Hall.

____. 1968. "The Theory and Measurement of Family Change." In Indicators of Social Change: Concepts and Measurements, ed. Eleanor B. Sheldon and Wilbert E. Moore, pp. 295-348. New York: Russell Sage Foundation.

____. 1970. World Revolution and Family Patterns. New York: 1970.

____. 1971. "Force and Violence in the Family." Journal of Marriage and the Family 33 (November): 624-36.

Gordon, L. A., and E. V. Klopov. 1972a. Chelovek posle raboty: Sotsial'nye problemy byta i vnerabochevo vremeni. Moscow: Nauka.

____. 1972b. Chelovek posle raboty: Sotsial'nye problemy byta i vnerabochevo vremeni, prilozhenie. Moscow: Nauka.

Gordon, L. A. and B. Levin. 1968. "Nekotorye sotsial'no-bytovye nosledstviya pyatidnevki v bol'shikh i malkykh gorodakh." Voprosy ekonomiki 4: 138-42.

Gordon, L. A. and N. M. Pimashevskaya. 1972. Pyatidnevnaya rabochaya nedelya i svobodnoe vremeya trudyashchikhsya. Moscow: Mysl'.

Gosplan SSSR. 1931. Vsesoyuznaya perepisi naseleniya 1926 goda, Vol. 51: Soiuz Sovetskikh Sotsialisticheskik Respublik. Moscow: Gosplan.

1935. Trud v SSSR, 1934: ezhegodnik. Moscow: Gosplan.

1936. Trud v SSSR: statisticheskii spravochnik, ed. A. S. Popov. Moscow: Gosplan.

Grant, Nigel. 1968. Soviet Education. London: Penguin.

Grazia, Sebastian de 1962. Of Time, Work, and Leisure. New York: Anchor.

Gregory, James S. 1968. Russian Land, Soviet People: A Geographical Approach to the U. S. S. R. New York: Pegasus.

Gromov, A. S., L. B. Gorikova, I. V. Krymskaia, and O. E. Chernetskii. 1969. "Differences in Grades Received By Male and Female Students at the Medical School in Rostov-on-Don." Sovetskoe zdravookhranenie, 1968, No. 3, pp. 21-24, as translated in Soviet Sociology 7 (4): 61-64.

Gross, Edward. 1968. "Plus ca change . . . ? The Sexual Structure of Occupations Over Time." Social Problems 16 (Fall): 198-208.

Grushin, B. 1967. Svobodnoe vremya: aktual'nye problemy. Moscow: Mysl'.

____. 1969. U. S. S. R.: The Problem of Leizure [sic]. Moscow: Novosti.

Grzhegorzhevskii, A. N., L. N. Revin, and G. Ya. Frolov (eds.). 1971. Proizvoditel'nost'truda: faktory i rezervy rosta. Moscow: Mysl'.

Habakkuk, H. J. 1968. "The Historical Experience on the Basic Conditions of Economic Progress." In Comparative Perspectives on Social Change, ed. S. N. Eisenstadt, pp. 29-45. Boston: Little, Brown & Co.

Havens, Elizabeth M. 1973. "Women, Work and Wedlock: A Note on Female Marital Patterns in the United States." American Journal of Sociology 78 (4): 946-61.

Heer, David M. 1972. "Recent Developments in Soviet Population Policy." Studies in Family Planning 3 (November): 257-64.

Hochschild, Arlie Russell. 1973. "A Review of Sex Role Research." American Journal of Sociology 78 (January): 1, 011-29.

Hough, Jerry F. 1969. The Soviet Prefects: The Local Party Organs in Industrial Decision-Making. Cambridge, Mass.: Harvard University Press.

Ilyin, A. 1972. "Sociologist's Letter on an Important Subject: How Is the Village to Grow Younger?" Komsomolskaya pravda, January 26, 1972, as translated in Current Digest of the Soviet Press 24 (5): 9, 18.

Inkeles, Alex, and Raymond Bauer. 1968. The Soviet Citizen: Daily Life in a Totalitarian Society. New York: Atheneum.

Ivanchenko. A. A. 1965. "Trudovye resursy ekonomicheskikh rayonov SSSR i problemy ratskional'novov ikh ispol'zovaniya." In Voprosy razmeshcheniya proizvodstva v SSSR, ed. N. N. Nekrasov, pp. 160-94. Moscow: Nauka.

Jacoby, Susan. 1970. "Women in Russia." New Republic 162 (April): 16-18.

Javeau, Claude. 1974. "Essai d'inventaire des problemes methodologiques lies aux enquetes de budget-temps." Unpublished paper delivered at the Eighth Work Congress of Sociology, Toronto, Canada.

Kharchev, Anatoly Georgievich. 1964. Brak i sem'ya v SSSR. Moscow: Mysl'.

_____. 1973. "Today's Family and Its Problems." Zhurnalist, November 1972, pp. 58-61, as translated in Current Digest of the Soviet Press 25 (1): 18.

Kharchev, Anatoly G., and K. L. Emel'yanova. 1970. "Brak: ideal i deistvitel'nost." In G. V. Osipov, Anatoly G. Kharchev, Z. A. Yankova (eds.), Sotsial'nye issledovaniya, No. 4: problemy braka, sem'i, i demografii. Moscow: Nauka. pp. 61-65.

Kharchev, Anatoly G., and S. I. Golod. 1969. "Proizvodstvennaya rabota zhenshchin i sem'ya." In Sotsial'nye problemy truda i proizvodstva, ed. G. V. Osipov and Ya. Shchepan'sky, pp. 439-56. Moscow: Mysl'.

Kingsbury, Susan M., and Mildred Fairchild. 1935. Factory, Family and Woman in the Soviet Union. New York: G. P. Putnam's Sons.

Knudsen, Dean. 1969. "The Declining Status of Women: Popular Myths and Failures of Functionalist Thought." Social Forces 48 (December): 183-93.

Kogan, D. M. 1970. "Svyazi sovremennoi gorodskoi sem'i s sel'skoi." Sovetskaya etnografiya (November-December): 105-10.

Kokarev, E. M., S. M. Havasardov, E. M. Shershakova, and V. V. Yankovskii. 197 . "Osobennosti ispol'zovaniya trudyashchikhsya malovo goroda no severe." Pp. 186-96 in V. I. Bolgov (ed.), Sotsial'nye issledovaniya, No. 6: problemy byudzheta vremeni trudyashchikhsya. Moscow: Nauka.

Kobanovskii, V. N. 1970. Kollektiv kolkhoznikov: sotsial'nov-psikhologicheskie issledovanie. Moscow: Mysl'.

Kolobov, L. S. 1964. Rezhimy pyatidnevnoe rabochei nedeli, sokrashchyushchie nochnye smeni. Moscow: Legkaya industriya.

Kolpakov, B. T. and V. D. Patrushev. 1971. Byudzhet vremeni gorodskovo naseleniya. Moscow: Statistika.

Kolpakov, B. T. and G. A. Prudenskii. 1966. "Opyt izucheniya vnerabochevo vremeni trudyashchikhsya." In Sotsiologiya v SSSR, ed. V. N. Fokin and M. A. Ryzhova, Vol. 1, pp. 208-26. Moscow: Mysl'.

Komarovsky, Mirra. 1967. Blue-Collar Marriage. New York: Vintage.

Kon, I. S. 1973. "Zachen nuzhny ottsy?" Literaturnaya gazeta, February 28, p. 11.

Kosarev, A. 1973. "Thoughts About Boarding Schools: Yesterday, Today and Tomorrow." Uchitelskaya gazeta, May 5, as translated in Current Digest of the Soviet Press 25 (39): 15.

Kozhevnikova, T. 1973. "Toward Universal Secondary Education: The Very Extended Day." Pravda, March 1, 1973, as translated in Current Digest of the Soviet Press 25 (9): 15-16.

Kosven, Mark Osipovich. 1963. Semeinaya obshchina i patronimiya. Moscow: Akademii Nauk SSSR.

Kryazhev, V. G. 1966. Vnerabochee vremya i sfera obsluzhivaniya. Moscow: Ekonomika.

Kryazhev, V. G., and M. B. Markovich. 1962. "Obizuchenie byudzheta vremeni trudyashchikhsya." In Metodologicheskie voprosy izucheniya urovnya zhizni trudyashchikhsya, No. 2, ed. I. Y. Pisarev, pp. 109-22. Moscow: Sotsal'no-ekonomicheskoi literatury.

Ksenofontova, V. V. 1969. "Career Plans of Eighth and Ninth Grade Students and Their Realization." In The Career Plans of Youth, ed. M. N. Rutkevich, pp. 46-55. as translated by Murray Yanowitz in Soviet Education 11 (3-5).

Kumachenko, Ya. S. 1966. Nekotorye ekonomicheskiye problemy povysheniya effektivnosti proizvodstva. Moscow: Nauka.

Kurgansky, V. 1967. Letter written to Komsomolskaya pravda, December 15, 1966, as translated in Current Digest of the Soviet Press 19 (11): 2.

Kushner, P. I. 1970. The Village Viriatino: An Ethnographic Study of a Russian Village from before the Revolution to the Present, translated and edited by Sula Benet. New York: Anchor.

Kuznetsova, Larisa. 1967. "Whose Job Is the Kitchen?" Literaturnaya gazeta, July 12, p. 12, as translated in Current Digest of the Soviet Press 19 (33): 7-8.

____. 1968. "The New Face of the Madonna." Literaturnaya gazeta, February 28, as translated in Current Abstracts of the Soviet Press 1 (2): 19-20.

____. 1972. "Razbitye chasy. Zhenshchina: sem'ya i rabota." Literaturnaya gazeta, June 28, p. 12.

_____. 1973. "Obeshchal zhenit'sya . . ." Literaturnaya gazeta, April 4, p. 12.

Labzin, A. L. 1965. "Stroitel'stvo kommunizma i ustraneneie ostatkov neravenstva ostatkov neravenstva v polozhenii zhenshchiny." Filosofskie nauki (1): 98-106.

Lapidus, Gail Warshofsky. 1975. "USSR Women at Work: Changing Patterns." Industrial Relations 14 (2): 178-95.

Laslett, Barbara. 1973. "The Family as a Public and Private Institution: An Historical Perspective." Journal of Marriage and the Family 35 (3): 480-92.

Lebedev-Patreiko, V. G. Rabinovich, and D. Rodin. 1933. Byudzhet vremeni rabochei sem'i. Leningrad: LNIIKKh. (Leningradskii Nauchno-Issledovalel'skii Institut Kommunal'nogo i zhilischnogo Khozyaislva i Stroilel'stva)

Lenin, V. I. 1964. The Development of Capitalism in Russia. 2d rev. ed. Moscow: Progress Publishers.

Lennon, Lotta. 1971. "Women in the U. S. S. R." Problems of Communism 20 (July-August): 45-58.

Levikov, Aleksandr. 1971. "An Interview About the Relationship of the Consumer and the Producer." Literaturnaya gazeta, February 17, p. 10, as translated in Current Digest of the Soviet Press 23 (10): 10-11.

_____. 1973. Primeny XX veka: srednii gorod glzami sotsiologov, zhurnalistov i gorozhan. Moscow: Sovetskaya rossiya.

Levin, B. M. 1971. "Svobodnoe vremya i razvitie bytovykh obshchnostei." In A. G. Kharchev and Z. A. Yankova (eds.), Sotsial'nye issledovaniya, No. 7: metodologicheskie problemy issledovaniya byta. Moscow: Nauka. pp. 104-17.

Lewin, M. 1968. Russian Peasants and Soviet Power: A Study of Collectivization. London: George Allen and Unwin, Ltd.

Libedinskaya, L. 1967. "Freedom for the Kitchen?" Literaturnaya gazeta, February 22, 1967, p. 12, as translated in Current Digest of the Soviet Press 19 (15): 13-14.

Lieberson, Stanley. 1969. "Measuring Population Diversity." American Sociological Review 34 (February): 850-62.

Liegle, Ludwig. 1975. The Family's Role in Soviet Education. New York: Springer Publishing Company.

Lipset, Seymour Martin and Richard Dobson. 1972. "The Intellectual as Critic and Rebel: With Special Reference to the United State and the Soviet Union." Daedalus (Summer): 137-98.

Litvinenko, L. T. 1971. "Mat' ne domokhozyaika." Zhurnalist (January): 40-43.

Litvyakov, P. P. 1969. Demograficheskie problemy zanyatosti. Moscow: Ekonomika.

Macpherson, C. B. 1962. The Political Theory of Possessive Individualism. New York: Oxford University Press.

Mandel, William M. 1975. Soviet Women. New York: Anchor Books.

Manevich, Yu. 1970. "Problems of Manpower Reproduction and Ways to Improve the Utilization of Labor Resources in the U. S. S. R." Voprosy ekonomiki, October 1969, as translated in Current Digest of the Soviet Press 22 (1): 14-18.

Markov, V. I. 1965. "Nekotorye voprosy ispol'zovaniya trudovykh resursov." In Problemy ekonomiki truda, ed. E. V. Kasimovskii, pp. 256-92. Moscow: Ekonomika.

Marok, Edenka. 1973. "Skol'ko stoit domokhozyaika?" Literaturnaya gazeta, December 19, p. 13.

Marx, Karl and Frederick Engels. 1968. Selected Works. New York: International Publishers.

Massell, Gregory J. 1968. "Law as an Instrument of Revolutionary Change in a Traditional Milieu." Law and Society Review 2 (February): 179-228.

"Materialy k izucheniyu byudzheta vremeni zhenshchin-rabotnits." 1959. Voprosy truda (4): 224-31.

Matthews, Mervyn. 1972. Class and Society in Soviet Russia. London: Penguin.

Mazur, Peter D. 1967. "Reconstruction of Fertility Trends For the Female Population of the U. S. S. R." Population Studies 21 (1): 33-52.

____. 1968. "Birth Control and Regional Differentials in the Soviet Union." Population Studies 22 (November): 319-33.

____. 1969. "Correlates of Divorce in the U. S. S. R." Demography 6 (August): 279-286.

____. 1973. "Fertility and Economic Dependency of Soviet Women." Demography 10 (February): 37-51.

Medlin, William K. 1960. Soviet Educational Programs. Washington, D.C.: U.S. Government Printing Office.

Mellor, Roy E. H. 1966. Geography of the U.S.S.R. New York: Macmillan.

Mialkin, A. V. 1962. Svobodnoe vremya i vsestoronnee razvitie lichnosti. Moscow: VPSh i AON pri TsK KPSS.

Mikhailyuk, V. B. 1970. Ispol'zovanie zhenskovo truda v narodnom khozyaistve. Moscow: Ekonomika.

Monich, Zinaida. 1973. "The Professional and Paraprofessional Component in the Structure of the Rural Population." In Part 1 of Intelligentsiia v struture sel'skovo naselenia, Minsk: Nauka i Tekhnika, 1971, as translated in Soviet Sociology 12 (Summer), 56-76.

Moore, Barrington, Jr. 1966. Social Origins of Dictatorship and Democracy: Lord and Peasant in the Making of the Modern World. Boston: Beacon Press.

Morton, Henry W. 1973. "Housing." In Handbook of Soviet Social Science Data, ed. Ellen Mickiewicz, pp. 122-35. New York: Free Press.

Musatov, Ivan Mikhailovich. 1967. Sotsial'nye problemy trudovykh resursov v SSSR. Moscow: Mysl'.

Nash, Edmund. 1970. "Women at Work: The Status of Women in the U.S.S.R." Monthly Labor Review 93 (June): 39-44.

Netsenko, A. V. 1964. Svobodnovo vremya i evo ispol'zovanie. Leningrad: Nauka.

Novoplyansky, D. 1972. "Reflections on Letters: Mamas and the Harvest." Pravda, June 14, p. 3, as translated in Current Digest of the Soviet Press 24 (24): 37.

____. 1973. "Follow-up on a Letter: Dispute Over Leave." Pravda, March 11, p. 3, as translated in Current Digest of the Soviet Press 25 (10): 27.

Novozhenyuk, V. M. 1971. "Nekotorye sotsial'no-ekonomicheskie problemy zhenskovo truda v sel'skom khozaistvo." In

Proizvoditel'nost' truda: faktory i rezervy rosta, ed. A. N. Grzhegorzhevskii, L. N. Revin, and G. Ya. Frolov, pp. 208-32. Moscow: Mysl'.

Nye, F. Ivan and Felix M. Berardo. 1973. The Family: Its Structure and Interaction. New York: Macmillan.

Ofer, Gur. 1973. The Service Sector in Soviet Economic Growth: A Comparative Study. Cambridge, Mass.: Harvard University Press.

Olson, David H., and Carolyn Rabunsky. 1972. "Validity of Four Measures of Family Power." Journal of Marriage and the Family 34 (May): 224-34.

Oppenheimer, Valerie Kincade. 1970. The Female Labor Force in the United States: Demographic and Economic Factors Governing Its Growth and Changing Composition. California: Institute for International Studies, University of California.

____. 1973. "Demographic Influence on Female Employment and the Status of Women." American Journal of Sociology 78 (January): 946-61.

Osipov, G. V. 1966. Industry and Labour in the U. S. S. R. London: Tavistock.

Osipov, G. V., and S. F. Frolov. 1966. "Vnerabochee vremya i evo ispol'zovanie." In Sotsiologiya v SSSR, ed. V. M. Fokin and M. A. Ryzhova, Vol. 2, pp. 227-44. Moscow: Mysl'.

Ovchinnikova, I. 1973. "Problems of Upbringing: Children from Birth to Three." Izvestiya, April 28, 1973 as translated in Current Digest of the Soviet Press 25 (17): 11-12.

Panova, N. V. 1970. "Voprosy truda i byta zhenshchiny." In Problemy byta, braka i sem'i, ed. N. Solovyev, Yu. Lazauskas, and Ya. Yankova, pp. 87-94. Vil'nus, Lithuania: Mintis.

Patrushev, V. D. 1962. "Studying the Time-Budgets of Working People." Vestnik statistiki 1961 (1), as translated in Soviet Sociology 1 (Summer): 38-43.

____. 1963. Intensivnost' truda pri sotsializme. Moscow: Ekonomicheskoi literatury.

____. 1966. Vremya kak ekonomicheskaya kategoriya. Moscow: Mysl'.

Pavlova, M. 1971. "Irena's Career." Literaturnaya gazeta, September 22, 1971, as translated in Current Digest of the Soviet Press 23 (43): 16-17.

Perevedentsev, V. 1971. "Budet li svad'ba." Literaturnaya gazeta, February 24, p. 13.

____. 1974. "Some Statistics on the Soviet Union." Literaturnaya gazeta, April 24, 1974, as translated in Current Digest of the Soviet Press 26 (18): 11.

Petrosyan, G. S. 1963. "O ratsional'nom ispol'zovanii vnerabochevo vremeni trudyashchiksya." Voprosy ekonomiki (6): 32-41.

____. 1965. Vnerabochevo vremya trudashchikhsya v SSSR. Moscow: Ekonomika.

____. 1966. "Opyt issledovaniya byudzhetov vremeni trudyashchikhsya." Ekonomicheskie nauki (1): 87-93.

Phillips, Derek L., and Kevin J. Clancy. 1972. "Some Effects of 'Social Desirability' in Survey Studies." American Journal of Sociology 77 (March): 921-40.

Pimenova, A. 1970. "Uslugi v sem'e." In Problemi byta, braka i sem'i, ed. N. Solovyev, Yu. Lazauskas, and Ya. Yankova, pp. 141-52. Vil'nus, Lithuania: Mintis.

____. 1971. "Novyi byt i stanovlenie vnutrisemeinovo ravenstva." In A. G. Kharchev and Z. A. Yankova (eds.), Sotsial'nye issleovaniya, No. 7: Metodologicheskie problemy issledovaniya byta. Moscow: Nauka. pp. 34-45.

Pirenne, Henri. 1966. "Stages in the social history of capitalism." In Class, Status and Power: Social Stratification in Comparative Perspective, ed. Reinhard Bendix and Seymour Martin Lipset, pp. 97-106. 2d. ed. New York: The Free Press.

Pisarev, I. Yu. 1962. Metodologicheski voprosy izucheniya urovnya zhizni trudyashchikhsya, No. 2. Moscow: Sotsial'no-ekonomicheskoi literatury.

Podkorytova, L. L. 1969. "School Children of an Industrial Center Choose Their Paths (Based on Data From Kamensk-Uralsk)." In The Career Plans of Youth, ed. M. N. Rutkevich, pp. 28-36, as translated by Murray Yanowitz in Soviet Education 11 (3-5).

Polyani, Karl. 1957. The Great Transformation: The Political and Economic Origins of Our Time. Boston: Beacon Press.

Poston, Dudley L., Jr., and Gordon C. Johnson. 1971. "Industrialization and Professional Differentiation by Sex in the Metropolitan Southwest." Social Science Quarterly (September): 331-48.

Prather, Jane E. 1971. "When the Girls Move In: A Sociological Analysis of the Feminization of the Bank Teller's Job." Journal of Marriage and the Family (November): 777-82.

Prudenskii, G. A. 1961. Vnerabochee vremya trudyashchikhsya. Novosibirsk: Sibirskovo otdeleniya AN SSSR.

____. 1962. "The Free Time of Working People in Socialist Society." Kommunist 1960 (15), as translated in Soviet Sociology 1 (1): 32-38.

____. 1972. Problemy rabochevo i vnerabochevo vremeni. Moscow: Nauka.

Rapoport, S. S. 1974. "Sotsial'nye probley svobodnovo vremeni." Sotsiologicheskie issledovaniya (2): 198-203.

Rashin, A. G. 1940. Formirovanie promyshlennovo proletariata v rossii-statistiko-ekonomicheskie ocherki. Moscow: Gosudarstvennoe sotsial'no-ekonomicheskoe izdatel'stvo.

____. 1961. "Dinamika promyshlennykh kadrov SSSR za 1917-1958 gg." In Izmeneniya v chislennosti i sostave sovetskovo rabochevo klassa, ed. D. A. Baevskii, pp. 7-73. Moscow: Akademii nauka SSSR.

Razina, A. 1975. "Serious Talk About the Little Ones." Pravda, December 14, 1974, as translated in Current Digest of the Soviet Press 26 (50): 24.

Reder, Melvin W. 1957. Labor in a Growing Economy. New York: Wiley.

Rigby, Thomas H. 1968. Communist Party Membership in the U. S. S. R., 1917-1967. Princeton, New Jersey: Princeton University Press.

Robinson, John P. 1967. "Social Change as Measured by Time-Budgets." Unpublished paper read at American Sociological Association annual meeting.

Rodman, Hyman. 1969. "Marital Power in France, Greece, Yugoslavia and the United States." Journal of Marriage and the Family 29 (May): 320-24.

Rowbothom, Sheila. 1972. Women, Resistance and Revolution: A History of Women and Revolution in the Modern World. New York: Vintage.

Rubinov, A. 1967. "The Industry of Good Services." Literaturnaya gazeta, March 29, 1967, p. 12, as translated in Current Digest of the Soviet Press 19 (15): 14-16.

Ryvkina, R. V. 1966. Sotsiologicheskie issledovaniya: voprosy metodologii i metodiki. Novosibirsk: Novosibirskii gosudarstvennyi universitet.

Sacks, Michael Paul. 1974. "Sex Roles in Soviet Russia: A Study of Continuity in the Midst of Change." Unpublished doctoral dissertation, University of Michigan.

Sadvokasova, E. A. 1968. "Rol' aborta v osushchestvlenii soznatel'novo materinstva v SSSR." In Izuchenie vosproizvodstva naseleniya, ed. T. V. Ryabushkn, pp. 207-24. Moscow: Nauka.

Safilos-Rothschild, Constantina. 1970. "The Study of Family Power Structure: A Review 1960-1969."

_____. 1971. Pp. 79-90 In Carlfred B. Broderick (ed.), A Decade of Family Research and Action, ed. Carlfred B. Broderick, pp. 79-90.

_____. 1972. "The Relationship between Work Commitment and Fertility." International Journal of Sociology of the Family 2 (1): 64-71, National Council on Family Relations.

Sahlins, Marshall David, and Elman R. Service (eds.). 1960. Evolution and Culture. Ann Arbor: University of Michigan Press.

Sannikova, A. P. 1970. "Izmeneniya v struture i chislennosti sem'i u rabochikh karel'skoi ASSR." Sovetskaya etnografiya 45 (4): 97-106.

Scheuch, Erwin K. 1972. "The Time-Budget Interview." In The Use of Time: Daily Activities of Urban and Suburban Populations in Twelve Countries, ed. Alexander Szalai, pp. 69-87. The Hague: Mouton.

Sharapov, V. 1969. "Novye pyatiletniy plna." Professionalnoe technicheskoe obrazovaniye (June): 10-11.

Shim, Eduard. 1967. "Ready, Heave!" Literaturnaya gazeta, February 1, 1967, as translated in Current Digest of the Soviet Press 19 (15): 12-13.

Shokin, Zory. 1971. "The Bachelor Yesterday, Today, Tomorrow." Literaturnaya gazeta, April 21, 1971, as translated in Current Digest of the Soviet Press 23 (15): 36-37.

Sirotkin, S. P., A. V. Solov'ev, and M. I. Skarzhinskii. 1968. Proizvoditel'nost truda i ispol'zovanie rabochevo vremeni v sotsialisticheskom obshchestve. Moscow: Vysshaya shkola.

Skolnick, Arlene. 1973. The Intimate Environment: Exploring Marriage and the Family. Boston: Little, Brown & Co.

Skuridina, L. D. 1966. "O nepolnom rabochem dne dlya zhenshchin-materei." Izvestiya siberskovo otdelenii (9): 19-24.

Slater, Philip. 1970. The Pursuit of Loneliness: American Culture at the Breaking Point. Boston: Beacon Press.

Slesarev, G. A., and Z. A. Yankova. 1969. "Zhenshchina no promyshlennom predpriyatii i v sem'e." In Sotsial'nye problemy truda i proizvodstva, ed. G. V. Osimov and Ya. Shchepan'sky. Moscow: Mysl'. pp. 416-38.

Smith, Page. 1970. Daughters of the Promised Land. Boston: Little, Brown.

Smith, Willard S. 1973. "Housing in the Soviet Union—Big Plans, Little Action." In Soviet Economic Prospects for the Seventies, pp. 402-27. Washington, D.C.: U.S. Government Printing Office.

Sonin, M. Ya. 1961. "Trudovye resursy domashnevo khozyaistva." In Trudovye resursy SSSR: problemy raspredeleniya i ispol'zovaniya, ed. N. I. Shishkina, pp. 143-56. Moscow: Ekonomicheskoi literatury.

____. 1965. Aktual'nye problemy ispol'zovaniya rabochei sily v SSSR. Moscow: Mysl'.

Sprey, Jetse. 1972. "Family Power Structure: A Critical Comment." Journal of Marriage and the Family 34 (May): 235-38.

Stinchcombe, Arthur L. 1965. "Social structure and organizations." In Handbook of Organizations, ed. James G. March, pp. 142-93. Chicago: Rand McNally.

____. 1968. Constructing Social Theories. New York: Harcourt, Brace and World.

Stone, Phillip J. 1972. "The Analysis of Time-Budget Data." In The Use of Time: Daily Activities of Urban and Suburban Populations in Twelve Countries, ed. Alexander Szalai, pp. 89-111. The Hague: Mouton.

Strumilin, S. G. 1957. Problemy economiki truda. Moscow: Gosudarstvennoe izdatel'stvo politicheskoi literatury.

____. 1964. Izbrannye proizvedeniya v pyati tomakh, Vol. 3: Problemy ekonomiki truda. Moscow: Nauka.

Sukharevskii, B. 1972. "Nepolnyi rabochii den': evo granitsy i effektivnost'." Literaturnaya gazeta, March 15, p. 10.

Sullerot, Evelyne. 1971. *Woman, Society and Change*. New York: McGraw-Hill.

Suprun, P. I. and A. I. Goncharenko. 1971. "Ispol'zovanie byudzheta vremeni trudyashchikhsya i rost proizvoditel'nosti truda." In *Proizvoditel'nost truda: faktory i rezervy rosta*, ed. A. N. Grzhegorzhevskii, L. N. Revin, and G. Ya. Frolov, pp. 183-207. Moscow: Mysl'.

Szalai, Alexander. 1972. "Introduction: Concepts and Practices of Time-Budget Research." In *The Use of Time: Daily Activities of Urban and Suburban Populations in Twelve Countries*, ed. Alexander Szalai, pp. 1-12. The Hague: Mouton.

Szalai, Alexander (ed.). 1972. *The Use of Time: Daily Activities of Urban and Suburban Populations in Twelve Countries*. The Hague: Mouton.

Takarskaya, N. 1967. "Zakrepleniye kadrov v promyshlennosti." *Ekonomicheskiye nauki* (4): 45-50.

Tatarinova, N. 1973. "Nauchno-technicheskii progress i trud zhenshchin." *Voprosy Ekonomiki* (11): 57-64.

Takarskaya, N. 1967. "Zakrepleniye kadrov v promyshlennosti." *Ekonomicheskiye nauki* (4): 45-50.

Taterinova, N. 1973. "Naucho-technicheskii progress itrud zhenshchin." *Voprosy Ekonomiki* (11): 57-64.

Tilly, Louise A., and Joan W. Scott. 1975. "Women's Work and Family in Nineteenth Century Europe." *Comparative Studies in Society and History* 17 (January 1975): 36-64.

Treiman, Donald J. 1970. "Industrialization and Social Stratification." *Sociological Inquiry* 40 (2): 207-34.

Troinitskii, N. A. (ed.). 1906. *Chislennost' i sostav rabochikh v rossii na osnovanii dannykh vseobshchie perepisi Rossiiskoi Imperii 1897*, Moscow: Gosudarstvennii ministr vnutrennikh delenii.

Trufanov, I. P. 1970. "Byudzhety vremeni kak instrument issledovaniya byta trudyashchikhsya." Pp. 128-149 In V. I. Bolgov (ed.), *Sotsial'nye issledovaniya*, No. 6: problemy byudzheta vremeni trudyashchikhsya. Moscow: Nauka.

Ts. S. U. See Tsentral'noe statisticheskoe upravlenie pri sovete ministrov SSSR.

Ts. S. U. RSFSR. See Tsentral'noe statisticheskoe upravlenie pri sovete ministrov RSFSR ezhegodnik.

Tsentral'noe statisticheskoe upravlenie pri sovete ministrov RSFSR. 1971. Narodnoe khozyaistvo R. S. F. S. R. v 1970 godu: statisticheskii ezhegodnik. Moscow: Statistika.

____. 1972. Narodnoe khozyaistvo R. S. F. S. R. v 1971 godu: statisticheskii ezhegodnik. Moscow: Statistika.

Tsentral'noe statisticheskoe upravlenie pri sovete ministrov SSSR. 1963. Itogo vsesoyuznoe perepisi naseleniya 1959 goda: R. S. F. S. R. Moscow: Gosstatizdat.

____. 1969a. Narodnoe khozaistvo SSSR v 1968 godu: statisticheskii ezhegodnik. Moscow: Statistika.

____. 1969b. Zhenshchini i deti v SSSR. Moscow: Statistika.

____. 1970. Women in the Soviet Union: Statistical Returns. Moscow: Progress Publishers.

____. 1971a. Narodnoe khozyaistvo SSSR v 1968 godu: statisticheskii ezhegodnik. Moscow: Statistika.

____. 1971b. Narodnoe obrazovanie, nauka, i kul'tura v SSSR: statisticheskii sbornik. Moscow: Statistika.

____. 1972a. Itogi vsesoyuznoi perepisi naseleniya 1970 goda, Vol. 1: chislennost' naseleniya SSSR. Moscow: Statistika.

____. 1972b. Itogi vsesoyuznoi perepisi naseleniya 1970 goda, Vol. 2: pol, vozrast i sostayanie v brake naseleniya SSSR. Moscow: Statistikia.

____. 1972c. Itogi vsesoyuznoi perepisi naseleniya 1970 goda, Vol. 3: uroven' obrazovaniya naseleniya SSSR. Moscow: Statistika.

____. 1973a. Itogi veseoyuznoi perepisi naseleniya 1970 goda, Vol 4, raspredelenie naseleniya SSSR. Moscow: Statistika.

____. 1973b. Itogi veseoyuznoi perepisi naseleniya 1970 goda, Vol. 6: raspredeleniya naseleniya SSSR po zanyatiyam. Moscow: Statistika.

____. 1974. Narodnoe khozyaistvo SSSR v 1973 g. Moscow: Statistika.

Tsimbalyuk, Victor. 1974. "Etot zagadochnye muzhchina." Literaturnaya gazeta, June 5, pp. 9-10.

Tumanov, I. P. 1964. Rabochee i svobodnoe vremya. Irkutsk: Vostochno-sibirskoe knizhnoe izdatel'stvo.

Turk, James L., and Norman W. Bell. 1972. "Measuring Power in Families." Journal of Marriage and the Family 34 (May): 215-23.

Ulam, Adam B. 1960. The Unfinished Revolution: An Essay on the Sources of Influence of Marxism and Communism. New York: Vintage Books.

U. S. Congress, Joint Economic Committee. 1962. Dimensions of Soviet Economic Power. Washington, D. C.: U. S. Government Printing Office.

1964. Annual Economic Indicators for the U. S. S. R. Washington, D. C.: U. S. Government Printing Office.

1965. Current Indicators for the U. S. S. R. Washington, D. C.: U. S. Government Printing Office.

1968. Soviet Economic Performance: 1966-1967. Washington, D. C.: U. S. Government Printing Office.

1970. Economic Performance and the Military Burden in the Soviet Union. Washington, D. C.: U. S. Government Printing Office.

U. S. Department of Commerce. 1969. Projections of the Population of the U. S. S. R., by Age and Sex: 1969 to 1990. Washington, D. C.: U. S. Government Printing Office.

Urlanis, B. 1971. "Babushka v sem'e." Literaturnaya gazeta, March 3, p. 11.

Vanek, Joann. 1973. "Keeping Busy: Time Spent in Housework, United States, 1920-1970." Doctoral dissertation, University of Michigan.

Vodzinskaya, V. V. 1970. "Orientatsiya na professii." In Molodyozh' i trud, ed. V. A. Yadova and V. I. Dobrynina, pp. 79-101. Moscow: TsK VLKSM.

Volga, N. 1970. "Issledovanie dinamiki razvitiya semei dlya sovershenstvovaniya tipov zhilishcha." In Problemy byta, braka i sem'i, ed. N. Solovyev, Yu. Lazauskas, and Ya. Yankova, pp. 50-61. Vil'nus, Lithuania: Mintis.

Volin, Lazar. 1970. A Century of Russian Agriculture: From Alexander II to Khrushchev. Cambridge, Mass.: Harvard University Press.

Vorozheikin, Evgenii Minaevich. 1973. Brak i sem'ya v SSSR. Moscow: Znanie.

Vostrikova, A. M. 1964. "Examination of Fertility, Marriages and Family in the U. S. S. R." In Studies of Fertility and Social Mobility, ed. Egon Szabady, pp. 214-28. Budapest: Akademiai Kiado.

Waldman, Elizabeth. 1974. "Children of Working Mothers." Monthly Labor Review, January, pp. 64-67.

Whyte, Martin K. 1971. "Rural Russia Today." In Sociological Realities: A Guide to the Study of Society, ed. Irving Louis Horowitz and Mary Symons Strong, pp. 28-34. New York: Harper and Row.

Wolf, Eric R. 1969. Peasant Wars in the Twentieth Century. New York: Harper and Row.

____. 1971. "Peasant Rebellion and Revolution." In National Liberation: Revolution in the Third World, ed. Norman Miller and Roderick Aya, pp. 48-67. New York: Free Press.

The Woman Question: Selections from the Writings of Karl Marx, Frederick Engels, V. I. Lenin and Joseph Stalin. 1951. New York: International Publishers.

Yankova, Z. A. 1970. "O semeino-bytovoi rolyakh rabotayushei zhenshchiny." In Sotsial'nye issledovaniya: problemy braka, sem'i i demografii, ed. G. V. Osipov, A. G. Kharchev, and Z. A. Yankova, pp. 76-87. Moscow: Nauka.

____. 1972. "Vse o zhenshchine." Literaturnaya gazeta, March 8, p. 12.

Yanovskii, V. V. 1968. "Fond i struktura svobodnovo vremeni trudyashchikhsya gorodov novovo tipa na krainem severe." In Naselenie i trudovye resursy severovostoka SSSR, ed. D. I. Valentei, pp. 59-71. Moscow: Nauka.

Yanowitz, Murray. 1963. "Soviet Patterns of Time Use and Concepts of Leisure." Soviet Studies 15 (July): 17-37.

Yanowitz, Murray, and Norton T. Dodge. 1969. "The Evaluation of Occupations in the Soviet Union." Slavic Review 28 (4): 619-43.

Yunina, Lyubov. 1971. "Only Romeos!" Literaturnaya gazeta, May 12, 1971, p. 12, as translated in Current Digest of the Soviet Press 23 (34): 28.

Yurkevich, N. G. 1970. Sovetskaya sem'ya: funktsii i usloviya stabilnosti. Minsk: Izdatel'stvo BGU imeni V. I. Lenina.

Zemstov, A. A. 1965. "Rezervy rost i ratsional'noe ispol'zovanie svobodnovo vremeni rabochikh." Voprosy filosofii (4): 61-69.

Zhuravlev, G. T. 1966. "Svobodnoe vremya trudyashchikhsya i evo izuchenie s primeneniem metodov variatsionnoi statistiki." In Sotsiologiya v SSSR, ed. V. N. Fokin and M. A. Ryzhova, Vol. 2, pp. 245-63. Moscow: Mysl'.

____. 1969. "Svobodnoe vremya i kul'turnaya zhizn' rabotnikov promyshlennovo predpriyatiya." In Sotsial'nye problemy truda i proizvodstva, ed. G. V. Osipov and Ya. Shchepan'sky, p. 367. Moscow: Mysl'.

Zlotnikov, R. A. 1970. :Svobodnoe vremya i obrazovanie." In V. I. Bolgov (ed.), <u>Sotsial'nye issledovaniya</u>, Vol. 6: problemy byudzheta vremeni trudyashchikhsya. Moscow: Nauka.

INDEX

ABOUT THE AUTHOR

MICHAEL PAUL SACKS is currently assistant professor of sociology at Trinity College in Hartford, Connecticut. He holds a Ph. D and M. A. in sociology from the University of Michigan and a B. A. from Queens College. He has studied Russian at Leningrad State University and at the University of Leeds.